RECAPTURING ANTHROPOLOGY

The publication of this book
was made possible by generous support
from the Brown Foundation

School of American Research
Advanced Seminar Series
Douglas W. Schwartz, General Editor

RECAPTURING ANTHROPOLOGY

Contributors

Lila Abu-Lughod
Department of Religion
Princeton University

Arjun Appadurai
Department of Anthropology
University of Pennsylvania

Richard G. Fox
Department of Anthropology
Duke University

José E. Limón
Department of English
University of Texas, Austin

Sherry B. Ortner
Department of Anthropology
University of Michigan

Paul Rabinow
Department of Anthropology
University of California, Berkeley

Michel-Rolph Trouillot
Department of Anthropology
The Johns Hopkins University

Joan Vincent
Department of Anthropology
Barnard College/Columbia University

Graham Watson
Department of Anthropology
The University of Calgary

Recapturing Anthropology

Working in the Present

Edited by

Richard G. Fox

SCHOOL OF AMERICAN RESEARCH PRESS
SANTA FE, NEW MEXICO

School of American Research Press
Post Office Box 2188
Santa Fe, New Mexico 87504-2188

Distributed by the University of Washington Press

Library of Congress Cataloging-in-Publication Data:
Recapturing anthropology : working in the present / edited by Richard
  G. Fox.
        p.   cm. — (School of American research advanced seminar series)
    Includes bibliographical references and index.
    ISBN 0-933452-77-2. — ISBN 0-933452-78-0 (pbk.)
        1. Anthropology—Methodology—Congresses.   2. Anthropology—
    Philosophy—Congresses.   3. Ethnology—Methodology—Congresses.
    4. Ethnology—Philosophy—Congresses.   5. Culture—Congresses.
    I. Fox, Richard Gabriel, 1939–   .   II. Series.
    GN33.R43   1991
    301'.01—dc20   91-26724
                                                                      CIP

CONTENTS

RECAPTURING ANTHROPOLOGY

Chapter 1

INTRODUCTION

Working in the Present

Richard G. Fox

> Let us suppose that there is some value in trying to shape an anthropology of the present. . . .
>
> Sidney Mintz, *Sweetness and Power*

HOW can anthropologists work in and write about the world at present? That question motivated a week-long advanced seminar at the School of American Research in Santa Fe, New Mexico, in June 1989.

Our group took the world "at present" not simply to mean the contemporary but also to refer to the peculiar: that is, we understood that fundamental and widespread changes had happened fairly recently in the world. Decentered, fragmented, compressed, flexible, refractive, postmodern—these terms are often used to represent the world today (cf. Harvey 1989). Our "present" appears to be substantially different from the "present" that our predecessors confronted, even just a short time ago.

Similarly, we recognized that the issue of "how anthropologists could work and write" is now more problematic than it was even a generation ago. The notion of "working" no longer comes down simply to choosing a methodology and an analytic scheme; the action of "writing" is now understood as much more than the mechanical process of "putting pen to paper" (a phrase whose very anachronism makes us recognize how different is the "world at present"). These new understandings of "work" and "writing" have put anthropology's claims to authority under siege. We believed that no anthropology of the present could ignore them; more-over, any anthropology of the present would have to build on their insights.

After complicating our initial question in these ways, we never ex-pected the seminar to develop a single answer. I am happy to report that it never did. There was consensus, however, on the central issue to which we should give attention. Despite different responses to questions about the nature of self and other, about the concept of culture, about the prac-tice of ethnography, about anthropology as a profession, about the history of texts, and about the character of local communities in a global society, we came to a common focus on strategies for recapturing anthropology's authority at present. I will discuss this common focus after making some brief comments on "predecessory" anthropologies of the present and on some current impediments to achieving such an anthropology.[1]

WHAT WORKED IN THE PAST

Anthropology's quest after the present goes back at least to the times just before and after World War II, when Robert Redfield, Ruth Benedict, and Julian Steward tried, in very different ways, to comprehend what were then called complex societies and their Great Traditions, national cul-tures, or levels of sociocultural integration. Such attempts involved state-ments not only about what the (present) world was like but also about what anthropology must be to study it.

There are for me two landmark works in the anthropology of *that* present. In 1956, Eric Wolf wrote of Mexico and other complex societies as webs of group relations linking local communities with the national level. For Wolf, an anthropology of that present had to track the brokers and brokering institutions that served as pivots between the local and national. About the same time, Sidney Mintz (1960) measured out an anthropology of the present in the course of one man's life and labor. We saw the many changes in Puerto Rican society over the first half of the twentieth century as Taso, Mintz's "worker in the cane," embodied, re-sisted, and, most of all, endured them.

Still another major work was *Reinventing Anthropology* (Hymes 1974), which asked, at a later and even more critical time, how the profession of anthropology must change in order to get a clean start. In introducing the volume, Dell Hymes argued that some professional traditions could even be scrubbed. He noted, for example, that anthropology departments con-tinued to defend the "four-field" approach, even though—or perhaps pre-cisely because—it was only a relic. Hymes also regretted that cultural anthropologists still strongly identified with the "primitive" world as ear-

lier anthropologists had imagined it—a world in which Western domination had no place and where the anthropologist need only locate—and
locate only—the "natives" to find a field site. "What it suggests," Hymes
(1974: 29) concluded, "is a trained incapacity to rise above one's professional subject and into the modern world." About the same time, Talal
Asad and his colleagues judged British social anthropology to be similarly
left inert by "the historical power relationship between the West and the
Third World" (Asad 1973: 19).

WORKING OUT THE PRESENT

Although proleptic and exemplary, these works encountered a present—in the world and in anthropology—rather different from today's.
Taso lived in a postwar Puerto Rico where insular paternalistic sugar es-
tates were giving way to Yankee agribusinesses, where migration to the
mainland was becoming an ever more important rite of passage, and
where even anthropologists—odd ones at that, because they had never
lived with the "primitives"—came to study. Wolf's Mexico was festooned
with closed corporate peasant communities; they were not pre-Colum-
bian survivals but the "weak weapons" of peasants on the margins of the
hacienda system. Hymes and Asad urged anthropologists to recognize
very much the same present, somewhat later on. Theirs was still the post-
war world of fully disappeared primitives and still-disappearing Western
colonies; of new nations and national identities and paths of development—and underdevelopment—abroad; and of new claims for representation and justice at home: a postwar world where the Vietnam War could
appear as the desperate parting shot of imperialism, mortally wounded
and on the run.

Scholars tell of a world at present that is very different. David Harvey
finds "a sea-change in cultural as well as in political-economic practices
since around 1972," which he relates to a new capitalism of flexible accumulation that has overwhelmed and compressed the globe (Harvey
1989:vii). Ernesto Laclau and Chantal Mouffe, in calling for a new radical
democratic politics, designate the present as a time when capitalism has
subsumed all social relations and the individual has become subordinate
to capital not only through wage labor but also at leisure, during education, in sex, and even at death (Laclau and Mouffe 1985: 160–61; also see
Rabinow 1986). Alvin Gouldner, Jürgen Habermas, and others writing
about late capitalism posit the formation of new classes and social movements under this stage of capitalist society. For these scholars, the present
is only an accumulation and perhaps, in terms of consciousness, an
exaggerated appreciation of the conditions that have been emerging in

capitalism for the last half-century. Frances McCrea and Gerald Markle, in reviewing this literature, synthesize it to explain the recent emergence of the antinuclear movement in the United States and globally (McCrea and Markle 1989:28–39).

Whatever its causes and character, our work is cut out for us by this world at present. Twenty years ago, Hymes could be pessimistic about the state of anthropology, yet be certain—and therefore ultimately optimistic—that reinvention was a real possibility. Today, Edward Said (1989) urges anthropology to reinvent itself just as passionately as Hymes did. Unlike Hymes, however, Said recognizes that there are no privileged positions, islands of objectivity, or places of greater "truth" for such a scholarship to attain. A reinvented anthropology, just as much as the anthropology it hopes to replace, will be—in fact, must be, according to Said—shot through with worldly interests, or what are called biases in the positivist lexicon. Reflexivity, relativity, and the rejection of a privileged position for science or scholarship represent a new age, quite unlike the present of even just a generation ago. Thus, when James Clifford (1988c:23, 213) similarly speaks of the need for new descriptions that emphasize the present's fragmentation and mix-up—which specify, for example, the presence of Anglo consumers of ceremony at Zuni Pueblo's Shalako celebration—he does not see them as milestones leading to a greater "truth." Like Said, Clifford judges such new representations as valuable in so far as they are critical, that is, contrary to the established portrayals.

The novelty of the world at present unmistakably works on the anthropologist in everyday life. Many examples—present-day stories of unprecedented culture shocks—kept coming up in the School of American Research seminar and appear in the contributions to this volume: for example, the anthropologist who heads halfway around the world to India only to find that the Hindu priest who is his chief informant has departed to serve parishioners (and to encounter other anthropologists?) in Houston, Texas. Surely this international travel "tag" played by Arjun Appadurai and Carol Breckenridge signals a new genre of "Nuerosis" for anthropologists in the field, one that will become ever more common. The world at present also increasingly has "halfie" anthropologists, as Lila Abu-Lughod defines herself—at the same time one who studies a people and one of the people so studied. This labor is made more difficult, as José Limón tells us, because such "indigenous" ethnographers often have to confront ostensible portrayals of themselves that are really representations of some Other in the ethnographies of their predecessors, who sometimes are also "indigenous" or "halfie." Still *other* anthropologists, as represented by Michel-Rolph Trouillot, ask "Europe and the West . . . to take the Other seriously" (Said 1989: 223) by not allowing the modern West to write off its culpability in quick-and-dirty confessions: the otherness constructed in the past cannot so easily be disembodied from present global relations.

Such cultural and professional contortions are ever present, and there is no way to make it back to a home base and escape them: the close-to-home constantly intermixes with the far-from-home, and often it is not worthwhile deciding which is which. I have this feeling when I watch Pro-Life protesters in North Carolina use present-day versions of Gandhian *satyagraha*, or when animal-rights activists preach a doctrine much like *ahimsa*. Sherry Ortner reports a similar sense of distance from the near as she studied her New Jersey "homeland." In this present we recognize many moments where the alien inhabits the familiar, or vice versa.

How does anthropology engage this world of fragmentary social relations, mixed-up but not interlinked culture, and metatheories that are imagined as shattered? Some anthropologists call for radically new works. They compress the archaeology of anthropology from its earliest professional stage right up to the present into a single horizon: the era of what they label the "realist" ethnography, one that they find unconvincing at best, dissimulating at worst (see Marcus and Cushman 1982; Crapanzano 1986). These anthropologists do not recognize the works on complex society from the 1950s or the calls for reinvention from the 1970s, which I mentioned earlier, as progressive, or even separate, stages of anthropology's development. Indeed, such development seems possible to them only in the present: anthropology has to be worked up almost from scratch; the present condition of the world both compels and enables radically novel works (Clifford 1988c: 23).

The contribution of these anthropologists, whom I refer to collectively and essentially (and therefore somewhat apologetically) as reflexivists or postmodernists, has been timely. Their critique makes recognition of the world at present and, in consequence, anthropology's difficulties in working within this world, its guiding interest. Ignoring this aspect of the reflexive or postmodern critique means we mistake it for irrelevant literary excursions, disinterested intellectual games, or, worst of all, professional opportunism. This critique therefore must enter into any consideration of an anthropology of the present.

WORKING OVER THE PAST

Clifford Geertz (1988: 1) states the major point of the reflexive or postmodern critique when he tells us that ethnography is "a kind of writing, putting things to paper." Rather than appearing as an objective scientific report, ethnography now appears as a scholarly construction. James Clifford (1986b: 118) further argues that what often passes for the "native point of view" in ethnography is only the assertion and certification of the anthropologist, who actually suppresses the collaboration of his "native" informants in the ethnographic fiction. By silencing the others that it supposedly represents, the ethnographic text reinforces the authority of the anthropologist as a professional.

Writing ethnography is always, therefore, an assertion of power, a claim to "authority" that, when successful, becomes an "authorization."

The postmodern critique has been especially good at uncovering the artifice—the literary conventions—used in ethnographic writing to legitimate anthropology. We are now much more aware—and wary—of the conventions by which we convince readers that we were really there and faithfully got the native point of view. We are much more suspicious of ethnography's claim to provide a tidy picture of the Other. Conventional representations of sudden baptisms into native society or other stories of the rapport we achieved in fieldwork are greatly suspect. Who now can tell "horror stories from the field"—the rabid dog that bit me in Tezibazar, the sheep's eye I ate in Vasilika—unselfconsciously? They represent a hackneyed genre even when they actually happened. By emphasizing that a realist ethnography is both constructed and authorized, these postmodern critics act to deauthorize it as the major product or "text" of cultural anthropology.

Few cultural anthropologists today, I believe, question the relativism underlying the postmodern critique. An ethnographic text, most of us would agree, works to construct the very society and culture under study. I imagine, too, that few anthropologists nowadays can ignore ethnography's loss of authority after the acts of authorship by which it has been constructed have been so astutely demystified. There is no question, then, that the postmodern critique has set an agenda for a critical debate about ethnographic authority and, by extension, about the present condition of anthropology.

There remains the question of how well this critique points us toward a new anthropology of the present. By their anguish, chagrin, condemnation, and accusations against it, some anthropologists validate the postmodern critique as an iconoclastic assault against anthropology, scholarship, or science as we now know it. Steven Sangren (1988) makes the postmodernists Goliaths of obscurantism and careerism. Jonathan Friedman (1987) and Nicole Polier and William Roseberry (1989), although more restrained, blow the critique up to large proportions. The postmodernists themselves do not hesitate to counsel us authoritatively about their radical purpose. George Marcus and Dick Cushman (1982:45), for example, contrast the failed genre of realist ethnography with a new, experimental ethnographic account that "leaves the world observed as open-ended, ambiguous, and in flux." James Clifford (1986b:109) agrees: "Much of our knowledge about other cultures must now be seen as contingent, the problematic outcome of intersubjective dialogue, translation, and projection."

Clifford therefore calls for a radical dialogic or polyphonic ethnographic text. Steve Tyler (1986:126) tells us, similarly, that postmodern ethnography rejects the realist ideology of the observer and the observed—"there being nothing observed and no one who is observer. There is instead the mutual dialogical production of a discourse, of a story of sorts." The "experimental moment" thus heralded has summoned forth numerous ethnographic texts pledged to a radical anthropology of the present.

Is this a new anthropology, truly *sans-culotte*, or only one that parades itself as such? Graham Watson (1987a) argues that the postmodern prescriptions do not solve the problem of reflexivity (there can be no solution, Watson claims) but conserve realist appeals to facticity and standard scholarly claims to authority. Paul Rabinow (1986) shows how historically naive about Western epistemology much of this critical literature is. When Marilyn Strathern (1987b:267) admits, seemingly with relief and perhaps even surprise, that the postmodern critique has not led to an ethnographic "jumble," should we not begin to worry about what it will lead to?

Consider the self-congratulation that the postmodern critique promotes under the guise of a disabling criticism. What conceit could be more satisfying to anthropologists than that their scholarly work—flawed though it may be—consists of doing and writing ethnographies? How better to satisfy our self-image as fieldworkers, above all, and to subsidize the fuzzy populism and reverse snobbery that often infuses that image?[2] The magic of fieldwork, the epiphany of the ethnographer, the sink-or-swim during an anthropological novitiate—all these antique conceits of anthropology are now embellished and modernized by an ostensibly self-critical reflexivity. The critique may make us aware of the "fictions," or narratives, that ethnographies represent, but its other message is that the production of anthropology still takes place through the same scholarly labor process by which our "ancestors" authorized the hallowed "anthropologyland" (to adapt a term from Bernard Cohn) we now inhabit—or put more honestly, the professional turf we (hope to) continue to control. By underwriting the craftsmanship of ethnographic writing, by representing field research as our "studio work," the postmodern critique coddles the artisan image by which we are deceived.

If self-reflection is to empower an anthropology of the present, then it must start not only by correcting the mystifications written into ethnographic texts but also by exposing the false consciousness that anthropologists often have about their scholarly work. The postmodern critique further ornaments, rather than redresses, the habit we anthropologists have of regarding ourselves as artisan workers, as independent craftsmen. Thus, it makes us aware of how artfully Evans-Pritchard first personified himself among the Nuer and then "disappeared" himself in favor of a scientific omniscience for the remainder of his text. The critique is silent, however, about how we mystify the nonartisan aspect of our labor—how we bury our funding sources in our texts even more carefully than we remove ourselves from the narrative. We only acknowledge the "support" (our preferred euphemism for "financing") of foundations and agencies in endnotes. Moreover, by showing the anthropologist to be too crafty an artisan—as, for example, in too neatly tying up the loose ends of culture into a realist ethnography—the critique willy-nilly reinforces our belief that such is our labor. Now all we need do is to reform our artisanship by a new consciousness based on postmodernism's own tropes: the End of Ideology (the demise of master narratives and grand theory) and the God That Failed (the failure of realist ethnography). Never mind new tools with which to craft different anthropologies. Never mind new work places—"shop floors" in which anthropologists should or must labor. Never mind the constraints upon how, where, and even whether we work. By ornamenting an artisan identity, the postmodern critique is idealistic about the future of anthropology (and therefore hardly pessimistic but most probably irresponsible). The craft of anthropology can continue to work in the world at present, it claims, if we adopt new mental templates. Anthropologists, like tapestry makers and rug weavers, need only select new cartoons.

A false consciousness about our scholarly labor can make us unrealistic about the work we have done and, at the same time, make us believe that we can do whatever comes to mind. Is anthropology at present an artisan craft, and was it ever one? If the answer is no, then the ethnographic field site, in the classic sense, was never the only work place in which anthropology was crafted. Yet we persist in a false and mystifying artisan identity—not only for ourselves, but even more strongly for the founding figures of anthropology, the Great Fathers in the Field.

For a very long time, this false consciousness has made us hostile to certain endeavors and fearful of others that we did not value as "real" anthropology. Consider our long-standing disdain for the "armchair" anthropologists of the late nineteenth century and the pejorative images we have of the ungrounded, "absentee" scholarship misproduced by these intellectual "rentiers." Those we now recognize as the heroes of the discipline labored overtime to promote an artisan identity for the fieldworking anthropologist: Malinowski all by himself fabricating a foreign world as he labored under detention; Boas single-handedly animating a museum diorama with the culture he collected. Have we learned too late from Ian Langham (1981) the truth about Radcliffe-Brown and his classic "fieldwork?" He actually collected Australian kinship terms from syphilitic aborigines forcibly interned in hospitals that were tantamount to mortuaries for them.

We should know better than to believe these myths that charter anthropology as artisanship. Ever since it became professionalized in the academy, the production of anthropology has come about not only through ethnographic craft, but also under "factory" conditions—for example, in university departments, at professional meetings, during academic conferences, and in libraries. We even admit the "industrial discipline" to be found in departments—teaching loads, tenure reviews, sabbatical policies, for example—and the way in which it sets conditions for the (non)production of anthropology. We comment adversely on the "time-motion" discipline enacted at major meetings: the ten-minute presentations in which we can say almost nothing, and the simultaneous sessions all of which we wish to attend. Do we really "craft" our next research project to NSF or NEH, or do we sell it?

Our images of such environments where factory production of anthropology takes place are invariably negative because they do not underwrite artisan images of anthropology. Instead, these other "shop floors" and the labor they require show us, in a way that the postmodern critique has not done, that we neither own nor control the means of our scholarly production. They thereby counter the notion that in the past we single-handedly created the context for our production and authority and that we are now at complete liberty to rewrite this context.

THE PRESENT WORK

The papers in this volume present radical views of the way in which anthropology gets produced in order to continue to produce it. Most of them begin by attacking what I have called the artisan image of anthropology, both in the past and at present. Some papers show the way in which the industry of anthropologists is disciplined outside of or away from the ethnographic work place. They then detail the effects on scholarship of these other sites of anthropology's production.

Michel-Rolph Trouillot argues that anthropology's construction of the Other was not, in fact, anthropology's own construction. Rather, anthropologists inherited a "savage slot" from Western philosophy and utopian thinking that long preexisted professional anthropology. Anthropology is constructed, and the labor of anthropologists disciplined by, the preexisting savage slot or definition of the Other, rather than vice versa. To castigate anthropology for its flawed construction of others, as the postmodern critique does, is fundamentally to misunderstand the agency and power directing our discipline; it is a curious instance of the victims blaming themselves.

Joan Vincent shows other ways in which the supposedly independent artisanship of the anthropologist is disciplined. A text, she urges, not only represents a politics in its contents, but it also works in a political context. This context conditions both the construction and the reception of the text. It decides which anthropology becomes authoritative and which discredited. If we try to read out the politics behind the production of anthropology by textual analysis alone, we miss the wider contemporary context in which an anthropology worked (or did not work). The postmodern critique, Vincent maintains, only substitutes texts without history for earlier anthropology's mistaken creation of people without history.

Another point of production for anthropology—the place especially important for the production of its current malaise—is in the demographics and micropractices of the academy, so Paul Rabinow argues. He shows that the generation of anthropologists now nearing retirement age, empowered by their seniority, face difficult decisions between "simple" reproduction of themselves or "expanded" reproduction of scholarship. Rabinow indicates the way in which the micropractices of the academy—for example, the practices surrounding a job candidate's visit—often secrete issues such as "who we anthropologists are and what should we become" in a habitus of conventional performance and evaluation. Rabinow thus offers a specific case of the contemporary conditions that Vincent argues give history (or deny it) to texts and theories in anthropology.

Graham Watson provides a case of what may get hidden under these micropractices: he calls attention to a scholarship that is curiously excluded from the postmodern critique's shortlist, namely, ethnomethodology. Watson argues that ethnomethodologists have contended with the construction of knowledge and other issues that concern postmodernists, but they did so earlier and in a more radical fashion. He is not inclined to explain the postmodernists' myopia in terms of the politics and micropractices set forth by Vincent or Rabinow or in terms of the compelling cultural category, the savage slot, argued for by Trouillot. Instead, Watson sees it as the result of the way in which anthropologists have gone about constructing their knowledge. This constructive labor, however, goes on within a larger scholarly workplace—one in which, Watson notes, the accumulation of academic capital depends at times on keeping competitive ideas out of the marketplace.

My paper gives another example of how the production of anthropology gets hidden under the artisan identity we have come to accept. I focus on "anthropologists without history," that is, an anthropology that has become as stereotyped, essentialized, and therefore deauthorized as any aborigine or indigene experienced in the works of classic ethnography. Boasian culture history, I assert, produced an anthropology that did not depend on ethnographic texts and that agonized over issues other than the Other. Its theme was the relationship between individual creativity and cultural constitution, not the grand encounter of the West with the rest.

The papers by Vincent, Fox, and Watson, then, give examples of those who, besides our interlocutors in the field, may be silenced as anthropology gets produced. By understanding the production of anthropology as involving industry, not just craft, we must also allow for sabotage, piracy, and espionage. Once these anthropologies are heard out, the three papers suggest, they can serve as new tools for the production of anthropology at present. The remaining papers carry on this effort.

José Limón discusses still another old, but generally unrecognized, tool in anthropology, one that most anthropologists do not craft themselves but are given—indeed, cannot refuse—and therefore one not fully under their control. This tool usually goes unrecognized by a textual critique. Limón shows the way in which what he calls "precursory ethnographies" are important parts of the scholarly machinery with which he has had to work. Whether these ethnographies are vilifications or glorifications, they mark off a work space that cannot be ignored in successor ethnographies. Limón poignantly describes his significant predecessor, Paredes, whose work championed the Mexican-American folk ballad as a vehicle of identity and resistance. Working with Paredes's celebration of the ballad, Limón discovered to his dismay, meant devaluing present-day Mexican-American music and dance. Limón turned to a new work place, the working-class dance hall, to find himself, but also to escape Paredes.

Lila Abu-Lughod also discusses an old tool in anthropology, but one much more familiar: the concept of culture. It, too, is not entirely of our making and certainly no longer under our exclusive control. In fact, anthropologists, Abu-Lughod insists, would do well to become alienated from this product of our labor, because then we would better realize the inequalities, dominations, and Orientalisms built into it. Since the culture concept depends on distinguishing self from other, Abu-Lughod believes that those anthropologists whose own identities confuse self and other—feminists and ethnic "halfies"—have a new tool with which to work out of the culture concept. She also suggests that anthropologists must transform their old workplaces, the ethnographic field locale, by writing "against culture" in it. This means writing about the everyday life of persons, not the cultural life of a people.

Sherry Ortner's paper also works from the distinction of self and other to define a new workplace for anthropology. We can best determine the inequalities and essentialisms built into anthropology's concept of the Other if we look at the way anthropology and its culture concept have been applied to ourselves. For Ortner, studying self works out to ethnography in New Jersey, among her former high-school classmates. Anticipating that study, she reviews in this paper what previous anthropologies of America did not say about ourselves, perhaps because they employed the concept of the Other. Ortner finds them remarkably silent on class relations but loud to report the division of society by gender and ethnicity—not at all by chance, she insists, because these two forms of social classification rest on the divisions of self and other with which anthropology likes to operate.

Arjun Appadurai suggests still another new workplace for anthropology. Arguing from personal experience that global processes now flow through the most localized of events, he wishes anthropologists to work on "ethnoscapes"—what, in effect, we live in nowadays. These ethnoscapes are new territories for the anthropologist, quite unlike the communities or societies we thought, once upon a time, we could encompass. Partly realized through global immigration, partly imagined through media exposure worldwide, these new points of production for anthropology, Appadurai persuades us, require a "macro-" or cosmopolitan ethnography. Such an ethnography would recognize that everyday life is now lived out globally and that the small community is the end point of a cultural jet stream. Starting from this new workplace, Appadurai then works back to the tools we will need for it. He suggests, for example, that we start with present ethnoscapes and work backward in time. In that way, we will be able to distinguish "genealogies," the local cultural patterns that provide spaces for global cultural forms, from "histories," the global processes that provide these forms.

WORK FOR THE PRESENT

Our papers give nine distinct versions of how and where anthropology might work today. During our seminar discussions, it became clear, however, that our individual approaches overlay a shared concern. We kept converging on the question, what can anthropology and anthropologists do to maintain or regain authority at present? Not one of us recommended a textualist strategy, that is, the crafting of "polyphonic," "dialogic," or other experimental formats. Instead, we argued about how anthropology could best "reenter" the real world (as Trouillot put it) or "recapture" (as I would say) the progressive character its basic concepts, like "culture," once had (see Fox 1985 and Kahn 1989 for critiques of reactionary uses of the culture concept).

"Reentry" and "recapture" helped remind us of the constraints operating on anthropology in the present. We are not completely free to work up radically new texts or whatever else comes to mind, as the postmodernists sometimes seem to suggest. We must reenter a world not of our making—one that, more likely, has made us. We must recapture our concepts when they have been imperialized by other disciplines or misconstructed in the world (as well as among ourselves), as happened earlier with the concept of "race." Recapture and reentry require an active confrontation with what we have become or what we have been made into at present; they are not furthered by an escapist postmodernism that proceeds as if admissions of guilt in the past could vouchsafe perfection in the future. Recaptured authority, instead, will depend on recognizing that our anthropology labors under an existing intellectual discipline, with many predecessory texts, and with a senior professional workforce so beset with doubt about its future reproduction that this fear alone often stymies productivity at present.

In determining strategies for recapturing anthropology's authority, we considered the following questions: Which came first, anthropology or the Other? Where should we initiate recapture: within the discipline of anthropology or outside it? Which concepts of anthropology should we try to recapture and which should we discard? Where will the struggle for recapture take place, how will it go on, and what are its chances of success? Underlying these questions was a general point. There is a complex and not yet fully uncovered history to anthropology's present condition, and depending on what stage or horizon we select to expose, we come upon different strategies for the present.

For illustration, let me begin with Trouillot's argument that the savage was a preexisting Western cultural category merely confirmed by anthropology. What Trouillot uncovers from the past surfaces in Appadurai's account of the present. When Appadurai urges anthropologists to recognize the ethnoscapes being created globally today, he acknowledges another world presently threatening to go beyond our scholarly capacities, a world that is remaking us whether or not we are willing. Both Trouillot and Appadurai portray an anthropology whose authority was (and will be) delegated by the world, rather than asserted in the profession. For them, reentry comes from an interested discovery of the world and its assertions, rather than from a critical exegesis of anthropology's texts and their professional claims.

Nevertheless, once in existence and suitably professionalized, anthropology and its culture concept could further confirm the savage slot, as Abu-Lughod argues, by attaching scientific authority to corrupted representations of others. Ortner gives a good example of this process when she contends that anthropology's concept of otherness, however it came about, made class a missing link in scholarship on America. Ortner's desire to get underneath an analysis based on gender, race, or ethnicity is another admonition to anthropologists that the culture concept has been grossly overworked. For Abu-Lughod, we are already too late to recapture a concept like culture; it is better to put it to rest and reenter the world as freshly as we can. Limón illuminates an equally unfortunate overuse of the culture concept: Paredes's concept of culture led him to judge present-day Mexican-American dance as corrupted and unauthentic, even though it serves as a "weapon of the weak." Limón confronted his predecessor's work, stripped romanticism and the overvaluation of the authentic from the culture concept he found in that work—and thereby recaptured the concept of culture.

How, then, can we begin the work of recapturing anthropology's authority? Trouillot's strategy, as I noted earlier, is to start outside anthropology, to unearth the regrettable history by which the culture concept validated a preexisting savage slot. Abu-Lughod suggests internal reform for our initial effort: we should fashion new tools within the field. Vincent hopes that we follow a mixture of these strategies, recognizing that anthropologists make something of the world, as in their construction of knowledge, but also understanding that they are made something (or nothing) by the world, as in the reception or refusal of their knowledge. Vincent, like Trouillot, believes that uncovering the past can recapture the present, but, along with Abu-Lughod, she thinks the effort has to be made first within the field, by exposing its history.

Appadurai and I suggest that anthropology may have to recapture authority by letting go of a diminished view of ethnography. We ask whether it is possible or even worthwhile to try to recapture ethnography from the "condescending veneration" that the postmodernists have accorded it. Appadurai's reentry for anthropology is global and transnational, letting the present world remake us and our concepts of fieldwork, cross-cultural comparison, and community. I also wish to retire ethnography, but I argue that one way to recapture authority is to return to culture history—a kind of anthropology that existed before ethnography exercised exclusive empire, that once had something important to say about the world, and that could be retooled to say something about the present.

Where will the struggle for recapture take place, and what are the odds on its success? Watson appears to be the most optimistic that direct intellectual competition can succeed, and he makes such a contest the very business of his paper. Limón shows the special circumstances of competition with a respected predecessor that led him to recapture the cultural resistance built into Mexican-American dancing. Vincent, although she is more concerned about the way in which political struggles determine the sorts of anthropologies that survive, is also cautiously optimistic that studying such past struggles will steady us at present.

Rabinow seems the least optimistic about the outcome of the struggle for recapture, perhaps because he locates it in the micropractices of the profession. It is a good deal easier to uncover the history of Western conceptions of otherness, as Trouillot wishes; or bare the hidden politics behind texts, as Vincent suggests; or write new narratives, as Abu-Lughod, Appadurai, and I want; or find new views of self by peeling off layers of otherness, as Ortner and Limón desire, than it is to reform the way in which job candidates are shortlisted, then wined and barbecued. Yet it is precisely the assembly line for reproducing anthropology that Rabinow exposes. Like Trouillot and Appadurai, Rabinow reminds us that there is a world in which anthropology operates and to which it must respond, quite apart from producing texts as claims to authority. Rabinow's world is so everyday and habitual, and yet so hegemonic, that it appears inescapable and nearly incontrovertible. Confrontations between "top candidates" and senior faculty are more likely to give rise to new rankings of the candidates and indigestion at the recruitment dinners than to recapture or reentry.

Perhaps, then, writing against culture, digging up the archaeology of anthropology, reenchanting the profession, globalizing the discipline, making it cultural-historical, revisiting the self, recognizing the predecessor, battling for ethnomethodology, or any of the other means of recapturing authority we suggest will only be labor lost. Perhaps, in a nightmarish vindication of Marvin Harris's cultural materialism, an anthropology of the present will only come about courtesy of a demographic transition—the mass retirement of the "elders" late in the twentieth century. The contributors to this volume and, I suspect, many other anthropologists, do not intend to be so patient.

Our industry in Santa Fe and in this volume is not only a matter of personal craft. We depended on a particular work place, the School of American Research, which hosted this seminar, and on the labors of Jonathan Haas, Douglas Schwartz, Jane Kepp, and Jane Barberousse before, during, and after the seminar. I thank them for their help and hospitality. This introduction has benefited greatly from critical readings by the other participants in the seminar and by Sidney Mintz, Jane Kepp, and Ernestine Friedl, to all of whom I am grateful. I also wish to thank the John Simon Guggenheim Memorial Foundation and the National Endowment for the Humanities, which provided support during the time I wrote the original proposal for the advanced seminar, and the Wenner-Gren Foundation for Anthropological Research, which provided funding for the participants' travel.

──────── *Notes* ────────

1. For the concept of the predecessory ethnography and ethnographer, see José Limón's paper in this volume.

2. Compare LaCapra's (1985:91) criticism of Darnton's "history in the ethnographic grain": "Darnton's binary opposition between the armchair and the archives recalls the tendentious contrast drawn by certain anthropologists between 'armchair' theorizing and fieldwork. In anthropology, this contrast has often fostered a self-mystified understanding of fieldwork as untouched by theory and in closest proximity to 'authentic' native experience—fieldwork as the virginally pure 'real thing'."

Chapter 2

ANTHROPOLOGY

AND THE SAVAGE SLOT

The Poetics and Politics of Otherness

Michel-Rolph Trouillot

ANTHROPOLOGY faces an unprecedented wave of challenges that require an archaeology of the discipline and a careful examination of its implicit premises. The postmodernist critique of anthropology, which is now the most vocal and direct response to these challenges in the United States, falls short of building that archaeology because it tends to treat the discipline as a closed discourse. In contradistinction, I contend that the internal tropes of anthropology matter much less than the larger discursive field within which anthropology operates and upon whose existence it is premised. A cultural critique of anthropology requires a historicization of that entire field. New directions will come only from the new vantage points discovered through such a critique.

CHALLENGES AND OPPORTUNITIES

Academic disciplines do not create their fields of significance, they only legitimize particular organizations of meaning. They filter and rank—and in that sense, they truly *discipline*—contested arguments and themes that often precede them. In doing so, they continuously expand, restrict, or modify in diverse ways their distinctive arsenals of tropes, the types of statements they deem acceptable. But the poetics and politics of the "slots" within which disciplines operate do not dictate the enunciative relevance of these slots. There is no direct correlation between the "electoral politics" of a discipline and its political relevance. By "electoral politics," I mean the set of institutionalized practices and relations of power that influence the production of knowledge from within academe: academic filiations, the mechanisms of institutionalization, the organization of power within and across departments, the market value of publish-or-perish prestige, and other worldly issues that include, but expand way beyond, the maneuvering we usually refer to as "academic politics." Changes in the types of statements produced as "acceptable" within a discipline, regulated as they are—if only in part—by these "electoral politics," do not necessarily modify the larger field of operation, and especially the enunciative context of that discipline. Changes in the explicit criteria of acceptability do not automatically relieve the historical weight of the field of significance that the discipline inherited at birth. More likely, the burden of the past is alleviated when the sociohistorical conditions that obtained at the time of emergence have changed so much that practitioners face a choice between complete oblivion and fundamental redirection. At one point in time, alchemists become chemists or cease to be—but the transformation is one that few alchemists can predict and even fewer would wish.

Anthropology is no exception to this scenario. Like all academic disciplines, it inherited a field of significance that preceded its formalization. Like many of the human sciences, it now faces dramatically new historical conditions of performance. Like any discourse, it can find new directions only if it modifies the boundaries within which it operates. These boundaries not only predated the emergence of anthropology as a discipline, but they also prescribed anthropology's role (and ethnography's ultimate relevance) to an extent not yet unveiled. Anthropology fills a preestablished compartment within a wider symbolic field, the "savage" slot of a thematic trilogy that helped to constitute the West as we know it. A critical and reflexive anthropology requires, beyond the self-indulgent condemnation of traditional techniques and tropes, a reappraisal of this symbolic organization upon which anthropological discourse is premised.

Anthropology's future depends much on its ability to contest the savage slot and the *thématique* that constructs this slot. The times are ripe for such questioning. More important, solutions that fall short of this challenge can only push the discipline toward irrelevance, however much they may reflect serious concerns. In that light, current calls for reflexivity in the United States are not products of chance, the casual convergence of individual projects. Neither are they a passing fad, the accidental effect of debates that stormed philosophy and literary theory.[1] Rather, they are timid, spontaneous—and in that sense genuinely American—responses to major changes in the relations between anthropology and the wider world, provincial expressions of wider concerns, allusions to opportunities yet to be seized. What are those changes? What are these concerns? What are the opportunities?

On sheer empirical grounds, the differences between Western and non-Western societies are blurrier than ever before. Anthropology's answer to this ongoing transformation has been typically ad hoc and haphazard. The criteria according to which certain populations are deemed legitimate objects of research continue to vary with departments, with granting agencies, with practitioners, and even with the mood shifts of individual researchers. Amid the confusion, more anthropologists reenter the West cautiously, through the back door, after paying their dues elsewhere. By and large this reentry is no better theorized than were previous departures for faraway lands.[2]

While some anthropologists are rediscovering the West without ever naming it, what "the West" stands for is itself an object of debate, within and outside the gates of academe. The reactionary search for a fundamental Western corpus of "great texts" by many intellectuals and bureaucrats in the English-speaking world is both the reflection of a wider conflict and a particular response to the uncertainties stirred by this conflict. Interestingly, few anthropologists have intervened in that debate. Fewer even among those thought to be at the forefront of the discipline have deigned to address directly the issue of Western monumentalism, with one or two exceptions (e.g., Rosaldo 1989). Even more interestingly, anthropological *theory* remains irrelevant to—and unused by—either side of the "great texts" debate, rhetorical references notwithstanding. Today, the statement that any canon necessarily eliminates an unspecified set of experiences need not come only from anthropology—thanks, of course, to the past diffusion of anthropology itself, but thanks especially to changes in the world and to the experiences that express and motivate these changes. Minorities of all kinds can and do voice their cultural claims, not on the basis of explicit theories of culture but in the name of historical authenticity. They enter the debate not as academics—or not only as academics—but as situated individuals with rights to historicity. They speak in the first person, signing their arguments with an "I" or a "we," rather than invoking the ahistorical voice of reason, justice, or civilization.

Anthropology is caught off guard by this reformulation. Traditionally, it approached the issue of cultural differences with a monopoly over native discourse, hypocritically aware that this discourse would remain a quote. It is too liberal to accept either the radical authenticity of the first person or the conservative reversion to canonical truths—hence, its theoretical silence.

Here again, silence seems to me a hasty abdication. At the very least, anthropology should be able to illuminate the myth of an unquestioned Western canon upon which the debate is premised.[3] In doing so, it would certainly undermine some of its own premises; but that risk is an inherent aspect of the current wave of challenges: its numerous opportunities are inseparable from its multiple threats. Nowhere is this combination of threats and opportunities as blatant as in the postmodern admission that the metanarratives of the West are crumbling.

THE FALL OF THE HOUSE OF REASON

Whatever else postmodernism means, it remains inseparable from the acknowledgment of an ongoing collapse of metanarratives in a world where reason and reality have become fundamentally destabilized (Lyotard 1979, 1986).[4] To be sure, the related claim (Tyler 1986:123) that "the world that made science, and that science made, has disappeared" is somewhat premature. The growing awareness among literati that rationality has not fulfilled its promises to uncover the absolute becoming of the spirit does not alter the increasing institutionalization of rationality itself (Godzich 1986:xvii–xix). Indeed, one could argue that the spectacular failure of science and reason, judged on the universal grounds that scholars love to emphasize, serves to mask success on more practical and localized terrains into which academics rarely venture.

But if the world that science made is very much alive, the world that made science is now shaky. The crisis of the nation-state, the crisis of the individual, the crisis of the parties of order (liberal, authoritarian, or communist), terrorism, the crisis of "late capitalism"—all contribute to a Western malaise and, in turn, feed upon it (Aronowitz 1988; Jameson 1984). Philosophers reportedly asked: can one *think* after Auschwitz? But it took some time for Auschwitz to sink in, for communism to reveal its own nightmares, for structuralism to demonstrate its magisterial impasse, for North and South to admit the impossibility of dialogue, for fundamentalists of all denominations to desacralize religion, and for reenlightened intellectuals to question all foundational thought. As the walls crumbled—North and South and East and West—intellectuals developed languages of postdestruction. It is this mixture of negative intellectual surprise, this postmortem of the metanarratives, that situates the postmodernist mood as primarily Western and primarily petit bourgeois.

These words are not inherently pejorative, but they are meant to historicize the phenomenon—an important exercise if we intend to have cross-cultural relevance. First, it is not self-evident that all past and present cultures required metanarratives up to their current entry into postmodernity. Second, if only the collapse of metanarratives characterized the postmodern condition, then some of the non-Western cultures that have been busily deconstructing theirs for centuries, or that have gone through megacollapses of their own, have long been "postmodern," and there is nothing new under the sun. Things fell apart quite early on the southern shores of the Atlantic, and later in the hinterlands of Africa, Asia, and the Americas. Third, even if we concede, for the sake of argument, that metanarratives once were a prerequisite of humankind and are now collapsing everywhere at equal rates (two major assumptions, indeed), we cannot infer identical reactive strategies to this collapse.

Thus, we must distinguish between postmodernism, as a mood, and the recognition of a situation of postmodernity. The acknowledgment that there is indeed a crisis of representation, that there is indeed an ongoing set of qualitative changes in the international organization of symbols (Appadurai, this volume), in the rhythms of symbolic construction (Harvey 1989), and in the ways symbols relate to localized, subjective experience, does not in itself require a postmortem. In that light, the key to the dominant versions of postmodernism is an ongoing destruction lived as shock and revelation. Postmodernism builds on this revelation of the sudden disappearance of established rules, foundational judgments, and known categories (Lyotard 1986:33). But the very fact of revelation implies a previous attitude toward such rules, judgments, and categories—for instance, that they have been taken for granted or as immutable. The postmortem inherent in the postmodernist mood implies a previous "world of universals" (Ross 1988a:xii–xiii). It implies a specific view of culture and of culture change. It implies, at least in part, the Enlightenment and nineteenth-century Europe.

In cross-cultural perspective, the dominant mood of postmodernism thus appears as a historically specific phenomenon, a reaction provoked by the revelation that the Enlightenment and its conflicting tributaries may have run their course. This mood is not inherent in the current world situation, but neither is it a passing ambience, as many of the postmodernists' detractors would have—even though it ushers in fads of its own. It is a mood in the strong sense in which Geertz (1973b:90) defines religious moods: powerful, persuasive, and promising endurance. But contrary to religions, it rejects both the pretense of factuality and the aspiration to realistic motivations. It seeks a "psychoanalytic therapeutic" from the "modern neurosis," the "Western schizophrenia, paranoia, etc., all the sources of misery we have known for two centuries" (Lyotard 1986:125–26).

"We," here, *is* the West, as in Michael Jackson and Lionel Ritchie's international hit, "We Are the World." This is not "the West" in a genealogical or territorial sense. The postmodern world has little space left for genealogies, and notions of territoriality are being redefined right before our eyes (Appadurai, this volume). It is a world where black American Michael Jackson starts an international tour from Japan and imprints cassettes that mark the rhythm of Haitian peasant families in the Cuban Sierra Maestra; a world where Florida speaks Spanish (once more); where a Socialist prime minister in Greece comes by way of New England and an imam of fundamentalist Iran by way of Paris. It is a world where a political leader in reggae-prone Jamaica traces his roots to Arabia, where U.S. credit cards are processed in Barbados, and Italian designer shoes made in Hong Kong. It is a world where the Pope is Polish, where the most orthodox Marxists live on the western side of a fallen iron curtain. It is a world where the most enlightened are only part-time citizens of part-time communities of imagination.

But these very phenomena—and their inherent connection with the expansion of what we conveniently call the West—are part of the text that reveals the dominant mood as eventuating from a Western *problématique*. The perception of a collapse as revelation cannot be envisioned outside of the trajectory of thought that has marked the West and spread unevenly outside of its expanding boundaries. Its conditions of existence coalesce within the West. The stance it spawns is unthinkable outside of the West, and has significance only within the boundaries set by the West.

If the postmodern mood is fundamentally Western in the global sense delineated above, what does this mean for an anthropology of the present? First, it means that the present that anthropologists must confront is the product of a particular past that encompasses the history and the prehistory of anthropology itself. Second and consequently, it means that the postmodernist critique within North American anthropology remains, so far, within the very thematic field that it claims to challenge. Third, it means that a truly critical and reflexive anthropology needs to contextualize the Western metanarratives and read critically the place of the discipline in the field so discovered. In short, anthropology needs to turn the apparatus elaborated in the observation of non-Western societies on itself and, more specifically, on the history from which it sprang. That history does not start with the formalization of the discipline, but with the emergence of the symbolic field that made this formalization possible.

THE SAVAGE AND THE INNOCENT

In 1492, Christopher Columbus stumbled upon the Caribbean. The admiral's mistake would later be heralded as "The Discovery of America," the quincentennial of which two worlds will soon celebrate. To be sure, it took Balboa's sighting of the Pacific in 1513 to verify the existence of a continental mass, and Vespucci's insistence on a *mundus novus* for Christendom to acknowledge this "discovery." Then it took another fifty years to realize its symbolic significance. Yet 1492 was, to some extent, a discovery even then, the first material step in a continuously renewed process of invention (Ainsa 1988). Abandoning one lake for another, Europe confirmed the sociopolitical fissure that was slowly pushing the Mediterranean toward northern and southern shores. In so doing, it created itself, but it also discovered America, its still unpolished alter ego, its elsewhere, its other. The Conquest of America stands as Europe's model for the constitution of the Other (Todorov 1982; Ainsa 1988).

Yet from the beginning, the model was Janus-faced. The year 1516 saw the publication of two anthropological precursors: the Alcalá edition of the *Decades* of Pietro Martire d'Anghiera (a paraethnographic account of the Antilles, and in many ways one of Europe's earliest introductions to a "state of nature" elsewhere) and one more popular edition of Amerigo Vespucci's epistolary travel accounts. In that same year too, Thomas More published his fictional account of an "ideal state" on the island of *Utopia*, the prototypical nowhere of European imagination.

The chronological coincidence of these publications, fortuitous as it may be, symbolizes a thematic correspondence now blurred by intellectual specialization and the abuse of categories. We now claim to distinguish clearly between travelers' accounts, colonial surveys, ethnographic reports, and fictional utopias. Such cataloging is useful, but only to some extent. In the early sixteenth century, European descriptions of an alleged state of nature in the realist mode filled the writings of colonial officers concerned with the immediate management of the Other. The realist mode also pervaded travelers' accounts of the sixteenth and seventeenth centuries, before settling in the privileged space of learned discourse with eighteenth-century philosophers and the nineteenth-century rise of armchair anthropology. Even then, the line between these genres was not always clear-cut (Thornton 1983; Weil 1984). The realist mode also pervaded fiction—so much so that some twentieth-century critics distinguish between utopias and "extraordinary voyages," or trips to the lands of nowhere with the most "realistic" geographical settings. On the other hand, fantasies about an ideal state increased in fiction, but they also found their way into theater, songs, and philosophical treatises.

In short, classifications notwithstanding, the connection between a state of nature and an ideal state is, to a large extent, in the symbolic construction of the materials themselves. The symbolic transformation through which Christendom became the West structures a set of relations that necessitate both utopia and the savage. What happens within the slots so created—and within the genres that condition their historical existence—is not inconsequential. But the analysis of these genres cannot explain the slots nor even the internal tropes of such slots. To wit, "utopia" has been the most studied form of this ensemble, yet there is no final agreement on which works to include in the category (Atkinson 1920, 1922; Andrews 1937; Trousson 1975; Manuel and Manuel 1979; Eliav-Feldon 1982; Kamenka 1987). Further, when reached, agreement is often ephemeral. Even if one could posit a continuum from realist ethnography to fictional utopias, works move in and out of these categories, and categories often overlap on textual and nontextual grounds. Finally, textuality is rarely the final criterion of inclusion or exclusion. From the 200-year-long controversy about the *Voyage et aventures de François Leguat* (a 1708 best-seller believed by some to be a true account and by others, a work of fiction) to the Castañeda embarrassment to professional anthropology and the more recent debates on *Shabono* or the existence of the Tasaday, myriad cases indicate the ultimate relevance of issues outside of "the text" proper (Atkinson 1922; Weil 1984; Pratt 1986).

That the actual corpus fitting any of these genres at any given period has never been unproblematic underscores a thematic correspondence that has survived the increasingly refined categorizations. In the 1500s, readers could not fail to notice the similarities between works such as Jacques Cartier's *Brief Récit*, which features paraethnographic descriptions of Indians, and some of Rabelais's scenes in *Gargantua*. Montaigne, an observant traveler himself within the confines of Europe, used descriptions of America to set for his readers issues in philosophical anthropology—and in the famous essay "Des cannibales," he is quick to point out the major difference between his enterprise and that of his Greek predecessors, including Plato: the Greeks had no realistic database (Montaigne 1952). Early in the seventeenth century, Tommaso Campanella produced his *Citta del sole* (1602), informed by descriptions that Portuguese missionaries and Dutch mercenaries were bringing back from Ceylon and by Jesuit reports of socialism within the Inca kingdom.

Utopias were both rare and inferior—by earlier and later standards—during the seventeenth century. Few are now remembered other than those of Campanella, Bacon, and Fénelon. But the search for an exotic ideal had not died, as some authors (Trousson 1975) seem to suggest. Fénelon's *Aventures de Télémaque* went into twenty printings. The *History of the Sevarites* of Denis Vairasse d'Alais (1677–79) was published originally in English, then in a French version that spurred German, Dutch, and Italian translations (Atkinson 1920). Utopias did not quench the thirst for fantasy lands, but only because relative demand had increased unexpectedly.

Travel accounts, of which the numbers kept multiplying, helped fill this increased demand for the elsewhere. Some did so with reports of unicorns and floating isles, then accepted as reality by their public, including some of the most respected scholars of the time. But most did so with what were "realist" pictures of the savage, pictures that would pass twentieth-century tests of accuracy and are still being used by historians and anthropologists. Du Tertre (1667), Labat (1722), and Gage (1648)— to take only a few recognizable authors writing on one hemisphere— familiarized readers with the wonders of the Antilles and the American mainland.

Outside of a restricted group of overzealous scholars and administrators, it mattered little to the larger European audience whether such works were fictitious or not. That they presented an elsewhere was enough. That the elsewhere was actually somewhere was a matter for a few specialists. The dream remained alive well into the next century. Montesquieu was so much aware of this implicit correspondence that he gambled on reversing all the traditions at the same time, with considerable aesthetic and didactic effect, in his *Lettres persanes* (1721). The elsewhere became Paris; the Other became French; the utopia became a well-known state of affairs. It worked, because everyone recognized the models and understood the parody.

The thematic correspondence between utopias and travel accounts or paraethnographic descriptions was not well camouflaged until the end of the eighteenth century. The forms continued to diverge, while the number of publications within each category kept increasing. Utopias filled the century that gave us the Enlightenment, from Swift's parodic *Gulliver's Travels* (1702) to Bernadin de Saint-Pierre's unfinished *L'amazone* (1795). But so did realistic descriptions of faraway peoples, and so did, moreover, cross-national debates in Europe on what exactly those descriptions meant for the rational knowledge of humankind. In the single decade of the 1760s, England alone sent expeditions like those of Commodore Byron, Captains Cartwright, Bruce, Furneaux, and Wallis, and Lieutenant Cook to savage lands all over the world. Bruce, Wallis, and Cook brought home reports from Abyssinia, Tahiti, and Hawaii. Byron and his companions carried back accounts "of a race of splendid giants" from Patagonia. Cartwright returned with five living Eskimos who caused a commotion in the streets of London (Tinker 1922:5–25).

Scholars devoured such "realistic" data on the savage with a still unsurpassed interest, while writing didactic utopias and exploring in their philosophical treatises the rational revelation behind the discoveries of the travelers. Voltaire, who read voraciously the travel descriptions of his time, gave us *Candide* and "Zadig." But he also used paraethnographic descriptions to participate in anthropological debates of his time, siding for instance with the Göttingen school on polygenesis (Duchet 1971). Diderot, who may have read more travel accounts than anyone then alive, and who turned many of them in paraethnographic descriptions for the *Encyclopédie*, wrote two utopias true to form.[5] Rousseau, whom Lévi-Strauss called "the father of ethnology," sought the most orderly link between "the state of nature" first described by Martire d'Anghiera and the "ideal commonwealth" envisioned by More and his followers. He thus formalized the myth of the "noble savage," renewing a theme that went back not only to Pope and Defoe, but to obscure travelers of the sixteenth and seventeenth centuries. Long before Rousseau's *Social Contract*, Pietro Martire already thought that the Arawak of the Antilles were sweet and simple. Magellan's companion, Pigafetta, claimed in 1522 that the Indians of Brazil were "*creduli e boni*" by instinct. And Pierre Boucher, writing of the Iroquois in 1664, had confirmed that "*tous les Sauuages ont l'esprit bon*" (Gonnard 1946:36; Atkinson 1920:65–70).

The myth of the noble savage is not a creation of the Enlightenment. Ever since the West became the West, Robinson has been looking for Friday. The eighteenth century was not even the first to see arguments on or around that myth (Gonnard 1946). The verbal duel between Las Casas and Sepúlveda on the "nature" of the Indians and the justice of their enslavement, fought at Valladolid in the early 1550s in front of Spain's intellectual nobility, was as spectacular as anything the Enlightenment could imagine (André-Vincent 1980; Pagden 1982). Rather, the specificity of eighteenth-century anthropological philosophers was to dismiss some of the past limitations of this grandiose controversy and to claim to resolve it not on the basis of the Scriptures, but on the open grounds of rationality and experience. But the debate was always implicit in the thematic concordance that had tied the observation of the savage and the hopes of utopia since at least 1516. Swiss writer Isaac Iselin, a leading voice of the Göttingen school of anthropology, criticized Rousseau's ideals and the state of savagery as "disorderly fantasy" (Rupp-Eisenreich 1984: 99). The fact that the Göttingen school did not much bother to verify its own "ethnographic" bases, or that it used travelers' accounts for other purposes than Rousseau's (Rupp-Eisenreich 1985), matters less than the fact that Rousseau, Iselin, Meiners, and De Gerando shared the same premises on the relevance of savagery. For Rousseau, as for More and Defoe, the savage is an argument for a particular kind of utopia. For Iselin and Meiners, as for Swift and Hobbes in other times and contexts, it is an argument against it. Given the tradition of the genre being used, the formal terrain of battle, and the personal taste of the author, the argument was either tacit or explicit and the savage's face either sketched or magnified. But argument there was.

The nineteenth century blurred the most visible signs of this thematic correspondence by artificially separating utopia and the savage. To schematize a protracted and contested process: it is as if that century of specialization subdivided the Other that the Renaissance had set forth in creating the West. From then on, utopia and the savage evolved as two distinguishable slots. Kant had set the philosophical grounds for this separation by laying his own teleology without humor or fiction while moving away from the *Naturinstink*. Nineteenth-century French positivists, in turn, derided utopias as chimeric utopianisms (Manuel and Manuel 1979).

The growing fictional literature in the United States also modified the forms of utopia (Pfaelzer 1984). To start with, America had been the imagined site of traditional utopias, Tocqueville's *feuille blanche*, the land of all (im)possibilities. Defining an elsewhere from this site was a dilemma. Ideally, its Eden was within itself (Walkover 1974). Not surprisingly, William Dean Howells brings *A Traveler from Altruria* to the United States before sending his readers back to utopia. Edward Bellamy chose to look "backward." More important, America's savages and its colonized were also within itself: American Indians and black Americans, only one of whom white anthropologists dared to study before the latter part of this century (Mintz 1971, 1990). With two groups of savages to pick from, specialization set in, and Indians (especially "good" Indians) became the preserve of anthropologists.

At the same time, a black utopia was unthinkable, given the character of North American racism and the fabric of black/white imagery in

American literature (Levin 1967). Thus the black pastoral (the unmatched apex of which is *Uncle Tom's Cabin* [1851]—but note that the flavor is also in Faulkner) played the role that *Paul et Virginie* had played earlier in European imagination.[6] But true-to-form utopia writers in North America moved away from the specter of savagery.

Other factors were at play. The nineteenth century was America's century of concreteness, when its utopias became reachable. Of the reported 52 million migrants who left Europe between 1824 and 1924, more than ninety percent went to the Americas, mostly to the United States. In the United States, and in Europe as well, decreasing exchange among writers, who were involved in different forms of discourse and seeking legitimacy on different grounds, contributed even more to giving each group of practitioners the sentiment that they were carrying on a different enterprise. As they believed their practice and practiced their beliefs, the enterprises indeed became separated, but only to a certain extent. By the end of the nineteenth century, utopian novelists accentuated formal interests while utopianisms were acknowledged primarily as doctrines couched in non-fictional terms: Saint-Simonism, Fabian Socialism, Marxism (Gonnard 1946). Travel accounts came to pass as a totally separate genre, however Robinson-like some remained. The "scientific" study of the savage qua savage became the privileged field of academic anthropology, soon to be anchored in distinguished chairs, but already severed from its imaginary counterpart.

The rest of the story is well known, perhaps too well known, inasmuch as the insistence on the methods and tropes of anthropology as discipline may obscure the larger discursive order that made sense of its institutionalization. Histories that fail to problematize this institutionalization—and critiques premised on that naive history—necessarily fall short of illuminating the enunciative context of anthropological discourse. To be sure, anthropologists to this day keep telling both undergraduates and lay readers that their practice is useful to better understand "ourselves," but without ever spelling exactly the specifics of this understanding, the utopias behind this curiosity turned profession.

It has often been said that the savage or the primitive was the alter ego the West constructed for itself. What has not been emphasized enough is that this Other was a Janus, of whom the savage was only the second face.[7] The first face was the West itself, but the West fancifully constructed as a utopian projection and meant to be, in that imaginary correspondence, the condition of existence of the savage.

This thematic correspondence preceded the institutionalization of anthropology as a specialized field of inquiry. Better said, *the constitutive moment of ethnography as metaphor antedates the constitution of anthropology as discipline* and even precedes its solidification as specialized discourse. The dominant metamorphosis, the transformation of savagery into sameness by way of utopia as positive or negative reference, is not the outcome of a textual exercise within the anthropological practice, but part of anthropology's original conditions of existence. Anthropology came to fill the savage slot of a larger thematic field, performing a role played, in different ways, by literature and travel accounts—and soon to be played, perhaps, by unexpected media, if one takes the success of "Roots," "Miami Vice," or "China Beach" on North American television, or the international sales of Saddam Hussein punching balls during the Gulf War, as indications of a future. That the discipline was positivist in a positivist age, structuralist in a context dominated by structuralism, is not very intriguing; and as Tyler (1986:128) notes acutely, the more recent "textualization of pseudo-discourse" can accomplish "a terrorist alienation more complete than that of the positivists." Thus, attempts at disciplinary reflexivity cannot stop at the moment of institutionalization, or emphasize the internal tropes of late modern ethnographies, even though some rightly allude to the correspondence between savagery and utopia or to the use of the pastoral mode in anthropology (e.g., Tyler 1986; Clifford 1986b; Rosaldo 1986). Such attempts are not *wrong*. But the primary focus on the textual construction of the Other *in* anthropology may turn our attention away from the construction of otherness upon which anthropology is premised, and further mask a correspondence already well concealed by increasing specialization since the nineteenth century.

Indeed, the savage-utopia correspondence tends to generate false candor. It rarely reveals its deepest foundations or its inherent inequality, even though it triggers claims of reciprocity. From Pietro Martire and Rousseau to the postmodernist contingent(s) of North American anthropology, the savage has been an occasion to profess innocence. We may guess at some of the reasons behind this recurrent tendency to exhibit the nude as nakedness. Let me just say this much: in spite of such old claims, the utopian West dominated the thematic correspondence. It did so from behind the scene, at least most of the time. It showed itself in least equivocal terms on just a few occasions, most notably in the philosophical jousts over American colonization in sixteenth-century Spain (Pagden 1982) and in the anthropological debates of the eighteenth century (Duchet 1971).

But visible or not, naive or cynical, the West was always first, as utopia or as challenge to it—that is, as a universalist project, the boundaries of which were no-where, u-topous, non-spatial. And that, one needs to repeat, is not a product of the Enlightenment, but part and parcel of the horizons set by the Renaissance and its simultaneous creation of Europe and otherness, without which the West is inconceivable. Thomas More did not have to wait for ethnographic reports on the Americas to compose his *Utopia*. Similarly, eighteenth-century readers of travel accounts did not wait for verification. Even today, there is a necessary gap between the initial acceptance of the most fanciful "ethnographies" and the "restudies" or "reassessments" that follow. The chronological precedence reflects a deeper inequality in the two faces of Janus: the utopian West is first in the construction of this complementarity. It is the first observed face of the figure, the initial projection against which the savage becomes a reality. The savage makes sense only in terms of utopia.

THE MEDIATION OF ORDER

Utopia itself made sense only in terms of the absolute order against which it was projected, negatively or not.[8] Utopias do not necessarily advance foundational propositions, but they feed upon foundational thought. Fictional "ideal states," presented as novels or treatises, suggest a project or a counterproject. It is this very projection, rather than their alleged or proven fanciful characteristics, that makes them utopias. Here again, we need to go back to the Renaissance, that fictional rebirth through which Christendom became the West, where two more snapshots may clarify the issue.

From the point of view of contemporaries, the most important event of the year 1492 was not Columbus's landing in the Antilles, but the conquest of the Muslim kingdom of Granada and its incorporation into Castile (Trouillot 1990). The gap between the three religions of Abraham had paralleled the sociopolitical fissure that split the Mediterranean, but because of that fissure, religious intolerance increasingly expressed itself in ways that intertwined religion, ethnicity, territory, and matters of state control. To put it simply, as Christendom became Europe, Europe itself became Christian. It is no accident that the fall of Muslim Granada was immediately followed by the expulsion of the Jews from the now Christian territory. It is no accident either that the very same individual who signed the public order against the Jews also signed Ferdinand and Isabella's secret instructions to Columbus. Indeed, nascent Europe could turn its eyes to the Atlantic only because the consolidation of political borders and the concentration of political power in the name of the Christian God presaged the advent of internal order.

Order—political and ideological—was high on the agenda, both in theory and in practice; and the increased use of the printing press stimulated the interchange between theory and practice. Thus, in 1513, three years before Thomas More's *Utopia*, Niccolò Machiavelli wrote *The Prince*. In retrospect, that work signified a threshold: some leaders of the emerging Western world were ready to phrase the issue of control in terms of realpolitik long before the word was coined. The Machiavelli era encompassed Erasmus's *Education of a Christian Prince*, Budé's *Education of a Prince*, and other treatises that shared an "emphasis on the workable rather than the ideal," a belief that "men's destinies were to some extent within their own control and that this control depended upon self-knowledge" (Hale 1977:305).

The seminal writings that inscribed savagery, utopia, and order were conceived in the same era. This simultaneity is but one indication that these slots were created against the backdrop of one another. In the context of Europe, the works that set up these slots were part of an emerging debate that tied order to the quest for universal truths, a quest that gave savagery and utopia their relevance. Looming above the issue of the ideal state of affairs, and tying it to that of the state of nature, was the issue of order as both a goal and a means, and of its relation with reason and justice. Campanella's *City*, the runner-up to *Utopia* in the critics' view, clearly engaged some of Machiavelli's proposals and those of contemporary Spanish philosophers (Manuel and Manuel 1979:261–88). Campanella, like More, also wrote in nonfictional modes. He commented on European political regimes, in terms of their ultimate justification. He proposed to various European monarchs a nonfictional plan of rule based on his religious and philosophical views. Indeed, the opinions expressed in his treatises got him thrown into a Spanish jail, where he wrote his fictionalized utopia (Manuel and Manuel 1979; Trousson 1975:39, 72–78). Sir Thomas More, in turn, was executed.

The relation between fictionalized utopias and matters of political power goes way back to the ancestral forms of the genre in ancient Greece (Trousson 1975:39). So do debates on the nature of otherness. But we need not take the naive history of the West at face value: Greece did not beget Europe. Rather, Europe claimed Greece. The revisionist historiography through which the Renaissance turned Christendom into Europe and gave it its Greek heritage is itself a phenomenon that needs to be placed in history. The distinctiveness of the Renaissance was, in part, the

invention of a past for the West.[9] It was also, in part, an emerging claim
to universality and to an absolute order inconceivable without that claim.
As Las Casas, Montesquieu, and Montaigne were quick to point out in
different terms and times, a major difference between Europe and ancient
Greece was the reality of the savage as experienced by Europe after 1492.
Unlike that of Greece and Rome, or that of the Islamic world, the West's
vision of order implied from its inception two complementary spaces, the
here and the elsewhere, which premised one another and were conceived
as inseparable.

In imaginary terms that elsewhere could be Utopia; but in the concrete
terms of conquest, it was a space of colonization peopled by others who
would eventually become "us"—or at the very least who *should*—in a
project of assimilation antithetic to the most liberal branches of Greek
philosophy. In that sense, order had become universal, absolute—both in
the shape of the rising absolutist state (quite opposed, indeed, to Greek
democracy), and in the shape of a universal empire stretching the limits of Christendom out into nowhere. Colonization became a mission,
and the savage became absence and negation.[10] The symbolic process
through which the West created itself thus involved the universal legitimacy of power—and order became, in that process, the answer to the
question of legitimacy. To put it otherwise, the West is inconceivable
without a metanarrative, for since their common emergence in the sixteenth century, both the modern state and colonization posed—and continue to pose—to the West the issue of the philosophical base of order.
As Edouard Glissant (1989:2) phrases it: "The West is not in the West.
It is a project, not a place," a multilayered enterprise in transparent
universality.

Chronological convergences again illustrate the point. At about the
time Machiavelli wrote *The Prince,* the Spanish Crown made known its
supplementary laws on American colonization, and the Medici clan in
1513 secured the papacy with the nomination of Leo X—the same Leo,
bishop of Rome, to whom Pietro Martire dedicated parts of his ethnography. Two years later, the accession of Francis I as king of France signalled
the self-conscious invention of the traditions constitutive of the French
nation-state—a self-consciousness manifested in the imposed use of the
French dialect and the creation of the Collège de France.[11] One year after
Francis's advent, Charles I (later Charles V) became king of Castile and of
its New World possessions, and Martin Luther published the theses of
Wittenberg. The second decade of the new century ended quite fortu-
itously with a semblance of victory on the side of order, that is, with

Charles's "election" to the imperial crown in 1519. But the condemnation of Luther (1520), rural agitation within Castile itself, and the so-called Oriental menace (culminating with the 1529 siege of Vienna by the Turks) kept reminding a nascent Europe that its self-delivery was not to happen without pains. The notion of a universal empire that would destroy, through its ineluctable expansion, the borders of Christendom became both more attractive in thought and more unattainable in practice.

The fictionalized utopias that immediately followed More's and over-lapped with the practical reshaping of power in a newly defined Europe were by and large reformist rather than revolutionary, hardly breaking new imaginary ground (Trousson 1975:62–72). This is not surprising, for, just as the savage is in an unequal relationship with utopia, so is utopia in an uneven relation with order. Just as the savage is a metaphori-cal argument for or against utopia, so is utopia (and the savage it encom-passes) a metaphorical argument for or against order, conceived of as an expression of legitimate universality. It is the mediation of universal order, as the ultimate signified of the savage-utopia relation, that gives the triad its full sense. In defense of a particular vision of order, the savage became evidence for a particular type of utopia. That the same ethnographic source could be used to make the opposite point did not matter, beyond a minimal requirement for verisimilitude. To be sure, Las Casas had been there, Sepúlveda had not; and this helped the cause of the *procurador*. To be sure, the Rousseauists were right and Göttingen was wrong about cra-nial sizes. To be sure, the empirical verdict is not yet in on the Tasaday. But now as before, the savage is only evidence within a debate, the im-portance of which surpasses not only his understanding but his very existence.

Just as utopia itself can be offered as a promise or as a dangerous illusion, the savage can be noble, wise, barbarian, victim, or aggressor, depending on the debate and the aims of the interlocutors. The space within the slot is not static, and its changing contents are not predeter-mined by its structural position. Regional and temporal variants of the savage figure abound, in spite of recurring tendencies that suggest geo-graphical specialization.[12] Too often, anthropological discourse modifies the projection of nonacademic observers only to the extent that it "disci-plines" them.[13] At other times, anthropologists help create and buttress images that can question previous permutations.[14] Thus, what happens within the slot is neither doomed nor inconsequential (Fox, this volume; Vincent, this volume). The point is, rather, that a critique of anthropology cannot skirt around this slot. The direction of the discipline now depends

	The West	The Rest	
The Observer			The Other
Culture			Nature
History			Stories

ORDER   SAVAGE
                 Noble
                 Barbarian
                 Wise
                 Evil

State: Justice   UTOPIA
                  Paradisiac
                  Communist
                  Innocent
                  Illusory
Thought: Reason

Here   Elsewhere

Figure 2.1. The symbolic organization of the savage slot, ca. 1515–1990.

upon an explicit attack on that slot itself and the symbolic order upon which it is premised (fig. 2.1). For as long as the slot remains, the savage is at best a figure of speech, a metaphor in an argument about nature and the universe, about being and existence—in short, an argument about foundational thought.

PORTRAIT OF THE ARTIST AS A BUBBLE

This brings us right back to the present. I have argued so far that to historicize the West is to historicize anthropology and vice versa. I have further suggested that the postmodern condition makes that two-pronged historicization both urgent and necessary. If these two arguments are correct, together they expose the unspoken assumptions of postmodernist anthropology in North America and reveal its inherent limitations. For the portrait of the postmodernist anthropologist that emerges from this dual exercise is not a happy one indeed. Camera and notebooks in hand, he is looking for the savage, but the savage has vanished.

The problem starts with the fated inheritance of the moderns themselves. The world that the anthropologist inherits has wiped out the empirical trace of the savage-object: Coke bottles and cartridges now obscure the familiar tracks. To be sure, one could reinvent the savage, or create new savages within the West itself—solutions of this kind are increasingly appealing. The very notion of a pristine savagery, however, is now awkward, irrespective of the savage-object. Lingering conditions of modernity make the notion a hard one to evoke in imagination, now that hordes of savages have joined the slums of the Third World or touched the shores of the West. We are far from the days when five Eskimos caused an uproar in London. The primitive has become terrorist, refugee, freedom fighter, opium and coca grower, or parasite. He can even play anthropologist at times. Televised documentaries show his "real" conditions of existence; underground newspapers expose his dreams of modernity. Thanks to modernity, the savage has changed, the West has changed, and the West knows that both have changed empirically.

But modernity is only part of the anthropologist's difficulty. Modern obstacles have modern (technical) answers, or so we used to think. The more serious issue is that technical solutions do not suffice anymore. At best, they can solve the problem of the empirical object by removing the Cokes and cartridges. At worst, they can fabricate an entire new face for savagery. But they cannot remedy the loss of the larger thematic field, especially since the savage never dominated this field. He was only one of the requisite parts of a tripartite relation, the mask of a mask. The problem is not simply that the masks are torn, that true cannibals are now rare. The problem is that now—as in Norman Mailer's *Cannibals and Christians* (1966)—both are equally good, or equally evil (Walkover 1974), if evil itself can be defined (Lyotard 1986).

This is altogether a *post*modern quandary. It is part of the world of constructs and relations revealed by our juxtaposed snapshots, and it is an intrinsic dilemma of postmodern anthropology. For if indeed foundational thoughts are seen as collapsing, if indeed utopias are arguments about order and foundational thoughts, and if indeed the savage exists primarily within an implicit correspondence with utopia, the specialist in savagery is in dire straits. He does not know what to aim at. His favorite model has disappeared or, when found, refuses to pose as expected. The fieldworker examines his tools and finds his camera inadequate. Most importantly, his very field of vision now seems blurred. Yet he needs to come back home with a picture. It's pouring rain out there, and the mosquitoes are starting to bite. In desperation, the baffled anthropologist burns his notes to create a moment of light, moves his face against the flame, closes his eyes, and, hands grasping the camera, takes a picture of himself.

TACTICS AND STRATEGY

Lest this portrait be taken to characterize the postmodernist anthropologist as the epitome of self-indulgence (as many critics, indeed, imply), let me say that narcissist labels characterize postmodernist anthropologists, as individuals, no better than they typify their predecessors or adversaries. Intellectuals as a group claimed and gained socially sanctioned self-indulgence long before postmodernism. Individual intent is secondary here. At any rate, anthropology's postmodern situation warrants more sober reflection than petty accusations of egomania across theoretical camps.

I may end up being both more lenient and more severe—thus risking the condemnation of foes and proponents alike—by saying that the perceived self-indulgence of the postmodernist anthropologists inheres in the situation itself. That is what makes it so obvious and such an easy target for opponents. If we take seriously the perception of an ongoing collapse of the Western metanarratives, the vacuum created by the fall of the house of reason in the once fertile fields of utopian imagination, and the empirical destruction of the savage-object, then the anthropologist who is aware of the postmodern situation has no target outside of himself (as witness) and his text (as pretext), within the thematic universe he inherits.

Once phrased in these terms, the dilemma becomes manageable. One obvious solution is to confront and change the thematic field itself and claim new grounds for anthropology—which is just what some anthropologists have been doing, though without explicit programs. But the dilemma, as lived by the postmodernists, is no less real, and the epiphany of textuality cannot be reduced to a mere aggregate of individual tactics of self-aggrandizement or preservation.[15] If electoral politics may explain either overstatements or the craving for new fads in North American anthropology and elsewhere, they say little of the mechanisms leading to specific choices among myriad possibilities. Why the text? Why the sudden (for anthropologists, to some extent) rediscovery of literature, and of some literature at that? However much the (re)discovery of textuality and authorial legitimation may be associated with midterm maneuvers, it also must be seen in another context. In that context—the thematic field delineated by order, utopia, and the savage—this emphasis on textuality represents a strategic retreat triggered by the perception of ongoing destruction. In other words, electoral politics alone cannot explain postmodernist anthropology. To propose viable alternatives, one needs to take the ideological and theoretical context of postmodernism seriously, more seriously than the postmodernists do themselves. One needs also to take more seriously both literary criticism and philosophy.

METAPHORS IN ETHNOGRAPHY AND
ETHNOGRAPHY AS METAPHOR

The recent discovery of textuality by North American anthropologists is based on a quite limited notion of the text. The emphasis on "the independent importance of ethnographic writing as a genre" (Marcus 1980:507), the dismissal of pre-text, con-text, and content, all contribute to reading the anthropological product as isolated from the larger field in which its conditions of existence are generated. Passing references aside, the course of inquiry on the relations among anthropology, colonialism, and political "neutrality," which opened in the late 1960s and early 1970s (e.g., Asad 1973), is now considered closed, because it allegedly revealed all its partial truths. Passing mentions of gender aside, feminism—as a discourse that claims the specificity of (some) historical subjects—is bypassed because it is said to deal only with "content."[16] Passing references to the Third World notwithstanding, the issues raised by Wolf's historicization of the Other (1982), an inquiry that inherently makes anthropology part of this changing world, are considered moot. Mentions of relations of textual production notwithstanding, the mechanisms and processes emphasized are those that singularize the voice of anthropology, as if anthropological discourse was either self-enclosed or self-sufficient.

Not surprisingly, the archaeological exploration that underpins the North American exercise in reflexivity tends to stop at the institutionalization of anthropology as a discipline in the Anglophone world, or at best at the delineation of a specialized anthropological discourse in the Europe of the Enlightenment. In spite of the professed renunciation of labels, boundaries are set in modern terms to produce a history of the discipline, albeit one with different emphases. The construction exposed is a discursive order *within* anthropology, not the discursive order within which anthropology operates and makes sense—even though, here again, this larger field seems to warrant passing mention. The representational

aspect of ethnographic discourse is attacked with a vigor quite dispropor-
tionate to the referential value of ethnographies in the wider field within
which anthropology finds its significance. In short, to use a language that
still has its validity, the object of inquiry is the "simple" rather than the
"enlarged" reproduction of anthropological discourse. Terminology and
citations notwithstanding, the larger thematic field on which anthropology is premised is barely scratched.

But if we take seriously the proposition to look at anthropology as
metaphor—as I think we can, given the thematic field outlined—we cannot just look at metaphors in anthropology. The study of "ethnographic
allegory" (Clifford 1986b; Tyler 1986) cannot be taken to refer primarily
to allegorical forms *in* ethnography without losing site of the larger picture. Our starting point cannot be "a crisis in anthropology" (Clifford
1986a: 3), but in the histories of the world.[17] We need to go out of anthropology to see the construction of "ethnographic authority" not as a
late requirement of anthropological discourse (Clifford 1983b) but as an
early component of this wider field that is itself constitutive of anthropology. Would that the power of anthropology hinged upon the academic
success of genial immigrants such as Franz Boas and Bronislaw Malinowski! It would allow us to find new scapegoats without ever looking back
at the Renaissance. But the exercise in reflexivity must go all the way and
examine fully the enlarged reproduction of anthropological discourse.[18]

Observers may wonder why the postmodernist experiment in U.S. anthropology has not encouraged a surge of substantive models. The question of time aside, the difficulty of passing from criticism to substance is
not simply due to a theoretical aversion to content or an instinctive suspicion of exemplars. After all, the postmodernist wave has revitalized substantive production in other academic fields. It has stimulated architects
and political theorists alike. At the very least, it has provoked debates on
and of substance. Further, some political radicals advocate the possibility
of militant practices rooted in postmodernism—although not without
controversies (Laclau and Mouffe 1985; Arac 1986; Ross 1988b). More
important, the implicit awareness of an expanding situation of postmodernity continues to motivate grass-roots movements all over the world,
with their partial truths and partial results. In fact, an anthropologist
could well read postmodernism, or at the very least the postmodern situation, as a case for the specificity of otherness, for the destruction of the
savage slot.

To claim the specificity of otherness is to suggest a residual of historical experience that always escapes universalisms exactly because history
itself always involves irreducible subjects. It is to reserve a space for the
subject—not the existential subject favored by the early Sartre and who

keeps creeping back into the mea culpa anthropology, but the men and women who are the subjects of history.[19] It is to acknowledge that this space of the historical subject is out of reach of all metanarratives, not because all metanarratives are created equal and are equally wrong (which is the claim of nihilism and always ends up favoring *some* subjects and *some* narratives), but because metanarrative claims to universality necessarily imply the muting of first persons, singular or plural, deemed marginal. To say that otherness is always specific and historical is to reject this marginality. The Other cannot be encompassed by a residual category: there is no savage slot. The "us and all of them" binary, implicit in the symbolic order that creates the West, is an ideological construct, and the many forms of Third-World-ism that reverse its terms are its mirror images. There is no Other, but multitudes of others who are all others for different reasons, in spite of totalizing narratives, including that of capital.

Many propositions follow from this statement, not the least of which is that a discipline whose object is the Other may in fact have no object—which may lead us to take a much needed look at the methodological specificity of anthropology. It also follows that the authenticity of the historical subject may not be fully captured from the outside even by way of direct quotes; there may be something irreducible in the first person singular. This, in turn, raises two related issues: that of the epistemological status of native discourse;[20] and that of the theoretical status of ethnography. I will turn to these issues, not so much in a purely abstract mode (though this may be also necessary), but as entwined with specific research projects.

First, anthropology needs to evaluate its gains and losses in light of these issues, with a fair tally of the knowledge anthropologists have produced in the past, sometimes in spite of themselves and almost always in spite of the savage slot. We owe it to ourselves to ask what remains of anthropology and of specific monographs when we remove this slot—not to revitalize disciplinary tradition through cosmetic surgery, but to build both an epistemology and a semiology of what anthropologists have done and can do. We cannot simply assume that modernism has exhausted all its potential projects. Nor can we assume that "realist ethnography" has produced nothing but empty figures of speech and shallow claims to authority.

Second, armed with this renewed arsenal, we can recapture domains of significance by creating strategic points of "reentry" into the discourse on otherness: areas within the discourse where the introduction of new voices or new combinations of meaning perturbate the entire field and open the way to its (partial) recapture.[21] This chapter is not the place to expand in the directions of these many queries, so I can only tease the

reader. But a few tasks seem to me urgent in this new context: an epistemological reassessment of the historical subject (the first person singular
that has been overwhelmed by the voice of objectivity or by that of the
narrator and that is so important to many feminists, especially Afro-
American feminists); a similar reassessment of nativeness and native discourse, now barely conceptualized; and a theory of ethnography, now
repudiated as the new "false consciousness." And for the time being, at
least, we need more ethnographies that raise these issues through concrete cases. Not so much ethnographies that question the author/native
dichotomy by exposing the nude as nakedness, but ethnographies (ethno-
historio-semiologies?) that offer new points of reentry by questioning the
symbolic world upon which "nativeness" is premised. At the very least,
anthropologists can show that the Other, here and elsewhere, is indeed a
product—symbolic and material—of the same process that created the
West.[22] In short, the time is ripe for substantive propositions that aim
explicitly at the destruction of the savage slot.

That it has not been so among the postmodernists of North American
anthropology is thus a matter of choice. In spite of a terminology that
intimates a decoding of "anthropology as metaphor," we are barely reading anthropology itself. Rather, we are reading anthropological pages, and
attention remains focused primarily on the metaphors in anthropology.
This recurring refusal to pursue further the archaeological exercise ob-
scures the asymmetrical position of the savage-other in the thematic field
upon which anthropology was premised. It negates the specificity of otherness, subsuming the Other in the sameness of the text perceived as
liberating cooperation. "We are the world"?

Anthropology did not create the savage. Rather, the savage was the
raison d'être of anthropology. Anthropology came to fill the savage slot in
the trilogy order-utopia-savagery, a trilogy which preceded anthropology's institutionalization and gave it continuing coherence in spite of in-
tradisciplinary shifts. This trilogy is now in jeopardy. Thus the time is
ripe—and in that sense, it is postmodern—to attack frontally the visions
that shaped this trilogy, to uncover its ethical roots and its consequences,
and to find better anchor for an anthropology of the present, an anthropology of the changing world and its irreducible histories. But postmodernist anthropologists pass near this opportunity looking for the savage in
the text. They want us to read the internal tropes of the savage slot, no
doubt a useful exercise in spite of its potential for self-indulgence. But
they refuse to address directly the thematic field (and thus the larger
world) that made (makes) this slot possible, morosely preserving the
empty slot itself.

Times have changed since the sixteenth century: one now is innocent until proven guilty. Thus, claims of innocence can take the shape of silence. Somehow, to my surprise, I miss the faithful indignation of a Las Casas.

──────── *Notes* ────────

My thanks to all those who commented on earlier versions of this paper, the participants at the Santa Fe Seminar, graduate students and faculty at Johns Hopkins University and at the New School for Social Research, and the readers for the School of American Research. Personal thanks to Kamran Ali, Talal Asad, Lanfranco Blanchetti, Ashraf Ghani, Ananta Giri, Richard G. Fox, Richard Kagan, and Eric Wolf, none of whom should be held responsible for the final product. An early version of this paper, "Anthropology as Metaphor: The Savage's Legacy and the Post-Modern World," appeared in *Review*, a Journal of the Fernand Braudel Center, vol. XIV, no. 1, Winter 1991.

1. For reasons of space, I cannot retrace here all the connections between recent debates in philosophy and literary theory and recent critiques of anthropology. Our readings are too parochial, anyway—to the point that any major thinker needs to be translated into the discipline by an insider. Anthropology has much more to learn from other disciplines, notably history, literary criticism, and philosophy, than the reflexivist interpreters assume. There are blanks to be filled by the reader with proper use of the bibliographical references.

2. Other reasons aside, long-term fieldwork in the so-called Third World, after the initial dissertation, is becoming more difficult and less rewarding for a majority of anthropologists. Unfortunately, issues such as the increased competition for funds to do fieldwork abroad or the growing proportion of two-career families in and out of academe only make good conversation. Practitioners tend to dismiss them in written (and therefore "serious") assessments of trends in the discipline. The sociology of our practice is perceived as taboo, but see Wolf (1969), whose early appeal for such a sociology fell on dead ears, and Rabinow (this volume).

3. In that sense, I take exception to Renato Rosaldo's formulation that the conservative domination "has distorted a once-healthy debate" (Rosaldo 1989: 223). What a certain kind of anthropology can demonstrate is exactly that the debate was never as healthy as we were led to believe.

4. See Graff (1977), Jameson (1984), Arac (1986), Lyotard (1986), Ross (1988b), and Harvey (1989) on conflicting definitions of postmodernism. I am not qualified to settle this debate. But if postmodernism only means a style, a bundle of expository devices, characterized (or not) by "double coding" (Jencks 1986), then it does not much matter to anthropologists—as long as they note that double coding has been part of the cultural arsenal of many non-Western cultures for centuries. On the connection between postmodernism and metanarratives, see Lyotard (1979, 1986), Eagleton (1987), and Harvey (1989).

5. The first consists of two chapters in *Les Bijoux indiscrets*. The second is the

fantastic *Supplément au voyage du Bougainville*, a primitivist utopia where Tahiti is the Other in more than one way, being both savage and female (Trousson 1975:140; Brewer 1985).

6. I owe my ideas on the black or plantation pastoral to conversations with Professor Maximilien Laroche and access to his unpublished paper on the subject. In Bernadin Saint-Pierre's successful *Paul et Virginie* (1787), whose setting is a plantation island, a group of maroon slaves surprises the two lovers. But to the heroes' amazement, the chief of the runaway slaves says, "Good little whites, don't be afraid; we saw you pass this morning with a negro woman from Rivière-Noire; you went to ask her grace to her bad master; in gratitude, we will carry you back home on our shoulders."

7. Some writers have made this point. Others have assembled the necessary information to make it, without always drawing the same conclusion from their juxtapositions. I have read over the shoulders of so many of them, and imposed my reading on so many others, that credits for this section and the next were sometimes difficult to attribute in the main text; but see Atkinson (1920, 1922, 1924), Baudet (1959), Chinard (1934), Duchet (1971), De Certeau (1975), Gonnard (1946), Todorov (1982), Trousson (1975), Rupp-Eisenreich (1984), and Droixhe and Gossiaux (1985).

8. My phrasing of this issue in terms of order owes to conversations with Ashraf Ghani. I remain responsible for its use here and its possible shortcomings. Empirical elements of an analysis of the role of order within the symbolic horizons of the Renaissance are plentiful in Hale's *Renaissance Europe: Individual and Society, 1480–1520* (Hale 1977).

9. Genealogies that trace the beginnings of anthropology to Herodotus (why not Ibn Battuta?) partake of that naive history. They serve the guild interests of the "discipline," its construction of tradition, authorship, and authority and the reproduction of the savage slot upon which it builds its legitimacy. Note, however, that it was only in the eighteenth and nineteenth centuries that Romantics and racists abandoned the ancient Greeks' own version of their cultural origins, denying the contributions of Africans and Semites to "civilization." Classical studies then invented a new past for Greece with an Aryan model (Bernal 1987).

10. From then on, descriptions of savagery would inscribe grammatically the absence in a way now all too familiar (and unquestioned) by anthropologists. The savage is what the West is not: "no manner of traffic, no knowledge of letters, no science of numbers . . . no contracts, no successions, no dividends, no properties . . ." (Montaigne 1952:94). This language is quite different from that of Polo (1958) or even from that of Pliny. But its immediate antecedents are in the very first descriptions of the Americas: Columbus, for instance, thought the "Indians" had "no religion"—by which he probably meant "none of the three religions of Abraham."

11. One cannot suggest that Francis I consciously foresaw a French nation-state in the modern sense, but the absolutist order he envisioned revealed itself

historically untenable without the invented tradition necessary for the symbolic construction of the nation. It is only by one of those ironies of which history is full that this tradition became fully alive at the time of the Revolution and was solidified by a Corsican mercenary with no claim to Frankish nobility, namely, Napoleone Buonaparte.

12. One suspects that the savage as wise is more often than not Asiatic, the savage as noble is often a Native American, and the savage as barbarian is often African or African-American. But neither roles nor positions are always neat, and the structural dichotomies do not always obtain historically. Jews and Gypsies, for instance, are savages "within" the West—an awkward position not accounted by the here/elsewhere dichotomy, but resolved in practice by persecution.

13. Anthropological insistence on, say, rebellion and resistance in Latin America, economic qua material survival in Africa, or ritual expression in Southeast Asia partakes of a symbolic distribution that predates chronologically and precedes epistemologically the division of labor within the discipline. A major limitation of the work of Edward Said is the failure to read "Orientalism" as one set of permutations within the savage slot.

14. My greater familiarity with Caribbean anthropology may explain why I find most of my positive examples in this corner of the world, but it is obvious to Caribbeanists that anthropology helped challenge the vision of the Antilles as islands in the sun peopled by indolent natives—a view popularized since the nineteenth century by racist yet celebrated writers such as Anthony Trollope (1859). How successful was the challenge is another issue, but forty years before "voodoo economics" became a pejorative slogan in North American political parlance, some North American and European anthropologists took Haitian popular religion quite seriously (e.g., Herskovits 1937b).

15. To be sure, in its current form, the alleged discovery of the text provokes transient hyperboles. We all knew that ethnography was also text if only because of the ABDs relegated to driving cabs when their lines could not see the light of day, or because of the careers destroyed when dissertations failed to sprout "publishable" books (the text/test par excellence?). That Marcus and Cushman (1982:27) "for simplicity . . . do not consider the very interesting relationship between the production of a published ethnographic text and its intermediate written versions" is not novel. Tenure committees have been doing the same for years, also "for simplicity," while we all continued to ignore politely the electoral politics that condition academic success.

16. See Clifford's (1986a:21) indulgent neglect of feminism on purely textual grounds: "It has not produced either unconventional forms of writing or a developed reflection on ethnographic textuality as such." Never mind that feminism now sustains one of the most potent discourses on the specificity of the historical subject and, by extension, on the problem of "voice." To be sure, some white middle-class women, especially in the United States, want to make that new-found "voice" universal, and their feminist enterprise threatens to become a new

metanarrative, akin to Fanon's Third-World-ism, or Black Power à la 1960. But it is at the very least awkward for Clifford to dismiss feminist and "non-Western writings" for having made their impact on issues of content alone.

17. In fact, I doubt that there is a crisis *in* anthropology as such; rather, there is a crisis in the world that anthropology assumes.

18. The limited exercises of the postmodernists would take on new dimensions if used to look at the enlarged reproduction of anthropology. For example, were we to rekindle the notion of genre to read ethnography (Marcus 1980), we would need to speculate either a metatext (the retrospective classification of a critic), or the sanction of a receiving audience of nonspecialists, or a thematic and ideological framework in the form of an archi-textual field (Genette, Jauss, and Schaffer, 1986). To speak of any of these in relation to ethnography as genre would illustrate enlarged reproduction and reexamine anthropology's own grounds.

19. I thank Eric Wolf for forcing me to make this important distinction.

20. The matter of the status of "halfies" (approached by Abu-Lughod in this volume) can be further analyzed in these terms. We need not fall into nativism in order to raise epistemological questions about the effect of historically accumulated experience, the "historical surplus value" that specific groups of subjects-as-practitioners bring to a discipline premised on the existence of the savage slot and the commensurability of otherness. At the same time, for philosophical and political reasons, I am profoundly opposed to the formulas of the type "add native, stir, and proceed as usual," so successful in electoral politics in and out of academe. Anthropology needs something more fundamental than reconstitutive surgery, and halfies, women, people of color, etc., deserve something better than a new slot.

21. The symbolic reappropriation that Christianity imposed on Judaism, or that liberation theology is imposing on Christianity in some areas of the world; the reorientation that the ecology movement has injected into notions of "survival"; the redirection that feminism has imposed on issues of gender; and Marx's perturbation of classical political economy from within are all unequal examples of "reentry" and recapture.

22. The anthropology of agricultural commodities as material and symbolic boundaries between human groups (along the lines opened by Mintz 1985b); the anthropology of the categories and institutions that reflect and organize power—such as "peasants," "nation," "science," (Trouillot 1988, 1989, 1990; Martin 1987) or the "West" itself (to renew with both Benveniste [1969] and Foucault); the anthropology of the transnational media and other forms of communication shaping the international organization of symbols—all can be fruitfully conceptualized within such a scheme.

Chapter 3

ENGAGING HISTORICISM

Joan Vincent

THE cutting edge of anthropology in the 1980s lay with criticism: historical, on the one hand, and textual, on the other. Criticism's chief characteristic, in both its postmodern and postmarxist forms, has been unsettlement, or "crisis"; its goals, displacement and the assertion of new orthodoxy. Yet its perception of temporal and emergent structuring within anthropology tended to render it at once timeless and anachronistic. It lacked a sense of "discontinuous histories."

This essay is a reading of one moment in the 1980s, written in the context of rethinking historicism.[1] I argue that anthropology must be both critical and attuned to the politics of its history. First, I sketch out what is involved in rethinking historicism, applying its commitments first to ethnographic texts conceived as process and then to today's critical moment in anthropology. In the 1960s, anthropology provided a transfer point among the humanities, a position occupied in the 1980s by literary criticism. I ask what happened, and suggest why this needs to be anthropology's concern right now. Finally, I attempt to show how the rehistoricization of an earlier era in anthropology allows us to repossess the past to talk to the present and future.

RETHINKING HISTORICISM

I am arguing here for an "anthropological political economy" (Roseberry 1989), over time, of the construction and reception of ethnographic texts. A key text about texts in the 1980s was *Writing Culture: The Poetics and Politics of Ethnography* (Clifford and Marcus 1986). Its great moment was to say that ethnographic texts in themselves, by their representation, have a politics. I would suggest that there are, in fact, two kinds of politics around the texts of ethnography; *Writing Culture* sensitized us to one, but there is another, perhaps less yielding, politics: the struggles that were not embedded in the texts themselves. What led to the texts and their making also had a politics. And this, of course, requires that we rethink their historicity.

A useful definition of "the new historicism" was provided by Marjorie Levinson in 1989. The reconstructed historicist project is conceived and conducted as a reflexive affair. Reflection, an act of mind, is set in the field of material production, its cultural mediations, and their hegemonic forms. A repossessing of the past is also, at one and the same time, a surgical operation on the present with, some would add, an eye to the future. Part component and part accompaniment of this historicism re-thought are certain practices more familiar to anthropologists than historicism itself. I will discuss five of these, which I will label skepticism, contextualism, processualism, criticism, and engagement. Along with the new historicism, they hold the potential of resituating metaethnography.

The first practice, skepticism, involves a questioning of the traditional idea in anthropology that an ethnographer is a producer, and ethnography, a product. From *Writing Culture* to *Works and Lives: The Anthropologist as Author* (Geertz 1988), anthropologists have written about ethnographers simply as ethnographers, existing in their own ethnographic presents, and in relation to one another. Skeptical historicism questions the validity of such a concentration upon the individual, whether as fieldworker or as author—on "magus-role" players, as Marilyn Butler puts it in her paradigm-breaking study of romantics, rebels, and reactionaries (1982). The role of the ethnographer is inflated when no imperatives are acknowledged other than the truth of her or his experi-ence. Skepticism questions the autonomy of ethnography as text. Indeed, it is tempting to account for its privileging as a reaction to the print explosion. A generation or two ago, as Peter Lawrence (1975) pointed out, it was possible for a scholar to read all the ethnographies that had been published and to place ethnographic knowledge within a consistent intellectual framework. Now, the volume is too great. Unable to master it, the anthropologist has been tempted into circumscribing ethnography, even to downplaying its significance. I would argue, however (and have documented in my own historicized account [1990] of how anthropologists have studied politics), that ethnography is critically important as the one vehicle above all others through which anthropologists represent and transform theory.

Contextualism, the second practice, involves understanding ethnography not as aesthetics or poetics, but as a historical phenomenon that must be associated with social, political, and material circumstances. In an earlier essay (1987), I set out to discuss the intellectual performance of Roy Franklin Barton in the context of his times and ours. Placing him alongside his fellow Edwardians, Bronislaw Malinowski and Franz Boas, I suggested that the study of these ethnographers in the context of their times advances an assessment of the critically distinctive, but many-layered, relationship between anthropology and colonialism. It certainly led me to a conceptualization of the role of ethnographers on the moving edge of capitalist expansion, and of the function of ethnographic writing in a larger scheme of things. (The narrowness of our understanding of our discipline, past and present, is treated most profoundly by Michel-Rolph Trouillot in his essay in this volume.)

The importance of reading the books an ethnographer read, trying to become familiar with the intellectual ethnoscape (as Arjun Appadurai put it during our seminar discussions) in which she or he lived, seeing where she or he fitted in—or did not fit in—seems self-evident. "The writer takes in thoughts and structures from a babel about him, and his text is a giving back into the same discussion; part, in short, of a social process" (Butler 1982:9). It is ironic that Butler, having written those words, looked to anthropology for her contextual model. "A book is made by its public, the reader it literally finds and the people in the author's mind's eye," she wrote. "Literature, like all art, like language, is a collective activity, powerfully conditioned by social forces, what needs to be and what may be said in a particular community at a given time—the field of the anthropologist, perhaps" (1982:9). This is far removed from the simple "dialogic relationship" that the interpretivists of the 1980s saw to be the essence of the ethnographic experience. It carries us from ethnography as text to ethnography as communal enterprise or instituted process.

Processualism, the third practice, involves recognizing the importance of the reader—that is, reception and reproduction. Hans Gadamer provides the text in this case: "[the] reader does not exist before whose eyes the great book of world history lies open. But nor does the reader exist who, when he has his text before him, simply reads what is there" (1976:304). The term Gadamer uses for the characteristic which the reader brings to the text is prejudice: there can be no view of past ethnography that is not affected by the prejudice of its readers.

Elsewhere I have scrutinized the processual paradigm at some length (Vincent 1986a, 1990) and applied it to the production, reception, and reproduction of a specific ethnography, Barton's *Ifugao Law* (1919). This book was written when Barton was an inspector of schools in the Mountain Province of the Philippines when it was under United States jurisdiction. I suggested (1987) that the intellectual designs of those who received Barton's ethnography into the academy and reproduced it, such as Robert Lowie and E. Adamson Hoebel, were reflected by selective packaging within their own nomothetic productions and by the representation—or misrepresentation—of his data in textbooks. Barton was especially vulnerable in this respect since he had not fitted his own work into any specific box: evolutionary, diffusionist, or protofunctionalist. Because he never held an academic post in which he trained students to reproduce the paradigm under which he operated, and because he seemed far happier "doing" ethnography than thinking about how others used his work, its reproduction served several equally legitimate but divergent ends. The scientific prejudice of any academic reader is, of course, historically specific, so that in writing about Barton's ethnography, it was necessary to situate not only my predecessors but myself.

Barton's *Ifugao Law* was an empowering text, but such ethnographies are rare and seem to be becoming rarer. The distinction between ethnographies that empower the reader—their rich, multivocal texts giving the reader an alternative analysis to fight back with—and those that do not is critical. In this respect, the critique of ethnography launched by *Writing Culture* missed its target, I would argue, but fell on fertile ground. Moving beyond textual criticism to the social production, reception, and reproduction of ethnographies enables us to anthropologize historicism and rehistoricize anthropology. Every text does, then, indeed become a network of resistances, situated within its "multiple, interacting contexts of creation and reception" (La Capra 1985:344).

Criticism, the fourth practice, involves the recognition that, if historicizing the discontinuities of history provides a means of repossessing the past in the name of the present and future, there is a particular value to be gained from historicizing and repossessing the "classics" of ethnography—those master works that have perdured. "The great writings . . . are not merely pieces of historical evidence, fossils in the ground, but living texts that we too are engaged with. Just as they had no first author, they have not found their last reader. To see these works within their cultural context is also to acknowledge their place in the world we still inhabit" (Butler 1982: 10).

Skeptical historicism discourages the notion that works enter a discipline and become classics solely because of the value of their ideas or the truth of their representations. Jane Tompkins (1985) has suggested how some works, but not others, come to be recognized as classics; whose interests are served when this is done; and what is involved. Since historical contexts are multiple and conflicting, when we find ourselves holding in our hands "classic" ethnographies, we know that we are about to read the victors in struggles for past and present recognition and the attribution of significance.

Fifth and finally, the new historicism, as Levison (1989) suggests, feeds upon engagement. All historicizations of anthropology are partial and partisan. *Writing Culture* did a fair job of drawing attention to the politics within the text, as our seminar clearly recognized, but it is necessary also to address the politics around the writing of the text, the politics of reading the text, and the politics of its reproduction. William Roseberry has recently taken George Marcus to task for the playfulness with which he approaches the essay as a genre in anthropology. What is missing from Marcus's endeavor, Roseberry suggests (1989: x–xi), is "the constant and sustained engagement with ethnographic subjects and the requirement that one embed one's observations, inferences, and interpretations within that engagement."

ON CRISIS AND CONTENTION

Today's crisis has a past. Anthropology required in the 1980s, I would argue, not an experimental moment but a sense of crisis: an educated knowledge of unending crisis, or contention. The recognition of a "critical moment" in a chain of critical moments allows us to avoid dehistoricizing "this year's heroic paradigm" (as one of our readers put it) and imbuing it with a centrality it does not possess. The major division within the discipline for the past decade has been between those who engage in practice and those who do not. It was ever thus.

For some, today's crisis is seen to be in anthropology itself, or more narrowly, in the departments which house anthropologists. Since academics are, indeed, both empowered and constrained by the formal institutions in which they produce, there is some truth in this. But it is a minor truth, because the crisis extends throughout the university system, the liberal humanism of "Western" civilization, the national authoritarian pronouncements of a William Bennett or Keith Joseph, and the utilitarian priorities of a George Bush or Margaret Thatcher.

Traditional university systems of knowledge production have been outflanked by post-1946 sciences and technologies that have to do with language: phonology and theories of linguistics; problems of communication and cybernetics; computers and their languages; problems of translation; problems of information storage and data banks; telematics and the perfection of intelligent terminals; and paradoxology (Lyotard 1984). Print capitalism, in short, is giving way to microchip capitalism.

Academic anthropologists can live with that. We can be nostalgic about an experimental moment in the human sciences in the 1960s; we can regret a fractionating within the discipline that makes cults of continents and sects of specialization; we can deplore that segmentary models of man that are also straitjackets for men (Wolf 1964)—even while we reap the harvest as liberal western educators enlarge the canon of civilization. Even more can we suffer the nightmare of the intellectuals: "a feeling that, far from being able to remake the world, all one [can] do [is] to cultivate a tiny garden or—to use a more modern parlance—to retreat into a small shelter, not only unable to cope with society, but also abdicating one's responsibility to participate in it" (Wolf 1964:15). Such an attitude reflects, Wolf noted, a repression of the romantic motive in anthropology. We can continue to cultivate our own "invisible colleges" (Crane 1972), globally reflecting the small world in which academics move. The departments that housed our disciplinary heritage and traditions appear derelict in comparison. This, I believe, is reflected specifically in Paul Rabinow's essay in this volume.

The critical moment, recognized, calls for engagement. In her inaugural lecture at Cambridge University, Marilyn Butler, whose scholarly expertise is in English literature, linked the present crisis in the humanities in Britain with the revolutionary 1960s. She did so, however, in an unexpected way. As critically sensitive as any Third World anthropologist to the policies of national governments and global economies, she suggested that "schools, like universities, are in crisis because everywhere scarce resources are being diverted into the re-equipping, or creation, of industry. The sixties revolution that matters worldwide is not the Parisian one that gave Western academics post-structuralism, but the South Korean one that turned a war-devastated country into another Japan. The precondition of that technological miracle was a restrained workforce, and the moral is not lost on other governments" (Butler 1989:65). And so Butler's lecture became a critique of Thatcher's Britain.

Speaking thus, on that academic occasion, Butler personified two crucial components of the new historicism: first, the recognition of crisis and, second, the readiness to equate criticism with intervention (Levinson 1989:8). This, I would suggest, is what anthropology offered the humanities in the 1960s and what critical literary studies offered them in the 1980s. In the eighties, a great deal of anthropology in the humanities—a blurred genre—lost its critical edge. Literary studies were perceived to be that "transfer point for renewal across a wide range of disciplines" (Arac 1989:1), and anthropology came to see itself as a discipline in disarray. A self-conscious reassertion of its character, engaging both ethnography and historicism, is already in the making in the 1990s.

BATTLES AND PARADISES LOST: DECONSTRUCTING
THE EDWARDIAN MOMENT IN ANTHROPOLOGY

At the heart of ethnography's darkness stands the mystic figure of Bronislaw Malinowski. Anthropology's leading historian, George W. Stocking, Jr., wrote in his paper "The Ethnographer's Magic" (1983:70–71), "Its hero is of course the Polish-born scientist Bronislaw Malinowski, who . . . spent two years living in a tent among the Trobriand Islanders, and brought back to Britain the secret of successful social anthropological research." Roger Sanjek's recent edited volume, *Fieldnotes: The Makings of Anthropology* (1990), attests to the centrality of Malinowski in the worldview of practicing ethnographers. No other individual receives as many citations in the volume's index; authors and readers share a common understanding not only of Malinowski's famous tent but also of his coming into Kiriwina, his diary, his "culture-outline" with its multicolored crayonning, his attention to "the imponderabilia of daily life," his functionalist creed, his analysis of "speech-in-action," his letters and advice to his students, his seminar, even his field notebooks that were made available to the neophyte field researcher at the London School of Economics and Political Science. Sanjek reminds us (1990:210) of Malinowski's published portrayals of his fieldwork methods, "heroically in *Argonauts* (1922:2–5), mock-humbly but more revealingly in *Coral Gardens* (1935, vol. I:317–40, 452–82)." In a similar vein, I, too, have singled out *Coral Gardens and their Magic* for particular attention, suggesting how Ireland, India, and eastern and southern Africa were uppermost in Malinowski's mind and how "Malinowski, the academic, was very much a participant in the political world" of his time (Vincent 1990:161). In short, given the inaccessibility of the past, the Malinowskian "charter" theory of myth and legend is being applied in all consistency, as Ernest Gellner has pointed out (1988:181), to anthropology's own history.

Yet it is not simply a Malinowskian view of the functional relevance of the past for the present that has generated our critical moment in anthropology today. Anthropology's rehistoricization would appear to be part of a more universal response within the academy. Wolf Lepenies and Peter Weingart, historians of science, have suggested that "the rapidly diminishing belief in the irresistible progress of Western civilization [has been accompanied by] a growing skepticism and a loss of disciplinary self-confidence" (1983:xvii). In most cases, reaction to crisis has taken the form of the rehistoricization of a discipline within the enabling structure of a critical evaluation of the history of science itself. Thus, in focusing now on "the Malinowski icon" (Sanjek 1990:187) contextualized within the Edwardian era, I am led not to founding figures and genealogy but to discontinuous history, perceiving today's anthropology to be a parenthesis in the anthropologies that might have been.

Anthropology's rehistoricization first required its deconstruction. Challenges to the received view occurred on both sides of the Atlantic at more or less the same time. Talal Asad's *Anthropology and Its Colonial Encounter* (1973) marked one strand; *Reinventing Anthropology*, edited by Dell Hymes (1969), another. They represented tensions between anthropology and, respectively, the colonialist and the capitalist as anthropology's "significant other." Because the Edwardian era—the era of Boas, Barton, and Malinowski, among others—saw the establishment of a new phase in both imperialism and the development of capitalism, it provides a heuristic starting point for my rehistoricist project. All of our moments, the poet said, are defined by the containment of the times they are not. The methodological assumption (Collini 1978) that initiated my research in the Edwardian archives was the propriety of asking why something did not happen.

R. R. Marett's student at Oxford, George Henry Lane-Fox Pitt-Rivers, described the era's crises in *The Clash of Culture and the Contact of Races* (1927). "The great world shattering changes of the past decade," wrote Pitt-Rivers, "the War, the Russian Revolution, the Treaty of Versailles, and the consequences of these events, have led men to question for the first time many of the previously unchallenged assumptions implicit in their own civilization, whilst it has prompted them to regard with real concern and a desire to understand civilizations unlike their own" (1927:xii). Looking closer to home, he might have evoked crises over Ulster nationalism and the Irish civil war, the suffragettes, the stock-market crash, labor militancy, and the decline of the Liberal Party. Pitt-Rivers's book was dedicated to Malinowski, and, writing in 1927, the "right sort of anthropology" he arrived at was functional.

In the course of the "long" contained Edwardian moment, which I take the liberty of stretching from 1901 to 1927 (Vincent 1989, 1990: 78–151), a great many anthropologists came to accept functionalism's principles of closure as a discipline. Yet for much of that time, anthropology was clearly recognized as "an unsettled science" (Stocking 1984:160, quoting Malinowski; cf. Nieboer 1900:xviii; Rivers 1913; Vincent 1986b). For those who were beginning to view themselves in these years as professional, academic anthropologists, three possible trajectories coexisted ambiguously, no one dominating.

Today, we are thoroughly familiar with two of these trajectories, evolutionism and functionalism, although we tend to view them as "theoretical stances" rather than as social movements. Their superstructural principles have been set out with considerable clarity, often in binary opposition. The third trajectory, diffusionism, has been so thoroughly stigmatized that we see it only through the eyes of those who had most to gain from detracting interest from it—evolutionists and functionalists. "The notion of the [diffusionist] triumvirate [Elliot Smith, William Perry, and W. H. R. Rivers] as a litany of futility has been accepted by generations of students," Richard Slobodin observed (1978:73). Particularly to the point is A. P. Elkin's observation (1974) that very few of those who deride Elliot Smith today have actually taken the trouble to read his rather large corpus of publications. Writing about W. H. R. Rivers, Slobodin was struck by "the startling volume of misinformation" (1978:viii) that he found.

A social movement within a discipline, Martin Rudwick (1985) has suggested, is like a ship in a bottle. It has to be understood through its mode of construction, the sequence of manipulations by which the model is inserted and made to appear permanent. In Edwardian Britain, there was not simply an alternative to functionalism in the form of evolutionism, but a positively "anti-functionalist movement" (Fortes 1976:475) that had to be overcome. To this movement belonged, among others, Daryll Forde, characterized by those in Malinowski's circle as "a human geographer with ethnological interests" (Fortes 1976:459); V. Gordon Childe, the archaeologist; and the folklorist, Lord Raglan, "that lovable, outspoken and original stalwart of non-academic anthropology" (Fortes 1976:463). Unlike those in the Malinowski circle, they belonged to a "post-war social and intellectual . . . fringe-of-Bloomsbury student set . . . amongst whom [they] made some lifelong friends, destined later to play leading parts in our scientific and cultural life," as Fortes coyly put it (1976:461).

Forde was trained as a cultural anthropologist by Alfred Kroeber at Berkeley, but more cause for his distancing and exclusion from

Malinowski's circle, I would suggest, was that he had been a student of Elliot Smith at University College, London. Forde's first published work, *Ancient Mariners* (1926), was inspired by diffusionist concerns. Twenty-two years later, as an established scholar who had subsequently carried out field research in West Africa, Forde used the occasion of his presidential lecture to the Royal Anthropological Institute to chide British social anthropologists for being too narrowly sociological and not taking material factors into account. All this, of course, makes the narrative and analysis of the construction of functionalism—the sequence of manipulations by which the paradigm was inserted into the discipline's mainstream and made to appear both superior and permanent—an intricate and complex adventure that, regrettably, cannot be embarked upon here.

Yet as Fortes's phrasing suggests, there was indeed a coherence in the opposition to functionalism that lasted from the first decade of the twentieth century to the 1950s. Childe's advocacy of the concept of culture and of Marxism and Raglan's fierce opposition to anthropology's becoming a science of primitives were but two voices among many. It is my belief that Childe actually parodied the opening paragraphs of Malinowski's *Argonauts of the Western Pacific* (1922) in *Man Makes Himself* (Childe 1936), substituting his own materialism for Malinowski's romantic idealism over the building of a native canoe. Lord Raglan engaged in a long exchange of paradoxes and orthodoxies in the correspondence columns of *Man*. He was provoked by the discipline's opposition to applied anthropology, often then called "practical anthropology," as well as by an innocuous suggestion that anthropologists work in European peasant communities, a proposal he strongly supported.

For young scholars at the time, the derogation of diffusionism was far from a fait accompli. In a doctoral dissertation for the London School of Economics in 1926, Gerald Camden Wheeler phrased the critical contestation of the times as one between evolutionary and diffusionist perspectives. He and his contemporaries saw the diffusionist perspective not as the heliolithic and kulturkreis theorizing of Elliot Smith or the German scholars, but as an ethnology that was historical, that dealt with complex as well as primitive societies and that recognized culture contact, movement, and change. "The study of cultures cannot but be followed from the historical standpoint," he wrote, "that is, they will be looked on as always in process of change in time and space. . . . Our aim can only be to trace processes of change, not to seek first beginnings. . . . If ethnology is essentially historical in method, we have to assume a theoretically endless possibility of movement, and of action and reaction, direct or indirect, between culture groups" (1926:xiv).

Wheeler carried out fieldwork in the Solomon Islands for over a year in 1908 and 1909, part of the time alongside Rivers and Arthur Hocart. In Alu, he was befriended by the German ethnologist, Richard Thurnwald. Wheeler's dissertation, published as *Mono-Alu Folklore* (1926), acknowledges his debt to Edward Westermarck. Today it is difficult to envision the London School of Economics as other than the cradle of Malinowski's functional anthropology, but its roster of instructors at the beginning of the century included Alfred Cort Haddon (1904–1909), Wheeler (1909–1910), C. G. Seligman (1910–1913), Rivers (1912–1913), Henri Junod (1920–1921), M. J. Aitken (1923–1929), Childe (1926–1927), and Raymond Firth (1926–1932). Malinowski himself began teaching there in 1913, three years before he obtained his doctorate in anthropology, and Raymond Firth was the first of his students to do so, thus initiating the reproductive phase in Malinowskian functionalism that lasted until World War II. Lecture course outlines for the period (Quiggin 1942; Stocking 1984; Urry 1985) reveal the transmission not simply of an emergent, triumphant Malinowskian functionalism, but of an uneasy blending of all three perspectives—evolutionary, diffusionist, and functional.

Anthropologists of all three trajectories were engaged in the large intellectual debates going on at the time. Specific tensions held together anthropology-in-the-making, the ritual classicists (especially Gilbert Murray, Jane Harrison, and F. M. Cornford), and the latter-day idealists, best represented, perhaps, by F. H. Bradley, Bernard Bosanquet, and D. G. Ritchie (Collini 1978). Among the contested and contesting European anthropologies, Arnold van Gennep's blistering attack on Emile Durkheim's study of elementary forms of religious belief (Lukes 1973) occurred at the very moment in 1912 when the young A. R. Radcliffe-Brown at Cambridge was turning aside from his mentor, Rivers's, strictures on the complexity of oceanic peoples, initiating what turned out to be "British anthropology's long affair with Durkheimianism" (Collini 1978: 35; Vincent 1986b).

In the Edwardian institutional contestation, however, it was Malinowskian functionalists who initially won the day. It was their definition of social anthropology as the study of small-scale society—ahistorical, *ethno*-graphic, and comparative—that brought closure to the discipline until the 1950s, even while their ethnography portrayed the contradictions of the colonial situation in which most of them worked. How did this come about?

The event to which I attach considerable importance was the Rockefeller Foundation's funding of prolonged and intensive field research into culture contact in sub-Saharan Africa by Malinowski's students—for, as George Stocking (1974) has so splendidly documented, explanations of dominance are to be found not in the valency of ideas but in academic power, control, and institutionalization, and, I would add, strategies of reproduction. Malinowski succeeded with Rockefeller where Rivers, some thirteen years earlier, had failed with Carnegie (Vincent 1990: 120). The complexity that Rivers insisted on recognizing in the contemporary settings in which anthropologists worked—even if they were depopulated Melanesian islands—lost out to selective and ahistoric representations of "savage," "primitive," and "tribal" societies. Romantically, ethnicization followed.

Thus it was during the Edwardian era, with battles lost, that anthropology became distinctively *ethno*-graphic, by which I mean that professional, academic anthropologists chose to define themselves as writing about "peoples" rather than, for example, polities, places, or problems. This choice would appear to have owed a great deal at the time to the primacy attached to language, and to the views of German ethnologists on the relation of language to culture. But these convictions themselves existed within the global context of thrusting nationalisms in central Europe, and of the expansionist, administrative, law-and-order phase of British and German colonialisms. Ethnicization developed within an intellectual ethnoscape certainly, but also within a nonintellectual one, as Michel-Rolph Trouillot indicates in his chapter in this volume. The first was made up of eugenicists, imperialists, critics of colonialism, Fabians, and sociologists; the second, the populations of territories in Melanesia and elsewhere, and all that Pitt-Rivers wrote about so eloquently in *The Clash of Cultures*.

The primary victor in these Edwardian struggles was Bronislaw Malinowski. From Max Gluckman to Clifford Geertz, Malinowski has exerted a compelling attraction for critics. The documentation, analysis, adulation, and controversy that surround him bulk larger than life—and yet, I would suggest, remain partial and incomplete. Here I appropriate Malinowski to advocate historicism over textualism and discursivity.

The presupposition that the words an ethnographer writes at any one time, in any one text, fully and clearly reveal his philosophical stance is clearly misleading. A more complex discussion of Malinowski's work than that undertaken by Geertz—the Harold Bloom of anthropological criticism—would seek to explain why Malinowski decided to leave certain projects fragmentary, and others unpublished. Unpublished work, such as Malinowski's posthumously published *A Diary in the Strict Sense of the Term* (Malinowski 1967), articulates a relation with a writer's internalized "public"—readers and critics—that shapes both theme and style. No "public voice" can, surely, be accorded to a work its author never published. Yet this was the text selected to represent Malinowski in *Works and Lives* (Geertz 1988).

Textual isolationism can surely be carried to an extreme. Malinowski's ethnography (like Roy Franklin Barton's discussed earlier) is trimmed to suit the needs of successive representations. His romanticism has been trivialized, and its rebelliousness obscured (Vincent 1986a; n.d.). Malinowski's interpretivist critics, collectively it would seem, fail to recognize his thickest description, his deepest ethnography, *Coral Gardens and their Magic* (Malinowski 1935). They overlook his field trips to Africa and Mexico and they ignore his statement that the greatest mistake he made in his ethnography was to neglect the colonial situation. Another way of making the same point is to ask, How do readerships become limited? How do certain texts, written by certain authors, come to represent bodies of anthropology both to a wider audience and to anthropologists themselves?

Critical substance requires that Malinowski be restored to the cosmopolitan European intellectual tradition in which he was raised, and to the Cracow and Leipzig in which he lived, once sitting across a cafe table from the exiled V. I. Lenin. *Malinowski between Two Worlds: The Polish Roots of an Anthropological Tradition* (Ellen, et al. 1988) begins to do just this, and will surely be followed by other works that subject Malinowski's career and publications to the canons of critical historiographical study. For Edwardian London, this effort would mean repossessing several other "lost" figures on the human scale: Edward Westermarck, R. R. Marett, John Linton Myres, Leonard Trelawny Hobhouse, Graham Wallas, and Harold Laski, all of whom played not insignificant parts in the works and lives of Malinowski, his colleagues, and his students (Vincent 1984, 1990). The Malinowski who is the creation of traditional histories of anthropological theory bears little resemblance to the Malinowski who figures in the perceptions and arguments of his Edwardian contemporaries—or who is ignored by them. His anthropology has to be placed within the context of the debates and struggles of his and their time. How else may his ethnography be read?

CONCLUSION

This essay has argued that we are, as always, at a critical moment in anthropology. It is a moment, like all moments, that taps a political process and is self-consciously aware that it does so. Why, then, this rehistoricization of the discipline *now*? I would suggest that the mystifying of the experimental moment and the minimalizing of anthropology (as if it were ethnography and nothing else) have created within some of the discipline's practitioners a failure of confidence.

More specifically, this essay has argued that many of those who, in the 1980s, advocated the application of literary techniques to ethnographic texts did not use the insights of literary criticism in a particularly trenchant way. The references in this essay alone suggest that they narrowed prematurely what literary criticism offered. I have suggested elsewhere (Vincent 1990) that ethnography—or, better, the monograph based on field research—has always been the foremost vehicle of critical challenge to anthropology's dominant paradigms. In undermining ethnography, one undermines theory.

Finally, this essay has attempted to suggest, in a somewhat cursory fashion (but see Vincent 1990 for an extended treatment of the theme), that anthropology has constantly struggled in its productions to resonate with the world in which its practitioners have lived. At one point during our advanced seminar, the human condition he was describing in the American southwest led José Limón to urge us all fully to appreciate that "power exists; power resides; history hurts." "Allow me my anguish," was Rolph Trouillot's response to another participant's well-meant effort to intellectualize his argument. In engaging historicism, I would suggest, critical anthropology begins to engage this world. Viewed historically, engaging historicism has become a step towards dismantling historically established oppositions between practice and theory, production and criticism. It has real and practical consequences.

——— *Note* ———

1. The essay I presented to the seminar bore the title "Beyond Ethnography: Palimpsest for the 1990s." In response to the suggestions of my seminar colleagues, I have retained only a portion of that essay and expanded more on my conversational interjections at our sessions, arguing the case for both a greater knowledge of the history of anthropology and historicism. I am grateful to Richard Fox for later making the relevant portions of our seminar's taped sessions available to me.

Chapter 4

FOR HIRE:

RESOLUTELY LATE MODERN

Paul Rabinow

BAUDELAIRE'S wonderfully ironic injunction—you have no right to despise the present—is not easy to live up to. It is worth the effort, however, as it helps us to navigate a middle course between retreating into nostalgia and fleeing into fantasy. Baudelaire's injunction carried a double imperative: to observe society and to give aesthetic form to one's observations. Baudelaire's modern artists, however, were not *flâneurs* observing disinterestedly from the outside, but participant observers giving form to the present and thereby transforming its obvious ugliness into a new beauty. "Baudelairian modernity is an exercise in which extreme attention to what is real is confronted with the practice of a liberty that simultaneously respects this reality and violates it" (Foucault 1984: 41). At the end of the twentieth century, such a project, such a self-formative practice, such a way of standing toward the world and oneself is, albeit with appropriate transformations, still our task. The task is to be resolutely late modern.

In this paper I sketch one set of late modern practices in the hope that after we have a clearer sense of who we are, we will be able to decide who we ought to be. The paper's first section juxtaposes Franz Boas's program for joining anthropology and modern life—in which anthropology's task was to provide a scientific analysis of society and then lead society forward in an enlightened fashion on the basis of those scientific insights—with Max Weber's diagnosis that modern life has made the hope for such a pedagogic anthropology little more than self-delusion. Using these influential interpretations of modernity as an analytic grid, I offer an ethnographic sketch of the micropractices of hiring in the elite academy as emblematic of contemporary muddling of truth, ethics, and power. Starting with Joan Vincent's distinction between the profession and the discipline (one uncertain, the other flourishing), I argue that especially today, when a generational change is taking place throughout the American university system, reproduction of the profession currently turns too much on the tacit norms not of truth but of "character." I propose that the issue of character is largely taken for granted and unthematized; by bringing it to light it can be analytically distinguished from the relations of truth and power and its importance debated on its own terms.

ANTHROPOLOGY AND MODERN LIFE

DIDACTIC SCIENCE

Franz Boas published *Anthropology and Modern Life* in 1928. It is an important statement for a number of reasons, not least of which is the archaeological strata of scientific, political, and ethical layers it contains. These strata provide us with perspectives on our current situation. Among the most revealing of them is the problem of the unevenness of progress in anthropology. Some dimensions of *Anthropology and Modern Life* simply are dated; Boas's case against racial hierarchies and racial thinking has thoroughly carried the theoretical day. Today his arguments sound timid and far too generous in their serious engagement with his racist opponents. Of course, racism has hardly disappeared, but it no longer is a scientifically credible position. This unambiguous case of scientific progress, however, highlights Boas's typical overvaluation of the socially beneficent power of science.

It seemed self-evident to Boas that the truth of his position would bring with it social enlightenment. "I hope to demonstrate that a clear understanding of the principles of anthropology illuminates the social practices of our times and may show us, if we are ready to listen to its teachings, what to do and what to avoid" (Boas 1928: 11). He was partially wrong. Louis Dumont (1970) has shown that the triumph of an ideology of egalitarianism and individualism resulted in a naturalization of difference. Despite the best efforts of anthropology, racism remains largely intact, although no longer *dans le vrai*. Still, such naturalization of difference is not the same thing as scientific respectability. The continuation of racism does not put the scientific validity of Boas's anthropology in question; rather it reveals the limits of science's relation to social change. Boas's stance of upright and self-assured didacticism today seems thin. This does not mean that the discipline of anthropology has not created a body of knowledge (it has). It does mean, however, that the relation between anthropology's scientific achievements and their political and ethical consequences is more ambiguous and complex than Boasian humanism allowed.

Boas's understanding of modernity was naive. "Generally valid progress in social forms is intimately associated with advance in knowledge. It is based fundamentally on the recognition of a wider concept of humanity, and with it on the weakening of the conflicts between individual societies" (Boas 1928:227–28). Woefully wrong as empirical predictions, such pronouncements exemplify a blindness about the imbrication of knowledge in the world. My intent is not to attack Boas. I believe he stands as an exemplary founding figure for American anthropology in its commitment to understanding otherness and defending pluralism as fundamental to the species as well as to modern democracy. My intent is simply, sixty years later,to point to a disaggregation of the scientific from the political and the ethical. My claim is that this disaggregation, this problematization, this detotalization, stands as a challenge to any thinker who wishes to remain within the tradition of the Enlightenment as a modern and not a countermodern.

AN UNBROTHERLY ARISTOCRACY

Max Weber, writing a decade before Boas, offered a more complex interpretation of the relations of truth, politics, and culture. Weber's insights into just how problematic these relations were becoming in the modern world provided him with a more precise and illuminating insight into just what sort of ethical beings we moderns were. His 1915 essay, "Religious Rejections of the World and Their Directions," is one of the darkest portraits of the place of Intellectuals, capital I, and Culture, capital C, within Modernity, capital M. In the essay, Weber outlines ideal types of the competing "spheres of value" (and there are more than the three that Jürgen Habermas [1984] has rationally reconstructed) as a contribution to "the sociology and typology of rationalism" (1915:322). Weber's interpretations of the cultural role of science in modernity (understood as an economic and cultural formation) are of specific interest for the issue of ethics and community we are exploring. Although Weber's sociological and historical interpretation of modernity remains more compelling than Boas's, it is arguably more metaphysical and German (as Nietzsche would say) than he suspected.

Weber was keenly aware that knowledge was a social phenomenon carried by specific groups who played a role in the construction of the social hierarchies of modern life. He clearly indicated the importance for European culture of what Pierre Bourdieu has called "distinction": "The barriers of education and of aesthetic cultivation are the most intimate and the most insuperable of all status differences" (Weber 1915:354). In Weber's view, however, the reproduction of privilege and power through these class-restricted qualities had consequences that extended beyond the socially odious status barriers. These consequences were cultural, and they permeated the very nature of the knowledge being produced.

For Weber, the rise and triumph of empirical science was at the very heart of the cultural crisis of meaning. "The triumph of science in the face of universally acknowledged inequality of suffering and the injustice of the world leads to a devaluation of the world per se which can take the form of a positing of values as timeless and not dependent on their concretion—as culture" (Weber 1915:354). Science, for Weber, was not a hallowed refuge of rationality and hope—he saw that view as an uncourageous clinging to a historically surpassed bourgeois *bildung*—but literally a distorted and distorting achievement with dangers on the ethical, cultural, and political planes. "Worldly man has regarded this possession of culture as the highest good. In addition to the burden of ethical guilt, however, something has adhered to this cultural value which was bound to depreciate it with still greater finality, namely senselessness—if this cultural value is to be judged in terms of its own standards" (1915:355). This is the famous crisis of meaning that has received so much attention in the Weber scholarship.

The grim evaluation of intellectual life left to us by the venerable Weber at the end of his days is not to be taken lightly. "The intellect, like all cultural values, has created an aristocracy based on the possession of rational culture and independent of all personal ethical qualities of man. The aristocracy of intellect is hence an unbrotherly aristocracy" (Weber 1915:355). So, too, as we shall see later, is the petite bourgeoisie of the intellect. Still, his claim that all personal ethical qualities of intellectuals have been divorced from their intellectual pursuits is, ethnographically speaking, too broad a claim. Weber's view of the triumph of value-neutrality and objective knowledge as having an "elective affinity" with a community of ethically unbrotherly individuals would be hard to dispute either historically or sociologically. That elective affinity, however, is not an iron cage. Weber himself may have too readily accepted this tendency as unalterable, rather than as the historically and culturally contingent one that it obviously is. Do I have to add that its being historically contingent does not make it less real and constraining?

Weber was led sociologically to somber reflections on the ethical and social consequences of the rationalization of the world through science and capitalism: "The routinized economic cosmos, and thus the rationally highest form of the provision of material goods which is indispensable for all worldly culture, has been a structure to which the absence of love is attached from the very root. All forms of activity in the structured world have appeared to be entangled in the same guilt" (1915:355). This sacrifice of love, or, we might simply say, of solidarity, on the altar of science had a particularly striking consequence for intellectual life: "Cultivated man who strives for self-perfection, in the sense of acquiring or creating cultural values . . . can become weary of life but he cannot become satiated with life in the sense of completing a cycle. . . . Viewed in this way, all 'culture' appears as man's emancipation from the organically prescribed cycle of natural life. For this very reason culture's every step forward seems condemned to lead to an ever more devastating senselessness" (Weber 1915:356). This is Weber at his most prophetic, his most German. However brilliant Weber's analysis of culture, his appeals to that lost age when men died satiated with life seems closer to bathos than pathos.

ETHNOGRAPHIC ELEMENTS

STAGE SIX: GENERATIVITY

By all accounts this is a particularly unsettled and factious period in the American academy. There are a number of structural reasons underlying this discontent. The institutions of higher education are at the beginning of a major generational renovation; for example, half the faculty at the University of California at Berkeley will retire in the next decade. Those who entered the academy during the years of massive expansion following Sputnik are now looking retirement in the eye. Who will replace them (if anyone) and how they will handle that change (to the extent that they have the power to do so) are major questions that are only now becoming thematized in diverse ways in different fields. The generation of academics who are now in their forties and were formed (to the extent that they were) by the upheavals and contestations, both political and intellectual, of the late sixties and early seventies are now poised to become *les héritiers*.

The older group is overwhelmingly white and male; the younger includes a few more women; neither includes many representatives of what are currently designated as ethnic minorities.

Joan Vincent (personal communication, 1989) makes an important distinction between the profession and the discipline. The problems of reproduction of the profession, in its institutional dimension—especially at the larger and more prestigious universities—is my object here. Even at the professional level, of course, the current changes are taking diverse forms. Many smaller (often newer) anthropology departments are flourishing. Some of the older departments planned ahead or have already navigated this transition with some grace. I am speaking from a department that is in the throes of a distinctly less than graceful transition in social and cultural anthropology, and this no doubt situates my view of the matter. Clearly, one danger is to generalize too broadly from local conditions. Another is to conflate the transition pains of the profession with what to my mind is an exciting and diverse moment in the discipline. Again, as Joan Vincent and George Marcus (personal communication, 1989) rightly point out, the control of departments and the formation of new problematics are not the same thing.

This structural and demographic conjuncture forms an important background condition to current debates within the disciplines, but it does not predetermine their content. It seems fair to say that the intellectual programs which the Sputnik generation put on the agenda are now in question. Whether it is cognitive anthropology or symbolic anthropology or some other sort, it seems uncontroversial to say not that they have failed (as much serious work continues to be done in these subspecialties) but only that they have not lived up to the programmatic hopes that corresponded to (and were in part generated by) the myriad new departments, journals, training grants, foundation programs, and so forth, that were handed to those entering into the university system at that time. Messianism (or programmatic optimism) and structural expansion, while hardly reducible one to the other, are obviously not unrelated. Hence, while there is a plurality of research agendas today, none is dominant, none has produced the long-heralded normal science, none seems any longer to hold out the promise that each embraced twenty or thirty years ago for dramatic, sweeping, and sustainable change. This state of affairs clearly troubles some more than others.

I believe that some of the grumpiness, even virulence, observable in the field today is a function of this double conjuncture: the problem facing many of these sixty-year-old white males (and those of whatever gender or biological age who identify with them) is one of generativity. Having had every advantage available during the longest sustained period of growth and prosperity that institutions of higher education have known, the question is open (both for them and for us) as to how to evaluate their contribution. In Erik Erikson's schema of the seven stages of life, the next-to-the-last stage is adulthood: generativity versus stagnation. Generativity "is the concern in establishing and guiding the next generation." It includes but encompasses productivity and creativity and is embodied in the virtue of care (Erikson 1950:266–74). The last stage in Erikson's schema is maturity. We are not there yet.

Lest I be accused of "ageism," let me make clear that I believe such a demographic situation only makes probable a conjunctural crisis of generativity in the Eriksonian sense; it does not ensure any particular outcome. Those nearing the end of their careers can as well be mentors, selectively encouraging new trends in their field, as they can be a kind of colonial police, viewing the new trends and their representatives as dangerous and foreign ("barbarian," "irrationalist," "nihilist," "narcissist," etc., terms that are now replacing "idealist," "positivist," "soft," hard," and the older, cold-war masculinist cluster of boundary-maintaining epithets), nostalgic for the good old days and vigilantly resentful of changing ways. Bruno Latour's maxim, "Irrationality is always an accusation made by someone building a network over someone else who stands in the way," might well be emblazoned above doorways throughout the groves of academe (1988b:259). I am not talking about psychology here (although there is much to be said on that score). Rather I am simply identifying a disharmonious conjuncture of power relations and cultural form.

The importance of these tacit standards is highlighted when new groups seek entry into the system. The resistance to women in recent decades, to Jews in earlier periods (and in many ways today), and to minorities of all sorts today is in part a function of their simply not sharing the taken-for-granted skills and customs of the game which the old boys (a cultural term, not a biological one) learned in graduate school, conferences, hiring meetings, faculty meetings, football games, suburban homes, bars, and the rest of the environment that constitutes middle-class academic life. It requires a conscious act of self-analysis and will to overcome these dispositions, which one has spent so long inculcating; is it a surprise that so few make the effort?

TABLE MANNERS: MICROPRACTICES OF REPRODUCTION

Among the rites of initiation, sacralization, and socialization that abound in the elite circles of the American academy—all the more important and abundant for their very unselfconsciousness—one of the most crucial is the visit of the short-list candidate. Overdetermined, as are all such examinations of what Pierre Bourdieu refers to as the dominated faction of the dominating class, the visit is an enactment and examination (in the Foucaultian sense) of "character," the crucial indicator of eligibility for future collegiality. My aim here is not to present a comprehensive analysis of this set of cultural practices, but merely to bring it from background to foreground and thereby to make it more available for understanding and evaluation. Above all, my aim is *not* to claim that these evaluation procedures are Machiavellian; generally speaking they are rather the opposite: embodied and unselfconscious practices and dispositions that Bourdieu calls *habitus*. It is precisely their dispositional quality that makes them so hard to change. In discussions with colleagues in other fields, it has become clear that the form of the "visit" varies from one academic field to the next in the American academy. More ethnography would not be hard to compile, as we have all engaged in these practices.

Reversing Groucho Marx's dictum that he would not want to belong to any club that would have him as a member, elite institutions, by definition, seek to hire someone worthy of themselves; and anyone they hire is, post factum, worthy of being a member of the club. It is the best who always choose the best from among the very best, since, in the final analysis, it is they who have the power of nomination in the twin sense of naming and choosing. Because what is at stake is distinction, and because there is a great security in older symbolic wealth, it is no accident that members of established elite institutions are vastly overrepresented on short lists at other older institutions. These obvious mechanisms of reproduction are particularly transparent in periods like ours (twenty-seven of Berkeley's thirty faculty members are full professors, and all thirty have tenure). A survey of the American Anthropological Association's *Guide* reveals that of the approximately 140 members of the Chicago, Berkeley, Harvard, Michigan, and Columbia departments, only two have degrees from universities below the top ten ranked departments (and their foreign equivalents)—one from Utah and one from Boston. To anyone familiar with the "pockets of stagnancy" found in these elite departments, any debate about meritocracy would be hard to take seriously except in sociological terms of the analysis of the mechanisms and practices of reproduction.

The situation is complicated by the fact that there is an awareness (sometimes acute, sometimes muted, but rarely a source of voluntary disqualification) that standards have changed during the last thirty years and the quantitative and qualitative demands for entry into the system are immeasurably higher now. Some of the severest critics and upholders of an often imaginary tradition will admit, if pressed, that they would never make the grade by current rules. Others eagerly assume the mantle of the institution, claiming glory they themselves have neither created nor sustained. While this is always the way elite institutions work, there is a certain friability to these claims today. When intellectual arguments break down (or never begin), there is often an appeal to the institutional investment already made in programs whose scientific worth is no longer defensible—scientifically.

A candidate's "work" is the ostensible site of the preliminary sorting performed by the search committee. It would be sociologically naive to say that the "work" is the only criterion invoked at this initial stage. Previously established reputation, placement in the contemporary cultural field, and advisers' power are all practically inseparable from the work. (Three or four hundred candidates are not sorted by blind meritocratic principles that ignore other sources of symbolic capital and distinction; remember the outcry that occurred when the panels for the annual meetings of the American Anthropological Association had to be submitted anonymously.) Nonetheless, credentials and production (the latter gains weight, obviously, the higher one is on the career ladder) have the most importance during the triage. Needless to say, when it comes to "work," the author has not been problematized in anthropology.

The weight of the candidate's work is downplayed, if not eliminated, in the final competition, exactly to the extent that there is consensus that the search committee has done its job well: by definition, all these candidates meet our standards or they would not be on our short list. Self-satisfying and self-justifying both for the individual department and the discipline as a whole (it would be scandalous for a major university to put a candidate from another major university on its short list who was not, at least post factum, worthy), such preselection, although certainly necessary for elite reproduction, is not sufficient to specify which of the elect will be chosen this time. The small group of candidates at the "senior," "rising star," and "entry" level who appear continuously on more than one short list affirms this pattern.

This self-affirming and largely predetermined consensus about eligibility leaves "character" as the definitive criteria to be deployed for the final selection. Confidential phone calls from chairs to chairs, and conversations over drinks at conferences, turn on whether so-and-so is "difficult," "aggressive," or "sexist," three of the hardest labels to shake, particularly when the candidate is never given a chance to defend himself. Michele Lamont, a Québécoise sociologist, has observed that in contrast to the French hiring game, in the United States "being cultivated brings with it no advantages" (1988:29). Rather, the key to success is the incorporation of American norms: "initiative, self-confidence, independence, problem-solving activism, adjustment to institutional demands, organization, de-termination, motivation" (Lamont 1988:29). In correct proportions, a streak of Babbitry can also be an advantage.

When a short list is finally established, all that is left to examine is character (although battles over definition of subfields may well continue if the short list is sufficiently heterogeneous and there is only a thin con-sensus on the position's definition). A truly dreadful talk will, of course, be harmful to a candidate, but such a bad show can never be taken to indicate a fundamental deficit in the candidate's intellectual abilities—which, after all, have already been established as first rate by the search committee. Other causes are frequently assigned: an accident ("she seems jet-lagged," "the flu is terrible this year," "he's getting complacent"), or the revelation of a more deep-seated (aren't they always?) character flaw. We can see the truth of this hypothesis in the vocabulary available to down-play the cognitive or scientific content of the talk; it is bad form to dictate explicitly what anyone who is already in the charmed circle can say. The "work" has already partially assured that whatever is in the talk is more likely to be judged on other grounds.

What is read in the talk is the candidate's character: Did she choose the right talk to give? Will this person be a "good" colleague? How will she relate to students? (The solicitude displayed for the welfare of students is in remarkable contrast to its rather lower profile in ordinary circumstances.) Is she "difficult"? How will she "fit in" in the broadest sense? These qualities are often judged from the manner in which the candidate responds to questions. The repertory of performative moves would be worth ethnographic explanation. Not answering questions at all ("Gee, I hadn't thought of that") is catastrophic; aggressive comebacks are merely dangerous and can ultimately be advantageous; and flattery is usu-ally safe. Evaluation is often cast in terms of teaching ability, the relevance of which is dubious to the extent that the context is so different in terms of power, stress, and a hundred other variables. But beyond teaching abilities—this is the ethnographic hypothesis—is found the character evaluation.

There is much to be said about the tour of offices. A foreign colleague observed that it was like visiting the State Department—first the China office, then Africa, India, and so forth. The degree of *adoubement*, or ritual respect, required depends on the rank and relative positions of those in-terviewing and those being interviewed. A delicate game consists of not presenting oneself as too knowledgeable or too critical or too sycophantic or too ignorant of the interviewers' work and status. The extent to which this art of symbolic navigation is a product of class and status socialization is revealed and highlighted by the entry of newer minorities into the arena, who, while mastering in diverse ways the codes of the academic world, reveal through breakdown (not having been raised in these bodily, linguistic, and paralinguistic practices) how habitual the "docility" in its strict sense really is. This woman is "too aggressive," that ethnic minority is hypocritical in his compliments, the New Yorker is arrogant, and so forth. It is dangerous for the candidate or her supporters to point out these class- and status-based prejudgments to the old boys, who, proclaiming their perfect neutrality, will almost never engage on this ground. Ah, the WASP (membership relatively open to those of good character), as Jim Clifford (personal communication, 1988) points out, the most unmarked and hence most ethnic of ethnic groups.

Apparently not all disciplines engage in the "office visit." This could be perhaps explained by the anthropological disposition to have informants come for interviews and the reluctance of more "humane" disciplines to display their examinations in so direct and bureaucratic a manner; no doubt many other reasons could be given, and it would be worth exploring them. In some cases it is the candidate who sits in an office and is visited, and in others it is the candidate who is mobile and must improvise composure during the interruptions of phone calls and students' poking their heads in. What is this all about?

If the office round is tiring, at least the encounter is dyadic, and a simple enactment of signs of *hommage* usually suffices. In fact, it is the wisest thing to do. Candidates who overplay flattery, especially at the expense of other members of the department, are playing a dangerous game, forgetting that gossip is fueled by the recirculating of such talk. The game is more complicated and less easily mastered with students, whose habitus is less embodied but with whom the power risks are lower— because student power exists only to the extent that it is an element in faculty strategies, however tacit they may be. Student support is a potential plus, but when it is too fervent it is frequently seen as a mark against the candidate, for either it implies that current faculty-student relations are less than ideal, or else it is read as a mask for the tactics of another faction or as a "demagogic" character flaw in the candidate.

However important the "talk" and the office visits may be, the "dinner" (more so than the "lunch," in which drinking is usually controlled, daylight pours in, and other obligations press on hosts and guests alike) is perhaps the trickiest event to manage, as it is the one whose rules are the least explicit for either the candidate or the hosts. The dinner for the most prestigious of candidates must demonstrate the hosts' distinction (often "the" French restaurant in town) or, in places like Berkeley or New York, with many such establishments, unusual ethnicity (food from a particularly obscure province of Thailand) or local renown or charm. The care taken in the choice must be obvious, or else made known to the candidate. The hosts may well be uncomfortable in such surroundings, given their more-than-frequently strapped budgets and often "militantly petit bourgeois" (the phrase is Leo Lowenthal's) life-styles.

Having those who sit in judgment feel uncomfortable (perhaps revealing their own insecurities about how they would fare in these circumstances today, should they ever get as far as the interview) is dangerous for the candidate. The hosts' discomfort can be indicated by nervous joking about the exoticism of the menu, which demonstrates their own "regular guy" status as well as the out-of-the-ordinariness of the event. (The *Oxford English Dictionary* tells us that "guy" means, among other things, "a person of grotesque appearance, especially with reference to dress.") It is up to the candidate to manage this discomfort by showing her appreciation of the expense and distinction being displayed, as well as her own comfort and solidarity with the "regular guy" status she will be expected to assume. A candidate "too familiar" with such fare may not be the good colleague, the ordinary guy (in American "the guys" is gender neutral) that the boys are searching for; but too much discomfort or too much familiarity and ease with the hosts' nervous joking is equally dangerous because it disparages the distinction of the restaurant and the event. Hence what is required is an uneasy deferral to others, indicative of a potential belonging but one that does not signal having already crossed the threshold of acceptance (which is often interpreted as a dangerous presumption and arrogance on the part of the candidate).

Amid the cascading nonsequiturs (discussions of traffic problems are a bad sign for the candidate, as they indicate that he or she has not yet succeeded in making the interviewers feel comfortable), the meal proceeds. Choices are tacitly posed: Should the candidate drink the wine or stick with a beer as some of the younger old boys are doing? Should she notice that a spouse is drinking coffee (the distinctive marker of American dining habits, aside from starting a meal with the salad) during the entire meal? (The Nobel Prize-winning French microbiologist, Francois Jacob [1988], recounts one of his first visits to America, when he was the speaker at a luncheon, and tells of his dismay, discomfort, and, finally, amusement at looking down the table during his talk at his colleagues eating their sandwiches and salads, as he attempted to eat his own food while answering questions from those finishing off dessert.) Then eventually, whether unannounced or staged, with the realization that this is a serious event, someone shifts the talk to the profession or the person's research. How to answer not too seriously but not too lightly becomes, often with dessert, the task. Energy flagging by this point: what's a soul to do?

Simultaneously trivial and encompassing—indeed deriving much of their power from being labeled trivial—these micropractices provide, as Michel Foucault, Pierre Bourdieu, ethnomethodology, and the new philosophy and sociology of science have demonstrated, a rich terrain to explore. An ethnography of doctoral examinations, tenure meetings, ad hoc committees, and a long list of other such institutionalized practices would, it seems evident, be worth examining in their own turn. The point of such inquiry would not only be to unmask Machiavellian tactics or blatantly partisan strategies, tasks for which we have other analytic tools, but to pose the constructive question of who we want to be. This proposal is not a political program, although it would certainly eventually have impact on power relations. Nor is it a question of positivists versus humanists; ethical questions are transverse to epistemological ones. It merely maintains that if we want ethical considerations to play a central role in the articulation of truth and power—and I think we do—then bringing such considerations into view is the necessary first step towards recognizing who we are today and setting out on the road to a better place. We have, after all, no right to despise the present.

Chapter 5

REWRITING CULTURE

Graham Watson

INTERPRETIVE anthropologists have committed excesses, but they have not committed enough of them. Their critical analysis of modernist ethnography remains inchoate, their predicament unresolved. To take their analysis as given would be unduly complacent; to attempt to move beyond it, premature.

True, interpretive anthropology has had a bad press. Critics accuse it of being "intellectually irresponsible" (Spiro 1986:275), of lacking "predict-ability, replicability, verifiability, and law-generating capacity" (Shankman 1984:264), and of indulging in "openly acknowledged freedom to engage in mystification and creative self-empowering fabrication unaccountable to any challenge of logic or fact" (Sangren 1988:414). They characterize it as "subjectivist" (Connor 1984:271), as involving "navel-gazing" (Jarvie 1988:428), and as leading us all to "the black hole of solipsism" (Friedman 1987:167). They allude darkly to "the close relationship between indi-vidual psychology and anthropology in the United States" (Aijmer 1988:424) and to the fact that "quite a number of American anthropologists are poets" (Caplan 1988:9). They conclude that it constitutes "a particular form of individualist, bourgeois ideology" (Sangren 1988:418), a retreat from the world into the text, which ignores the interesting questions and reports "no-thing" (Rabinow 1988:359). They complain that interpretive anthropologists "proudly proclaim the relativity of everything except their own position" (Friedman 1987:164) and that their writing "seriously misrepresents the activity of ethnography" (Carrithers 1988:19). To cap it all, they say it is "already old-hat" (McDonald 1988:429) and that its jaded Priest-King awaits ritual slaughter (Leach 1989:137).

Well, yes, perhaps, but such excesses reveal interpretive anthropology to be not a radical enterprise but a reformist one. Its critical analysis remains incomplete in that it leaves realist notions of representation essentially intact.[1]

James Clifford (1983b:130) argues, with considerable justification, that "interpretive anthropology demystifies much of what had previously passed unexamined in the construction of ethnographic narratives, types, observations, and descriptions." Note, however, what still remains unexamined. Consider Clifford Geertz's amused comment (1988:1, 2):

> the most intense objection [to concern with "how ethnographic texts are constructed"] . . . is that concentrating our gaze on the ways in which knowledge claims are advanced undermines our capacity to take any of these claims seriously. Somehow, attending to such matters as imagery, metaphor, phraseology, or voice is supposed to lead to a corrosive relativism in which everything is but a more or less clever expression of opinion . . . Exposing how the thing is done is to suggest that, like the lady sawed in half, it isn't done at all.

Here Geertz equates—or seems to; his observation is characteristically deniable—"attending to such matters as imagery, metaphor, phraseology, or voice" with "how the thing is done" and "how ethnographic texts are constructed." That will not do. All honor to him for insisting (Geertz 1988:27) that ethnographers *write* and that "the separation of what someone says from how they say it . . . is as mischievous in anthropology as it is in poetry, painting or political oratory," but he and all who follow him, beguiled by Gallic gallimaufry, are remiss in being inattentive to the deeply germane work produced by those social scientists whose very project it is to describe how people collectively constitute a sense of an external and objective reality. I mean, of course, ethnomethodology.

Let me rephrase that. Ethnomethodology is divided into warring camps (Atkinson 1988), and I cannot vouch for all of them. I am interested, primarily, in the notions of indexicality and reflexivity, as expounded by Harold Garfinkel in 1967 and currently used by the constructivist sociologists of scientific knowledge in Britain (e.g., Barry Barnes, Harry Collins, Michael Mulkay, Steve Woolgar, Steven Yearly). Indexicality refers to the context dependency of meaning; reflexivity, to the way in which accounts and the settings they describe elaborate and modify each other in a back-and-forth process. Adopting these notions enables us to do two things. First, it enables us to press relativism well beyond the point to which most interpretive anthropologists have been willing to take it. The consequence, paradoxically, is to bring relief to those suffering epistemological hypochondria, to allow us all to get on with the business of reporting the world we know, and to do so without indulging in arch literary experiments. Second, it makes available for study the work in which laymen and professionals alike engage when we produce facts, determinate meanings, and definitive versions. It is work at which we are all adept but which is ordinarily invisible to us; we neither recognize it nor remark upon it. Yet it is the cake on which "such matters as imagery, metaphor, phraseology, and voice" are but the icing.

To characterize such matters as icing on the cake is not to dismiss them as insignificant. The point is to broaden the scope of inquiry to encompass matters systematically disregarded both by interpretive anthropologists and their critics.

Adopting indexicality and reflexivity will not induce us to embrace solipsism. While I hold no brief for ethnomethodology in its entirety, I think it only fair to observe that ethnomethodologists are concerned not with individuals or subjectivities but with courses of coordinated action. Pierre Bourdieu's (1977: 3, 81, 96; 1989) tarring ethnomethodology with the brush of subjectivism and voluntarism misrepresents its entire character. Ethnomethodology aspires to replace the prevailing Parsonian motivational approach to the analysis of social action with a procedural approach to the topic (Heritage 1987: 226). It asks not why but how.[2]

While ethnomethodologists take as their principal puzzle the comprehensibility of society, rather than the fact that people act in stable and regular ways, they have no difficulty in accounting for either structures or constraints. They insist that structures and constraints exist only in the practices of participants. To them structure is not an agent; it is not external to social encounters and it does not constrain them; rather it is located *in* them. Participants constitute structures, then orient themselves to them as if they had an objective existence prior to and independent of their discourse. They invoke structures in order to make sense of, and to render morally accountable, their actions and those of others: that is the aggregating mechanism.

When anthropologists likewise reify structures, they unreflectingly build into their explanatory apparatus the very commonsense reasoning ethnomethodologists set out to investigate. Granted, such has been the influence of Edmund Leach (1965), Frederick Barth (1969), and Pierre Bourdieu (1977) that anthropologists are less inclined than formerly to treat behavior as determined by rules, but "the system" or "objective structures" are still routinely said to "impact on" practice and to "produce" habitus. Exactly how is never specified. In Bourdieu's work, as Michael Moerman remarks (1988:57), how the material conditions of a social class produce habitus is left to unexplicated procedures of socialization during unexamined experiences presumed statistically to predominate among children of a given social class. But I digress.

To begin. All utterances have certain inherent and inescapable properties called indexicality and reflexivity. In principle these properties make incoherent the very notion of plain fact, definitive account, or determinate meaning. That is bad news for judges, oracles, anthropologists, and all obliged by their folk to produce verdicts, infallible predictions, and sustainable generalizations. Presumably, that is why we resist it so; but it is by attempting to come to grips with unpalatable truths that advances are made.

   The first unpalatable property of utterances is that meaning is invariably context-dependent, that is indexical. An utterance has a meaning only as part of a language. Even as part of a language it has no plain, literal sense. Its sense depends on the context in which it is uttered, who said it, when, to whom, in respect of what, and so on. (To make the point: any utterance whatsoever could, in principle, be intended or understood ironically.) So meaning is always contingent: this conclusion constitutes a radical extension of philosophy's treatment of the class of terms such as "we" and "they," whose meaning depends on the context of their use. No escape from the contingency of meaning is provided by defining one's terms. Definition merely displaces the problem sideways, for the defining terms themselves have to be defined, and so on.

   While the meaning of utterances is inherently unstable, we do not normally hear them that way; we normally hear them as having a sense that is stable to the point of being obvious. This is not because of any property of the linguistic system of which they are a part, but because they are already embedded in a context that provides them with a meaning, which we then take to be stable and obvious (Fish 1980:309). It follows that the search for determinate meanings is a wild goose chase. Such is the magnitude of the problem—in principle insurmountable—that in practice has to be overcome somehow by ethnographers and other scientific investigators whose business it is to propose generalizations that are sustainable and to formulate accounts that correspond to "the way things actually are." They are required to accomplish what is literally impossible.

People routinely produce what for practical purposes count as definitive accounts and sustainable generalizations. Being less concerned with first principles than with dealing with the practical matters at hand, people produce accounts that, although inevitably flawed, are good enough to be getting on with. That is what ethnographers do. Upon analysis, each and every account ethnographers produce can be seen to be inherently and irremediably defective.

For example, when, in their 1943 book *The Realm of a Rain Queen* (my favorite ethnography), the Kriges maintain that the social organization determines whom one shall marry (a proposition central to their work and therefore closely argued), they never land on a bedrock of plain truth that does not require further interpretation; every supposedly determinate term they substitute for indeterminate ones turns out to be itself indeterminate, and they are, formally at least, on the slippery slope of infinite regress. To avoid that regress they inevitably have recourse to ad hoc commonsense (and predominantly nonliterary) procedures that in principle are fallible but in practice are sufficient.

The tightest form in which their proposition is stated reads, "The fundamental rule is that a man must marry . . . his 'cattle-linked cross cousin'" (1943:142). This looks straightforward enough, but in fact each of the terms "must," "marry," and "cross cousin" is troublesome. The "must" of the rule has to be interpreted in the light of the Kriges' observation that 40 percent of the Lovedu men do *not* marry the cattle-linked cross-cousin "born for them." The Kriges cope with this trouble by five principal strategies.

First, they "ad hoc" previously unstated provisos. For example, a girl should not, according to the rule as given, marry her father's sister's husband; yet the Kriges report that they have found "a suggestive number of cases of this marriage" and argue that "these vestiges may reflect a rather different system, not unknown in tribes further north which Lovedu *munywalo* [bride-price] arrangements have reshaped" (1943:143).

Second, they bring apparent exceptions under the auspices of the rule by elaborating upon it as they go, leaving the reader to infer that the latest elaboration is what the rule meant all along. For example, the case of a man marrying not his cattle-linked cross-cousin, but his cattle-linked cross-cousin-once-removed, is "merely a variation upon the fundamental theme" (1943:147).

Third, they invoke a previously unstated metarule. For example, a man need not marry his cattle-linked cross-cousin provided that he obeys the even more fundamental rule that "where a man receives cattle [as from some kinsman other than his father] he must send brides" (1943:146). When this metarule is breached, as in the case of a man marrying his parallel cousin (thus reversing cattle-bride reciprocities), a previously unstated meta-metarule is invoked: everything, the Kriges state, "is subject to the supreme principle that 'if they agree', the rigidity of the rule may be relaxed" (1943:156). If any particular arrangement "seems to contradict *munywalo* dispositions," why then, "the culture is full of apparent contradictions testifying to its flexibility and to the subjection even of institutional arrangements to the desire for agreement and compromise" (1943:152).

Fourth, they preserve the principle by admitting exceptions. For example, the fact that parallel-cousin marriages are found "should not surprise us. There are irregularities in every sphere of culture, and the rules of mate selection are particularly liable to upset because of the complex interrelations that arise in the social system" (1943:142).

Fifth, they assert that things are too complicated to spell out in the brief space available. For example, they write, "unfortunately we shall have space merely to glance at the larger features instead of examining closely the exquisite workmanship and superlative ornamentation" (1943:141), and "the whole subject of substitution is too large for adequate treatment here" (1943:159).

I do not wish to suggest that the Kriges have employed sleight-of-hand. The skills they deploy are licit; indeed, they are part and parcel of the empiricist enterprise. The aim of the empiricist is to reduce all possible readings to one—the one that is unassailable by virtue of its correspondence to a supposed free-standing reality. Such a single reading can be reached *only* through the exercise of skills such as those I have thrown into relief.

The point is nicely put by Lawrence Wieder (1971:129) in this dismissal of a rulelike semantics:

Ethnomethodological studies of the employment of criteria have found that the use of such ad hoc procedures as elaborating the sense of a rule so that how the rule fits in this case can be seen, reconstructing some feature of an event so that it can be seen that it fits the prescription of the rule, ignoring some aspect of an event that does not fit the rule, and proceeding to classify an event while some "critical" aspects are left undetermined are essential, unavoidable practices. Whenever persons are confronted with having to make a choice and cannot rely on leaving this case in the status of undecided they will employ these practices.

Such practices are not confined to ethnography; they are what ordinary, competent members of society do; they are what scientists and mathematicians do (Livingston 1986; Gilbert and Mulkay 1984; Yearley 1981). A particularly elegant illustration of their ubiquity is the history of Euler's theorem of polyhedra, which Barry Barnes and John Law (1976: 233) describe as "one big exercise in repairing indexicality."

Such practices are an indispensable part of the craft of our own science, yet the manual writers systematically overlook them. A widely used field manual, for instance, begins with the claim that it contains "everything required to begin research, collect data, analyze what you find, and write up your report" (Spradley 1980:v), but nowhere does it provide instruction about how to constitute facts. One reason, I suggest, is that to do so would be letting a particularly embarrassing cat out of the bag. Showing how the thing is done does indeed suggest that it is not done at all. To show *how* a fact is constituted is to show *that* it is constituted. To show that a fact is constituted is to show that it is not a fact in the sense intended: it is not a thing encountered, having an existence prior to and independent of the writer's discourse.

This brings us to the second essential and inescapable property of all utterances which, in principle, renders impossible the formulation of definitive accounts: reflexivity. Reflexivity, as the ethnomethodologists have it, refers to the way in which accounts and the setting they describe mutually elaborate and modify each other in a back-and-forth process. Accounts, which describe a setting, are made up of expressions that derive their specific sense from that setting. It is important to note that accounts are not interpretations superimposed on a preexisting reality; rather, they are constitutive of that reality; they make it what it is.

Lawrence Wieder's (1974) field study of a rehabilitative house for paroled drug addicts is perhaps the classic analysis of the mutually elaborative relationship between accounts and setting. According to inmates, staff, and sociologists, relations among inmates, and between inmates and staff, are governed by the "convict code," which prohibits inmates from cooperating with staff, showing enthusiasm for their proposals, or accepting the legitimacy of their rules. Inmates who cooperate with staff invite being beaten to death. All involved describe, explain, and interpret particular instances of inmate behavior by characterizing them as instances of conformity with the code, which is understood to be context-independent, and to exhibit the Durkheimian properties of exteriority and constraint.

The code is used not only to interpret actions but to alter them. It is not like the commentary to a travelogue, which purportedly stands outside the setting it describes, but is, rather, deeply embedded in a stream of interaction, the course of which it affects. When an inmate interrupts staff talk with the observation "you know I won't snitch," that observation not only formulates staff talk as an attempt to get the inmate to act as an informer, and not only explains why he cannot comply, but it also terminates the conversation and functions as a denial of cooperation. The code is thus not merely an account of a way of life, it is also a method of persuasion and justification.

The code is reflexively tied to its setting in that it both lends sense to that setting and obtains its sense from its place within it. Invoking the code provides an unequivocal meaning for actions whose meaning is in principle indeterminate; at the same time, the intrinsically vague maxims of the code (e.g., "do not snitch") derive their specific sense from the settings in which they appear. It is by observing instances of behavior in conformity with the maxim "do not snitch" that we learn what the maxim means.

Clearly, this conception of reflexivity differs importantly from conceptions of it current in interpretive anthropology. In anthropology, reflexivity is a variable—and a morally loaded one at that—mostly referring either to self-reflection or to a deliberate display of the work which the writer puts into the construction of his or her text. In the ethnomethodological perspective, on the other hand, all utterances, without exception, are reflexive. Being reflexive is not something we choose to do; it is something our discourse unavoidably is.

One difference between the conception of reflexivity that I am expounding and those current in anthropology is that, whereas in some early forms of ethnomethodology the institutionalized distinction between subject and object is collapsed (the two being seen as intimately bound up with one another), in anthropology the dualism is preserved.

Interpretive anthropologists trumpet revolutionary relativism, but they hold fast to an absolutist ontology. Those who accept at face value interpretive anthropologists' self-characterization will greet this assertion with skepticism. Everybody knows Geertz roundly declares that membership in the interpretive school entails a commitment to a view of ethnographic assertion as "essentially contestable," that anthropological interpretations are fictions "in the sense that they are 'something made'," and that the notion of brute fact is a delusion; nevertheless, his ontology is wholly realist, for he presupposes a reality which obtains prior to and independently of his descriptions of it (see Crapanzano 1986:68–75; Dwyer 1982:260–63; Watson 1989). He preserves a distinction between a reality of plain fact and contestable interpretation.

Nowhere does Geertz entertain the notion that facts are as much the product of interpretive procedures as are interpretations themselves. In "Deep Play: Notes on the Balinese Cockfight," he reports and simultaneously constitutes "facts" whose status as facts is "unmistakable" and about which he has obtained "exact and reliable data" (1975b:437, 426). In "Thick Description: Toward an Interpretive Theory of Culture" (1975a:16) he offers the possibility of sorting "real winks from mimicked ones." In "Anti Anti-Relativism" (1984:275) he argues that "it was not relativism . . . that did in absolute motion, Euclidean space and universal causation. It was wayward phenomena. . . ." Geertz thus shares the ontological outlook of Albert Spaulding, who, in his Distinguished Lecture to the annual meeting of the American Anthropological Association (1988:70), pronounced the "postmodern brand" of anthropology incompatible with his own, the "scientific."

Where stands James Clifford with regard to the dualism of subject and object?[3] Like Geertz, he equivocates. (At least he seems to; his phrasing leaves uncertain precisely what is being asserted.) His observation (1986a: 25) that "no one can write about others any longer as if they were discrete objects or texts" may be construed as recognition that reflexivity is indeed an essential property of all accounts, as may his characterization of culture as "contested, temporal, and emergent" (1986a:19). But his reference to "truthful, realistic accounts" (1986a:25), and his claim that "ethnographic truths are . . . incomplete" (1986a:7)—which implies, perhaps, the existence of complete truths—suggest a failure of nerve. He observes (1986a: 24) that the authors of *Writing Culture* "do not suggest that one cultural account is as good as any other," but he does not spell out what he means by a good account. Have appeals to "how reality actually is" been renounced as bases for evaluation, or have they not?

So, we can now situate "reflexive" anthropology along a continuum: at one end is an ontology-cum-epistemology according to which our accounts of reality *mirror* reality, and at the other end is one according to which our accounts *constitute* reality. "Reflexive" anthropology lies, it appears, not at the constitutive end of the continuum, but near the middle. According to the interpretive theory of the relationship between accounts and reality, accounts do not passively reflect a world presumed to be out there; they are, rather, actively constructed interpretations of it. The ontology is realist; it suggests a real world about which various interpretations can be made. So interpretive anthropology, far from being radical, is essentially conservative; it shores up and reinvigorates the realist genre it allegedly supercedes. Its seemingly radical break with realist notions of representation—hailed by Jay Ruby (1982b:126) as a "new paradigm" and by Clifford (1986a:22) as "a conceptual shift, 'tectonic' in its implications"—is but a diversion from the daunting task of grappling with the implications of indexicality and reflexivity.

I do not ironize idly. It is not my purpose to disparage the likes of James Clifford and George Marcus, whose scholarship commands my respect. What I want to do is to give their project an enthusiastic push towards successful completion. That entails clarifying the muddle.

It seems to me that anthropologists have three options. First, we can continue as before, meeting trouble halfway, attempting to contain and manage recurrent and obstinate methodological problems rather than addressing fundamental issues. We can ignore essential reflexivity, or pronounce it irrelevant, or try to defuse it (see Watson 1987a). This option becomes increasingly untenable as the epistemological researches of Malcolm Ashmore (1989) and Steve Woolgar (1988) gain currency. Second, we can opt for a return to a realist ontology-cum-epistemology. This is seductive but hopelessly antiquated. And third, we can opt for a relativist ontology-cum-epistemology. This option may be embraced either in the form of a radical ontology-cum-epistemology, or in the form of a methodological imperative.

In a radical ontology-cum-epistemology, the word and the world are one. This is not as daft as it may appear. We cannot demonstrate "reality" or part of it without employing description or ostension. "Reality" is simply not available independently of these procedures. What we have, and all we have, is not some supposed free-standing reality but merely the accounting procedures that purportedly indicate it.

Arguably, the more prudent course may be to abandon the notion of an objective reality, or at least to remain silent about it, thereby following Wittgenstein's (1922:189) proposal in the last line of the *Tractatus*: "Whereof one cannot speak, thereof one must be silent." The history of science consists of one version after another of what the facts are. What is accepted as plain fact today may be demoted to artifactual status tomorrow. So when is the inventory of reality to be taken (Tibbetts 1988:123)?

The history of Piltdown Man is instructive. Piltdown Man was at first inconceivable, then a discovery, then a fraud, now a prank—for how long (Brannigan 1981)? As each status became established, history was rewritten: this was how it had been "all along." As for the Tasaday, first characterized as a stone-age people, then as a fraud, then as "the empirical confirmation of a mythical apprehension of otherness" (Dumont 1988: 270), they are now suing their ethnographers for misrepresentation.

Now, were I to see an express train rushing toward me, I would be aware that "express train rushing toward me" is the product of my interpretive activities, and that people with a different interpretive repertoire—people, perhaps, whose culture knows no train—might reach a different conclusion. Nevertheless, I would get out of the way. Likewise, were an Azande to fall ill, then he or she would take appropriate evasive action by consulting the oracle. To the Azande, witches are as real as express trains are to me. Both witches and express trains are phenomena that we apprehend as encountered and that cannot be wished away.

It may be no use attempting to adjudicate between different realities by referring to the facts, because what the facts are taken to be is the result of argument rather than its warrant (Fish 1980:338). Put another way, every reality reflexively preserves itself by legislating in advance what will count as evidence (Pollner 1974). So it could be argued, even if we were somehow to apprehend an ultimate reality (the express train, the witches), we could never be sure that we had succeeded in doing so, because the relationship between that reality and our means of grasping it is one we can conceive of only from within the reality in which we find ourselves.

A philosophical conundrum as perennial as this is not going to be resolved here. Fortunately, it is not necessary to embrace a radically relativist ontology or epistemology. It is sufficient—and necessary—to adopt a radically relativist stance as a methodological imperative. If we want to know how people, including ethnographers, come to constitute their worlds, then it is necessary to suspend judgment on the status of informants' knowledge claims, lest we find ourselves accounting for what we take to be our informants' true beliefs in terms of their correspondence to what we hold to be real. Our anthropology of knowledge would then become merely the anthropology of erroneous belief, while the work done in constituting "true knowledge" as "true knowledge" would remain hidden from us (Barnes and Bloor 1982:23).

This stance does not entail judgmental relativism. To say that all forms of knowledge are equally efficacious for a particular purpose is nonsense. Nor does this stance absolve us from the necessity of discriminating among the competing truth claims of fellow analysts, or deprive us of the capacity to do so. Nothing I have said invalidates available mechanisms; it merely redescribes them. It redescribes them as mechanisms that are locally valid: conventional, not arbitrary. This redescription would constitute a problem if, and only if, the possibility obtained that there could become available to us a mechanism cleansed of the contingencies of culture and of history. Since the possibility is a chimera, the notion that our mechanisms for resolving disputes are "merely" locally valid is untroublesome.

Knowing that our evaluative criteria are culturally and historically contingent does not diminish the conviction with which we cling to them and, moreover, has no practical consequences. The reason for that, as Stanley Fish (1980: 370) observes, is that the position he advocates and I endorse "is not one that you (or anyone else) could live by. Its thesis is that whatever seems to you to be obvious and inescapable is only so within some institutional or conventional structure, and that means that you can never operate outside some such structure, even if you are persuaded by the thesis."

None of us can plausibly propose that our utterances are immune to the methodological troubles that we discern in the utterances of others. Indexicality and reflexivity are as indexicality-and-reflexivity-ridden as any other concepts. This is not a defect of the position I am advocating but a reiteration of it. The charge of *tu quoque* (so are you!) has no force. But knowing that one's utterances are reflexive while nevertheless being obliged even in saying so to employ realist language—a mode that implicitly denies its own reflexivity—leaves us in a quandary.

We have few options. One is to press on regardless, deconstructing others' utterances while privileging our own. Perhaps that is the only way to stay in the social science game. It seems to be the course advised by several leading sociologists of scientific knowledge. Barnes (1981a: 493) declares himself a relativist but nevertheless intrepidly employs realist prose because "it is a marvellous instrument. . . . On the left we have the vast complexity of reality, . . . on the right we have but a few thousand symbols, plus some competence in using them, and notably the competences of the realist mode. Somehow, with the miserable resources on the right we cope with the immensities on the left." Which assumes that the reality on the left is not a creature of the symbols on the right.

Harry Collins (1983: 102) recommends that "an awareness of one's own procedures is a valuable methodological astringent, but when we are doing the sociology of science, as opposed to talking about it, it is as well not to suspend the taken-for-granted rules of the method of sociological research adopted." Such recommendations have been indignantly rejected by Woolgar (1988: 100) as "ontological gerrymandering," effected "by means of a rhetorical boundary between the constituting behavior of others—to be regarded as strange and worthy of analysis—and the textual activities of the author—to be taken for granted as unworthy of attention."[4]

Objecting on other grounds to the kind of instrumental conformity advocated by Collins, Anna Wynne (1988:102) poignantly observes that it

> has profound epistemological consequences. For the data are very
> seductive. . . . Before you know where you are they have con-
> vinced you that they *are* reality. . . . The data not only are the
> reality of talk preserved on tape, but analysis based on them is
> about the world outside the talk.
>   This conclusion is deeply ironic in that it itself exemplifies how
> we reflexively create reality from what we take to be documents
> of it.

How can this seduction be forestalled? One way, alas hardly practi-
cable, might be to abandon assertive languages in favor of one like Balinese. Joanna Overing (1985:18, 19), summarizing Mark Hobart's work in
the same volume, observes that "in Balinese epistemology language is recognized as polysemic and double-edged, always affected by perceptions,
interests, and intentions of both speakers and listeners." Moreover, "the
Balinese view the world as a transforming one, and in a continual state of
becoming something else. . . . transforming worlds fit ill with a law of
identity, a law of non-contradiction, and a law of the excluded middle."
Perhaps the next best thing to abandoning assertive languages might
be to abandon unduly assertive literary forms, like the standard, rhetoric-
ridden scientific paper, such as you are now reading. Probably the best
known attempt to do this for anthropology is Kevin Dwyer's *Moroccan
Dialogues*. Dwyer (1982:257) quite rightly complains of the "contempla-
tive" premise of the scientific attitude, in which observation "is an objective
act that in no way influenced the object's true significance, a significance
that existed prior to the act of observing it." But his proposed solution, to
emphasize the dialogic nature of work in the field and thus to respect the
integrity of the Other's voice, is no solution at all. It is an attempt to play
chess with oneself, making the moves for both black and white pieces.[5]
In the work of those analysts of scientific discourse who are part of
the New Literary Forms movement we find an array of experiments such
as have not been attempted in even the most self-conscious writing in
anthropology (e.g., Taussig 1987): writing in the form of plays, parodies,
Nobel Prize acceptance speeches, and multiple voices, complete with sub-
versive commentaries and self-deprecatory footnotes—all intended to
disrupt readers' normal reading practices (see, for example, Mulkay 1984;
Ashmore 1988). These make prodigious demands of their readers, and I
imagine that only a small minority of readers who are urgently interested
in matters epistemological are likely to persist with them; the rest, once

the novelty has worn off, will drift back to more familiar forms of writing. In New Literary Forms we can see the future of interpretive anthropology, and it does not work.

It is significant that the authors of New Literary Forms are doing the sociology of science, not science itself. They cater to a sophisticated readership with a penchant for theoretical controversy, for whom the object of interest is epistemology rather than news from the laboratory. It is highly doubtful that practicing scientists working within the paradigm of normal science and looking to technical journals for the results of research would have much patience with them. But such patience is required of anthropologists researching current field monographs in the hope of gleaning news. Sometimes it seems as if the entire genre has been hijacked by those whose primary purpose is not to offer news but to interrogate our means of representation. Better the division of labor that obtains between science and the sociology of science: let participants be participants and analysts analysts.

That is not to disparage the efforts of the experimenters. They are important as catalysts. For the writer is not alone in his or her endeavor but is, rather, participating in a collaborative enterprise. The Kriges would not impress us so were it not for the cooperation of the publishing house (which lends the nobility of its name and ensures that the cloth covers of the book are expensively textured and soberly colored), the librarian (who places the book in the anthropology shelves rather than on those reserved for science fiction), and the teacher (who secures it a place in the anthropology-class reading list). Above all, the Kriges rely on readers' skills in filling out and making sense of scientific discourse, a peculiar one in which data are presumed autonomous, interpretations are either confirmed or disconfirmed by facts that are independently specified, and the discovery of orderliness and the production of definitive accounts are normal and expectable.

Once readers renovate their reading skills, become familiar with reality construction procedures, and know that "facts" are merely shorthand for temporarily stable reifications of these procedures, then writers are once again free to return to that marvelous instrument, realist prose, because, read under the auspices of indexicality and reflexivity, realist prose is no longer the same prose. A gestalt switch occurs. Reality construction procedures, hitherto backgrounded, spring into prominence.[6]

By these remarks I do not propose to license business as before, the business of disinterestedly reporting a reality out there, for the genie of essential reflexivity cannot be put back in the bottle. I reiterate my previous (1987a:35) recommendations that writers be aware of techniques used by others to establish their authority and achieve the appearance of a separation between their objects of study and their methods of studying them, that they be aware that they are probably using the identical methods for identical purposes, and that they ensure that their readers are fully and continuously alerted to them. I propose, merely, that the onus of reconstructing the writer-reader relationship be shifted, in large part, from the writer to the reader.

What is to be gained by placing the notions of indexicality and reflexivity on the agenda? Placing them on the agenda helps us to see at least some interpretive anthropologists' critical analyses of modernist ethnography as inchoate, as having been pressed only to the point where "interpretations" are admitted to be contestable while "facts" remain as givens and where, in consequence, anthropologists' accounts remain privileged insofar as they may be represented as, or understood as, corresponding to an objective reality: Geertz's "real winks."

It helps us also to see current insecurities, precipitated by the realization that interpretations are inherently contestable, as misplaced, for "facts" are constituted in precisely the same way as "interpretations." The distinction between the two is social rather than epistemological. Facticity is a status, not a state. It follows that there are no epistemological problems peculiar to "interpretive" discourse. There being no special problems, there is no need for special solutions. The novel textual formats of "interpretive" anthropology are redundant solutions to imagined problems.

We gain the freedom to get on with it without continually being laid low with the bouts of epistemological hypochondria to which interpretive anthropologists are subject. We can employ realist prose as a heuristic, knowing that what we write is never not indexical and never not reflexive: what is the point of fretting over the inevitable? Like the medical student newly aware of germs in the drinking water, we are no worse off, merely better informed.

To Ian Jarvie's taunt (1987: 273), "The *real* question in all this is what has happened to truth," we may offer, as rejoinder, Bruno Latour's vigorous assertion (1988a: 156), "Relativist sociologists are not sawing the branch upon which they sit because they are not seated on it, and no one is or has ever been: the strength of any science, and indeed of any argumentation, has never come from non-local, non-human and non-historical allies. . . ."

We can stop worrying about problems allegedly peculiar to anthropology by virtue of its subject matter. There is nothing *especially* futile about trying to write authoritative accounts of other cultures. Geertz got

it right (1988:144) when he referred to the "un-get-roundable fact that
all ethnographical descriptions are homemade, that they are describer's
descriptions, not those of the described." However could we have thought
otherwise? We speak only from within an interpretive community, with
no time out; our discourse is always perspectival, never synoptic. All we
(or anybody else) can offer is interpretations; this is so whether we are
dealing with other cultures or with our own. Arthur Frank (1985:114)
observes:

> Interaction is the problem of interpreting some presence of the
> other when presented with the text of that other's conversation
> and action, and the essence of that text is to be indexical, reflex-
> ive, and so forth. One social actor cannot 'know' another; he can
> only suggest interpretive possibilities, glosses, out of which the
> other is constituted.[7]

Taking on board indexicality and reflexivity not only furnishes us with
the intellectual tools required to extricate ourselves from the cul-de-sac
"interpretive" anthropologists have led us into, but it also enables us to
relocate culture and cultures in our conceptual schemes. In effect, it enables us to rewrite culture.

Anthropologists, like laymen, have tended to assume that there exist,
prior to and independently of our discourse, collectivities called cultures
that we must identify and describe (LeVine and Campbell 1972: ch. 7).
The effect of the anthropological enterprise, so described, is identical to
that of the lay enterprise. It is to systematically obfuscate the work
performed by participants in constituting and maintaining from moment
to moment the very collectivities which they—and we—represent as
encountered.

Having constituted cultures, the layman proceeds to impute agency to
them. He represents culture not as his accomplishment, but as his master.
His behavior, he tells us, is determined by the rules he is subject to by
virtue of his group membership. And, incredibly, anthropologists—those
of an earlier generation, at least—built this folk explanation of the deter-
minants of social behavior into their own explanatory apparatus. They
wrote as if, say, a North American Indian behaves like an Indian because
he is governed by Indian mores, or worse, because he *is* an Indian. What
this folk-cum-anthropological explanation does is systematically conceal
from us the fact that rules do not and cannot determine behavior. They
cannot determine behavior because both their meaning and their application are inherently and irreparably problematic. Meaning is problematic
because it is indexical. Application is problematic because no rule can

exhaustively specify all the conditions under which it is to be applied. Rules are, however, invoked by both actors and anthropologists as an interpretive resource in accounting for behavior. Indians who attribute to Indian custom what might to Euro-Canadians seem a casual attitude to time and work, and whites who attribute their superordination to Euro-Canadian habits of application and initiative, have both learned that people may be prompted to tolerate recurrent vexations by being per-suaded that those who vex them act not out of personal malice but out of constraint by a primordial and compelling culture for which no one in particular is accountable. And in thus shrugging off responsibility for what they do, laymen have received the endorsement of us anthropolo-gists who, besotted with our reified models of culture, seem incapable of identifying warm bodies when we see them.[8]

Our preoccupation with the exotic is a form of institutionalized in-competence in that it systematically blinds us to the everyday; it leads us to adopt the native's point of view, oblivious to the fact that that point of view encompasses unexamined everyday methods of attributing meaning and constructing reality (Silverman 1985: 106). Adopting indexicality and reflexivity frees us from dependence on the native as an expert on his culture who knows what he is up to and who unproblematically recounts that to the researcher. It underscores the facts that the native, as much as the ethnographer, is in the business of constituting meaning (Sharrock and Anderson 1982) and that culture, far from being a given framework that lies behind and is expressed in activities, is, rather, like the convict code, a flexible repertoire of interpretive resources drawn upon by partici-pants in accounting for action.[9]

The literature I have drawn on in this paper is hugely relevant to in-terpretive anthropology. It has been readily available for more than twenty years. It has had considerable impact on literary studies, from which in-terpretive anthropology has taken so much. It has influenced the work of a number of anthropologists (e.g., Bilmes 1976; Cohen and Comaroff 1976; Handelman 1978; Liberman 1985; Moerman 1988; Watson 1981) and has inspired at least one essay which has helped transform the field of intergroup relations: Michael Moerman's (1968) essay on the Lue. So one might ask why interpretive anthropologists have disregarded it. To the complaint that Harold Garfinkel's work is absent from the bibliogra-phies of Jay Ruby's *A Crack in the Mirror* (1982a) and David Parkin's *Se-mantic Anthropology* (1982), I now add that it is absent also from the bibliographies of Clifford and Marcus's *Writing Culture* (1986) and An-thony Jackson's *Anthropology at Home* (1987).

The notion that a point of view gains or loses currency because it "is" true or not carries little conviction, for we live in a global village of competing truths—one in which, moreover, that which is plausible today was not so yesterday and might not be again tomorrow; hence current searches for the social, rather than the rationalist, bases of belief. These searches become a search for the social *causes* of belief, or less forthrightly, for that which "sheds light on" belief; and it is seldom that causes of belief are not traced to supposed interests of some kind, however delicately and indirectly indicated, as in Joan Vincent's proposal, in this volume, to place ethnography in the political and economic context of its time.

The search for explanation in terms of underlying interests comes easily to us, both in our capacity as laymen (we are adept at attributing motives) and as social scientists (we are adept at ironizing), so it is tempting to press on, to advance "explanations" in terms, perhaps, of micropolitical processes (Rabinow, this volume), or disciplinary ethnocentrism (Watson 1984), or career ambitions and class interests (Sangren 1988), without first reflecting on the theoretical adequacy or inadequacy of this form of explanation.

The Edinburgh school of the sociology of scientific knowledge vigorously pursues the search for interests that underlie the plausibility of "true knowledge" (Barnes 1978; Bloor 1976), but the legitimacy of the search is contested by the school of York (Woolgar 1981). Woolgar argues that explanation in terms of underlying interests is flawed in two basic respects. First, it is in principle defeasible: you can never make the purported underlying interests stick, for alternative interests can always be nominated; besides, while an action may advance one perceived interest, it may prove contrary to another. Second, because accounts and the setting they describe mutually elaborate and modify each other in a back and forth process, an alleged underlying interest is an integral part of the setting it purports to explain. This is a trouble for participants (and for the Edinburgh school) because the effectiveness of an account depends on the routine denial of the interdependence between the alleged underlying interest and the actions it is said to explain. The interests of participants have to be made to seem independent of the actions from which they have been constructed; only then is it possible to argue for the prior existence of the interests and hence to imply that the actions resulted from these preexisting interests. Woolgar concludes that, rather than duplicate participants' practices by utilizing the notion of underlying interest as an interpretive resource, we should study the ways in which participants' engage in the practical management of their trouble. He has a point.

To conclude, I propose that we take on board the notions of indexicality and reflexivity, which will lead us to relocate the notions of culture and of underlying interest in our conceptual schemes and will open the way for a refocusing of attention on the ways in which our informants constitute their realities. This modest proposal lacks the glamor of those current perspectives whose adherents see themselves as radical. However, in that it constitutes a refusal to multiply studies unreflectingly within terms set by lay reasoning and, rather, places these very terms in question, it shows that such self-understandings are, if not entirely specious, at least in need of qualification. For we have inherited from philosophy much, much more than Rolph Trouillot's "savage slot," and our inheritance is both more encompassing than that of José Limón's Paredes and more constraining than any of the isolated concepts, such as "the Other," that were at the center of so much discussion in our advanced seminar. So, what may be said about interpretive anthropology may be said also about nascent "radical" orthodoxies: they are, in one critical respect, part of the problem, not the solution. If there be any truth to the claim that anthropology is in danger of becoming an intellectual dinosaur, the cause of the decline is to be sought not in the demise of indigenous people but rather in the fact that anthropologists balk at participating in the cognitive revolution generated by ethnomethodology.

─────── *Notes* ───────

I am indebted to Michael Ashkenazi, Augustine Brannigan, Leslie Miller, Karla Poewe, and Rod Watson for reading an earlier version of this paper, and to Usher Fleising for his generosity in making available the time in which to write it.

1. Ontological gerrymandering? See note 4.

2. A readable introduction to ethnomethodology is Benson and Hughes (1983). For an attempt to dispel some of the more common misconceptions about the subject, see Sharrock and Watson (1988).

3. Clifford, Geertz, and Marcus might protest that they do not constitute a coherent category. My reason for collecting them together is that they share an interest in how anthropologists achieve their effects through writing, and they have all (if I have understood them) failed to press their analysis to the point where all meanings are seen to be inherently unstable, never, in principle, to be retrieved from that state by even a partial correspondence to a supposed free-standing reality that exists prior to and independently of their accounts of it.

4. Ontological gerrymandering is rife. Gilbert and Mulkay (1984) report that scientists give an empiricist account of their own results while describing as contingent those of their rivals. Barnes (1981b) remarks that ethnographers tend to account for reports they deem accurate in terms of their correspondence to nature, while accounting for reports they think fantastic in terms of the cultural setting of their production. Hollis and Lukes (1982) consider what for them are

the puzzling sources of relativism while taking for granted their own use of rationality.

5. Dwyer (1982:225) records his informant, the Faquir, as saying "I know that these questions serve your purposes, not mine," but he interjects a footnote (1982:226) that characterizes the Faquir's words as evidence to the contrary: "The Faquir had said almost the exact same thing, that his work was important for others and not for him, when he described his term as village mogaddem." We shall never know how the Faquir might have responded. He does not write footnotes.

6. Sharrock and Watson (1988:60) assert that the relationship between ethnomethodology's point of view and that of any other sociology is such that "they are discrete and alternate, not additive, ways of seeing things . . . [So] it would make absolutely no sense for ethnomethodology to urge other sociologies to improve themselves by taking on board its concerns. . . ." This assertion may be understood—with the aid of a little ontological gerrymandering—as a function of the development of ethnomethodology as a professional specialism. Such a contingency should not inhibit other disciplines from borrowing ethnomethodology's notions. We can absorb the implications of essential reflexivity and then "forget" them, much as an artist "forgets" the artistic anatomy he has mastered.

7. This does not mean that anything goes. As Fish notes (1980:356), "The mistake is to think of interpretation as an activity in need of constraints, when in fact interpretation is a *structure* of constraints."

8. This passage, in a slightly different form, has previously appeared in Watson 1987b.

9. Of course something like this has been said before, notably by Comaroff (1978); but then, he has declared himself a partisan of ethnomethodology.

Chapter 6

FOR A NEARLY

NEW CULTURE HISTORY

Richard G. Fox

To study the plot without studying the characters will never make
sense of the drama of human life.

R. R. Marett, *Anthropology*

. . . historicity is neither an end nor by itself a means but a condition which must be recognized at every step.

Alexander Lesser, *The Pawnee Ghost Dance Hand Game*

NOWADAYS in America and the other core regions of late capitalism, life and death have ceased to be discreet conditions, easily discerned.
At either end of the life span—and sometimes, by misfortune, in between—we worry about whether humanity inhabits individual bodies
and when it has come or gone. There is an equivalent disquiet today about
ethnography's condition. Is ethnography alive (although it may require
massive scholarly transfusion)? Or is it brain-dead (but we anthropologists, patients and practitioners at once, simply cannot pull the plug)?

I speak here of "ethnography" as a text, not as a field method.[1] For
over half a century, such texts have embodied the findings and incorporated the authority of the anthropologist by telling anthropology's essen-
tial(ist) story—that most modern triangle—of the grand encounter
between the West and the rest, with the anthropologist as hypotenuse (to
adapt a phrase from Tom Lehrer).

The ongoing reflexive or postmodern critique exemplifies current anthropology's morbid fascination with the ethnographic text. This critique
argues that we have read ethnography's vital signs wrongly for many years.
The ethnographies that appear most vital to us—from the Trobriands

of Bronislaw Malinowski to Clifford Geertz's Bali, let us say—already suffered gravely from misrepresentation of others as Other, or so the critique tells us. The Malinowskian text depended on the convention that the anthropologist had "been there." As a narrative of empathy, it gave a false concreteness to a "there" that was constructed only in the presence of the anthropologist. Such texts in fact acknowledged the anthropologist's presence only to prove that he or she had made an effective entrée. The Geertzean text used a related convention: culture comprised a subtle code that only the canny anthropologist could decipher. Whereas the Malinowskian text may have rendered the Other as "always capitalized, always singular" (Geertz 1985), the Geertzean text bestowed an equal apotheosis on the ethnographer, who could speak, oracularly, of worlds otherwise unknown.[2]

Ethnography's strength, therefore, was actually its weakness: its claims to report authoritatively on other cultures depended on standard figurations, or "indigenations," asserted by the West—for example, the (spiritual) Oriental or the (pristine) native or the (professional) scholar. Anthropology's grand encounter with the Other was only an introduction to alter ego in the bush.

In spite of this critique, or perhaps because of it, some anthropologists hope to revive ethnography with "reflexive," "polyphonic," or "dialogic" devices. The question is: do they preserve life or only stave off death? The long quotations from informants, the emphasis on the dialogue between an ethnographer and an interlocutor, the Babel of many native voices—these new devices may only further burden an already overstressed text form. Hooking the ethnographic text up to such life-saving devices can never cure it of its "essential reflexivity," as Graham Watson (1987a) calls it—which is also its essential malaise: that it takes the native point of view out of context and reconstructs it elsewhere—no matter how extended the quotations from informants, how intensive the dialogue between interlocutors, or how many the voices the ethnography speaks for. Such new devices, perhaps inadvertently and no doubt unfortunately, may revive ethnography artificially (in the original meaning of the word). Similarly, the postmodern critique, by continuing to beat the drums for (what may be) the dead or dying, only succeeds in preserving one text form, ethnography, as central to anthropology or even identical with it.

Perhaps it is time to take the postmodern critique very seriously, perhaps more seriously than some of those who propose it do, for they seem to allow that the ethnographic text somehow can be patched up. Perhaps, too, now is a good time to consider whether the faults found with the so-called "realist ethnography" in fact adhere to any ethnography. Should we now allow ethnography death with dignity (and perhaps with more honor than the postmodern critique bestows)—if that is what is in store for it—and look at other possible texts, at other ways of narrating our understandings, and at other stories worth telling? Can we learn to celebrate encounters other than those mediated by the ethnographer on the spot? Can we textualize encounters, for example, mediated by histories of domination and resistance, which helped produce the alter egos ethnographers found when they went looking for others. New texts, or nearly new ones, such as the culture history I propose in this paper, need not, probably dare not, abandon all the conventions that characterized the fieldwork done by anthropologists and were textualized in the ethnography, especially the concern for everyday life, participant observation, cultural relativism, and, most recently, self-reflection. New texts, however, can augment these conventions of fieldwork with other textual concerns, such as historical process, individual intention, and the relations from afar that structure inequality in local, everyday life.

The nearly new culture history I propose is resolutely realist, although not naively so. It is therefore no less a fiction or construction than an ethnography, but it avoids some of the fictions involved in constructing the old ethnography. It does not, for example, tie up the loose ends of culture into a neatly wrapped ethnographic package. This culture history is a chronicle of intentions, contingencies, and relationships: among people, in a culture, over time. It therefore makes no claim to be a portrayal "from life," as ethnography did. Being a history, it recognizes that it is a dramatization; it has a never-ending plot and innumerable characters. Obviously, it is a construction, but of a particular sort: the historian, as Paul Ricoeur (1984:26) notes, wants "this construction to be a reconstruction."

Nevertheless, such a culture history conserves current anthropology's intention of getting the native point of view in the broad sense because it confronts questions that ethnography, even in postmodern form, often finesses. Ethnography has never questioned that there are others to be met in the course of fieldwork, among whom the anthropologist figuratively pitches camp. Culture history pursues the question of who these others are and how they have come to be. In a recently completed study of the culture history of Gandhian utopia (Fox 1989), I looked at a set of cultural meanings that condensed over a century from individual utopian visions. Through this culture history, I hoped to understand what has made India "other" and makes Indians others whom anthropologists study. How well can we possibly know our interlocutors in the field if we do not have this history in mind?

Ethnography also finesses the question of where anthropologists should pitch their tents. It too often specifies a physical location—an inhabited jungle clearing, a village community, an urban barrio—in place of an intellectual position (cf. Fox 1972). Ethnography then has to claim authority on the basis of "having been there" and the special empathy it creates. Otherwise, how could it justify its construction of "fieldwork" as meaning physical, rather than scholarly, placement? Culture history avoids these fictions about empathy; it need not take "fieldwork" to mean space instead of stance.

This culture history authorizes an anthropology that intellectually occupies the middle ground between the individual and culture, between personages and processes, as I shall soon explain. It responds to the postmodern critique neither by denying it nor by adopting "experimental" ethnographic texts that may only be vainly trying to raise the dead. It responds by promoting formally "realist" texts that do not suffer from ethnography's ills. In the next section I show why this culture history is not entirely new. In the section after that, I show how it may help renew anthropology by helping to pluralize it, so that we get *anthropologies*, "never singular, never capitalized."

THE OLD CULTURE HISTORY

Our received images of Franz Boas portray him either as an archempiricist or as only an overly cautious investigator (perhaps depending on whether we studied with Leslie White or not). Neither image, however, prepares us to believe that Boas would ever chastise (a subfield of) anthropology for its fear of generalization. Yet Alexander Goldenweiser reports that Boas once said, "A man who finds one potsherd . . . passes with us as an archaeologist, one who finds two potsherds, as a good archaeologist, one who finds three, as a great archaeologist" (Goldenweiser 1933:158, n.1).

Can this revelation prepare us for Alfred Kroeber's (1935:543) even more surprising assertion that Boas was not interested in cultural phenomena?

We usually remember that anthropology was not invented in Malinowski's tent and that it existed even before it came of age with Margaret Mead in Samoa. But do we remember the full force of the intellectual struggles that engaged our predecessors? Here we confront a statement by Boas that by our image of him and the "Boasian school," he should never have willingly made. Kroeber tells us something we expect even less: that Boas was not a Boasian, at least by our received image of them.

Before ethnography became anthropology's text—that is, before Malinowski's dictum became anthropology's credo—other texts and anthropologies existed. Robert Thornton (1983) argues that ethnography only replaced such earlier texts in Africa—where they consisted of travel and missionary accounts and, later, ethnographic surveys "from the verandah"—after an active intellectual struggle (also see Vincent's paper, this volume). Malinowski and his fellow ethnographers not only developed ethnography as a text to serve their claims to authority, they also developed it to vanquish other texts they regarded as inferior and less truthful. Consider again A. R. Radcliffe-Brown's "rewriting" of his Andaman field research (see note 1).

Although the equivalent struggle in the United States was not as openly conflictful, probably because it involved different cadres (perhaps also cohorts) of Boas's students, it nevertheless went on. One Boasian, Alexander Lesser, for example, disowned what he took to be the functionalism of two other students of Boas, Margaret Mead and Ruth Benedict, and their rejection of culture history (see Mintz 1985a:45–51). (Radcliffe-Brown disowned them, too, because they were not *his* kind of functionalist.) Papa Franz himself noted the difference, although more gently, in his foreword to Mead's book on Samoa (Mead 1928:7–8). He contrasted her study of "the way in which the personality reacts to culture" with what he took to be the mainstream in anthropology, namely:

> modern descriptions of primitive people [that] give us a picture of their culture classified according to the varied aspects of human life. We learn about inventions, household economy, family and political organization [etc.]. . . . Through a comparative study of these data and through information that tells us of their growth and development, we endeavor to reconstruct . . . the history of each particular culture.

Nearing the end of his life, Kroeber (1954:766) lamented that "from about 1920–25 on, the book-minded and verbal-minded . . . increasingly entered [anthropology], in addition to the natural historian and the explorer type of personality or the aesthetically sensitive, from among whom the profession had until then been largely recruited" (see also Kroeber 1956:306–307). Kroeber complained (1954:767) that the current generation of anthropologists had forgotten just how recent the social science emphasis in anthropology was. (For the growing impact of social science on anthropology in the 1930s, see Stocking 1976:11–13.)

We need not accept Kroeber's disgruntlement to recognize that a major change occurred in American anthropology at about the same time as, and along roughly similar lines to, the "revolution in anthropology," as

Ian Jarvie (1974) calls it, perpetrated by Malinowskian ethnography in Britain.[3] After the revolution, Boas and the early Boasians become "historical particularists" or "American culture historians"—devitalized, essentialized, and homogenized like the Oriental, the "native," or any "other" loser.[4]

Anthropology, much like the Other, is too often always singular, always capitalized in common conception. We need to restore the vitality of anthropologies other than ethnography, just as much as we have tried to pluralize and lower-case "orientals" and natives. What texts did early Boasian anthropology hope to authorize, if not ethnography? What questions did their culture history address? What was the "agonistic field" (Latour and Woolgar 1979), that is, the controversy and confrontation that marked off their intellectual terrain?

My intention is to show an anthropology that was vital and productive and textualized before the apotheosis of ethnography—and before the ethnographic "study" or "report," as it was then called, gave authority to one anthropology. I maintain that it can help provide a text (there are others, such as the stories of "ethnoscapes" and "everyday life" that Appadurai and Abu-Lughod propose in this volume) by which to pluralize current anthropology and therefore to reproduce another anthropology as ethnography's hold grows weaker. In the meantime, it deserves respect as a kindred discipline, better than the "poor relation" status some histories of anthropology give it.

This paper therefore initially steps backward in time, eventually to move forward with *an* anthropology.

HISTORY OR SCIENCE?

The first question that exercised the early Boasians was whether they did history or science. Very early in his career, Boas contrasted a science of history, which explained phenomena without dissolving them into abstract laws or principles, with a science of physics, which valued deriving general principles more highly than understanding discrete phenomena. Boas claimed that both approaches were worthy, but his major efforts in cultural anthropology went into justifying historical studies. Boas used a cultural anthropology based on a science of history to combat a cultural evolution that adopted the approach of physics (see Boas 1888; also Lesser 1981; Stocking 1968:154–55; Handler 1983:209). Cultural evolutionists, Boas asserted, made up laws before they had worked up data. Boas perhaps held to this "methodological puritanism," as George Stocking, Jr. (1976:7) calls it, because he thereby rationalized his predilection

for history by a seemingly contradictory appeal to scientific methodology.[5] Much later, Boas observed that it was not possible "to solve an
intricate historical problem by a formula" and that research by American
anthropologists was a "mass of detailed investigations" (Boas 1920:
311–314).

This "natural history" perspective, as Marian Smith (1959) and Solon
Kimball (cited in Lesser 1981) labeled it, was even more sharply defined
by Kroeber, who called it "history" and strongly contrasted it with what
he termed "science" (Kroeber 1915:283). History, Kroeber argued, tries
"to preserve . . . the complexity of individual events . . . while also constructing them into a design which possesses a certain coherence" (Kroeber 1938:79). Kroeber (1935) specified the aim of historical science as
"descriptive integration," which recognized process in history as "a nexus
among phenomena treated as phenomena." Edward Sapir (1917:446)
similarly argued that "historical science thus differs from natural science,
either wholly or as regards relative emphasis, in its adherence to the real
world of phenomena, not, like the latter, to the simplified and abstract
world of ideal concepts. It strives to value the unique or individual, not
the universal."

Although the Boasians fought over what their "history" or "historical
science" should be, as I shall soon show, they were quite clear, and fairly
united, about what it was not. It was not sociology, which, as Kroeber
noted, greatly overlapped with anthropology in subject matter but differed markedly in scholarly origins. Sociology followed the physics model
and therefore was nothing like (Kroeber's) anthropology (that is, American anthropology as of 1936; see Kroeber 1936a:76). Neither was Boasian
historical science like British social anthropology, which also followed the
physics model (see Smith 1959:40 and Kimball, cited in Lesser 1981:10).
The confrontation between Kroeber (1936b) and Radcliffe-Brown (1935)
over kinship terminologies illustrates the difference well. It was clear to
both of them that they did radically different, although perhaps complementary, scholarships.

Boas and his early students often squabbled, as one of them accused
another of ripping phenomena out of context or of historical reconstructions that were more fanciful than factual. Whereas Stocking (1976:8)
sees these confrontations as family squabbles, I prefer to view them as
serious intellectual engagements. Familial disputes can be extremely intense, sometimes precisely because of the familiarity. Similarly, whereas
Stocking treats the divergent views among the Boasians as dominant and
recessive (subordinate) traits within a single scholarly gene pool, I want
to emphasize their intellectual controversy as substantial and developing,

not artifactual and inherent. These squabbles in fact betokened attempts by the Boasians to distance their historical science from the physics they disliked. They were not tributes to empiricism or inductivism; rather, they were efforts to work out canons for the descriptive integration that Kroeber extolled, the culture history that they all pursued. The issue was how much real history would enter their accounts and how much they would depend on historical reconstruction.

This polemic created unexpected fellowships and strange confrontations. Paul Radin and Alfred Kroeber, who in most other respects fundamentally disagreed (as I shall soon detail), both chastised Boas for not doing history. Boas claimed to use historical methods, Radin (1929:16) said, but he did not study actual historical sequences. For example, Radin supposed that Boas would take the current distribution of patrilineal and matrilineal societies as a given rather than investigate the possible history by which a present-day patrilineal society might once have been matrilineal, or vice versa. Kroeber's judgment also was that Boas lacked a concern with actual histories—whence Kroeber's assertion that Boas was not interested enough in phenomena. The problem, Kroeber somewhat more charitably put it, was that Boas employed a historical method only to provide negative instances against overgeneralizations (mainly by the evolutionists). Boas, Kroeber asserted, did not do history.

This confrontation was very significant for the further development of culture history. By taking exception to Boas, Kroeber and Radin were pushing culture history toward a greater development. Boas, as they maintained, had not really been interested in actual historical events or sequences. In his famous study of design elements on Alaskan needle cases, for example, Boas (1908:564) set out various evolutionary and determinist theories about how designs develop, such as the possibility that realistic representations can degenerate over time into purely conventional designs. He then argued (1908:588–89) that the decorative forms are the "results of the play of the imagination under the restricting influence of a fixed conventional style," the origin of which he cannot account for. Boas thus could argue persuasively against seriating designs with no known history on the basis of an assumed evolutionary sequence from the realistic to the conventional (Boas 1908:592). Here, as Kroeber indicated, Boas expertly used the canons of historical method to dispute evolutionary sequences—but without doing history himself. Another instance was Boas's disclaimer in *Primitive Art*: there were insufficient data, he asserted, on the history of individual art styles; there was only sufficient information "to determine the dynamic conditions under which art styles grow up" (Boas 1927:6). In still another instance, Boas used

Elsie Clews Parsons's historical argument that the Spaniards had greatly influenced Zuñi culture against Frank Cushing's environmental determinism (Boas 1920:317).

The use of historical method to provide negative instances was the established form of Boasian culture history. Robert Lowie's *Primitive Society* and Goldenweiser's study *Totemism* are good examples of history used against evolutionary generalizations and, in the former case, against economic determinism and Marxism. In a review of *Totemism*, Lowie (1911:189) commented that this study was "based on methodological principles which are becoming the common property of all the active younger American students of ethnology."

Kroeber and Radin, in rather different and contradictory ways, wanted to take culture history forward from negative instances to positive chronicles. Radin (1933:42–43 ff.) argued for a culture history based on singularities, a sequence of individual events and real happenings. Kroeber was not content with the particular. He wanted a culture history whose theory was based on "integrative reconstructions," which went beyond Radin's "one damn thing after another" by allowing for historical structures, or patterns. Kroeber contrasted his concern for historical structures with what he considered Boas's interest in "structural interrelations" (Kroeber 1935:541–42). Lesser (in Mintz 1985a:41), attempting to prove that Boas was indeed theoretical, gives us some instances of what Kroeber disliked. Lesser shows that Boas sometimes pursued lawful statements, as, for example, that dangerous undertakings produce ceremonial behavior or that cultural complexity is related to population. These statements of process or structural relationships removed from any historical context led Kroeber to identify Boas with Radcliffe-Brown (as in "the equivalence of siblings"), and to disown them both. Not process, but pattern was Kroeber's goal: "a pattern is not a process; it is a descriptive representation of a constellation having its basis . . . in the reality of phenomena" (Kroeber 1935:567).

How much "real" history should there be in culture history? Today, we might see this squabble among the Boasians as unnecessary; we would probably agree with Ricoeur that any history is a reconstruction. There was a larger issue involved in this dispute, however, although the Boasian agonists did not clearly perceive it. The question was whether or to what extent culture was integrated. Ethnography as a text requires a firm assertion of cultural integration: there can be no grand encounter unless the Other essentially exists; there must be Tiwi culture, not Tiwis.

Boasian culture history left it an open question. For the early Boasians, cultural diffusion over time made cultural integration variable at best and ultimately problematic (cf. Kroeber 1936b; Lesser 1935). Disparate pieces, shreds and patches, or "loose ends" we might now say, could accumulate in a culture. They were held together by the "genius" of the people but they were not necessarily functionally integrated. Eskimos and Anglo-Americans, markedly different in technological complexity, could share a kinship terminology, according to Boas. Goldenweiser contrasted the "technical rationality," that is, the "common sense and cold reasoning," that primitive peoples sometimes displayed with their equal penchant at other times for "philosophical irrationality," that is, for "fantasy and logical irresponsibility" (Goldenweiser 1933:161).

Real history was the main protection against the assumption that culture was synchronically integrated. Kroeber's reconstructions of patterns struck other Boasians, I suggest, as untrustworthy because they removed this protection. His "ahistory" prepared the ground for the assertion of synchronic psychological integration by Benedict and Mead. Curiously, Kroeber (1938:557) claimed that Mead and Benedict did history even though they did not use time as a factor. That they provided a detailed picture of a cultural pattern evidently convinced him. Other Boasians assimilated Mead and Benedict to Radcliffe-Brown, even though Benedict rejected his understanding of culture as an organism. For Lesser (Mintz 1985a:45–51), the emphasis Benedict and Mead gave to psychological integration and synchrony was akin to Radcliffe-Brown's social anthropology, and he seems perplexed that Radcliffe-Brown denied the relationship. What was missing from Mead and Benedict, Radcliffe-Brown recognized, was Durkheim's social teleology. What they all shared, Lesser realized, was an integrationist approach to culture that rationalized ethnography and did away with culture history.

"Agonistic fields" in scholarship seem always to require corners into which people are pushed or paint themselves. Given their ultimate closeness, the early Boasians found fault with each other only from what may appear to us as odd directions—it came about as they tried to narrow down their culture history. At the same time (roughly) that Radin accused Boas of insufficient interest in history, Boas accused Kroeber of too much unsubstantiated historical reconstruction, and Kroeber accused Boas of inattention to historical particulars. Kroeber pushed Boas into one corner by overemphasizing the one small part of his scholarly production that linked him to Radcliffe-Brown. Boas had also been cornered by taking too restrictive a view of culture history: that it should mainly provide negative instances against evolutionism rather than integrative statements about cultural patterning. Radin painted himself into another corner, opposite to both Boas and Kroeber, by disowning any synthesis of the historically particular. Kroeber brushed Radin and Boas aside, but, by looking for historical constants, he ended up in just as awkward a position. His age-area hypothesis (Kroeber 1923:128), for example, by assuming an invariant history of cultural diffusion, abrogated the very history of particulars that he otherwise advanced. There were other dead ends: even Kroeber himself admitted that his immense trait-listing project did not produce the historically integrative understandings he desired; Clark Wissler (1923), in his notion of the "universal pattern" by which all cultures could be understood, also substituted a structural principle for actual historical accounts.

These particular squabbles, these premature attempts at closure, should not obscure the fact that the early Boasians disagreed on specifics because they agreed in general. Their basic disagreement was over how to do this culture history, and more specifically, how to judge when it was done properly; it was not over whether something else should be done. The early Boasians did break sharply with the textual conventions of their predecessors, the evolutionists. They wrote about cultures, not culture. Boasian texts also differed considerably from later ethnographies, even though they too told of cultures. The Boasians reported on cultures as collections of cultural traits—the collection labeled Pawnee or Crow had accumulated as a result of a particular history. Later ethnographers presented cultures as totalities; rather than historical deposits, the Trobriands or Samoa adhered as a result of structural or psychological integration.

What then was this historical science that the Boasians proposed as anthropology's distinctive scholarly undertaking? Rephrasing the Boasian terminology in today's vocabulary, we might say that their "natural history" implied a realist approach to knowledge (Bhaskar 1979; Isaac 1987), as against the positivist approach that Boas labeled "physics" and Kroeber called "science."[6] That is, they did not believe that social phenomena could be understood by constructing ideal types, conceptual frameworks, or any other heuristic that decomposed phenomena, that classified data out of context—that, in other words, analyzed social realities by creating conceptual models or classifications of them. Their theory and explanation were to emerge from analyzing the real—that is, existing—relationships among social phenomena, and specifically the historical patterns that came about because cultures made contact, culture traits moved and were adopted, and new cultures came about. In this respect, they stood apart from the evolutionists.

Their culture history also would tell whether or to what extent the parts of a culture interrelated, rather than assuming that they did. On this issue, they differed with the structural integration of Radcliffe-Brown and the psychological integration that Benedict initially proposed and Mead perfected. Anthropology was to be the study of the shreds and patches of culture, as Lowie said, but that included how cultures came to be shredded and patched—in terms of both the actual historical relationships and thence the general patterns that emerged from them.

INDIVIDUAL CREATIVITY AND CULTURAL CONSTITUTION

The question of how cultures came to be shredded and patched involved the role of the individual in culture change: how did individual creativity interact with existing cultural patterns to create culture? This question also involved the kind of anthropology the early Boasians would author and thereby authorize. What would be central to their culture history? Would it be texts that told of individual genius or of cultural constitution, or elements of both in some specific relationship?

On this point, there was an agonistic field. In the middle was Edward Sapir, who wished to allow for individual creativity but also for the formative power of cultural patterns.[7] According to Richard Handler (1983), Sapir solved the dilemma of cultural form against individual creativity by positing that some given form is necessary for individual expression, but that creativity comes from changing the form rather than giving in to it. For Sapir, "genuine" culture existed where forms and institutions were integrated and harmonious. They were not imposed by tradition or history; rather, they were alive to the interests and desires of individuals. "Spurious" culture, by contrast, was imposed and trite, overwhelming the individual with formal patterns, or it was simply barren, not giving the individual anything on which to exercise creativity (see Handler 1983:225–227). For Sapir, culture history would presumably be a chronicle of successful or failed individual cultural innovations within given cultural forms, either genuine or spurious.

Still, there was a strong underlying cultural determinism in Sapir's thinking, at least early in his career. He wrote, for example, that "an individual's mind is so overwhelmingly moulded by the social traditions . . . that the purely individual contribution of even markedly original minds is apt to seem swamped in the whole of culture" (1917:441), although even here he recognized that individuals do have "directive power, . . . culture-moulding influence" (Sapir 1917:442).

How could culture be formative and yet the individual be directive? That question, so directly put in Sapir's work, became the narrative for Boasian culture history and made their texts distinctive from later ethnographies. It was a narrative convention most often honored in the breech, however, as I shall shortly argue for Radin and Kroeber.

Goldenweiser was another Boasian in the middle. He argued that individuals not only carry civilization but also feed it. He also spoke, not too clearly, of the "biographical" individual, formed by culture but made unique by individual experiences (Goldenweiser 1917:449). Boas occupied this middle ground, too, but in typical fashion, he used individual creativity to support negative-case arguments against evolutionary sequences. There could be no invariant reconstruction of primitive decorative techniques, Boas (1908:588–89) asserted, because the "play of the imagination" produced unpredictable forms. Boas (1908:592) concluded that "one of the most important sources in the development of primitive decorative art is analogous to the pleasure that is given by the achievements of the virtuoso." Similarly, Lowie used individual creativity to negate assertions that primitive peoples lacked individuality (Lowie 1937: 220 on Lévy-Bruhl) and to falsify arguments for the "superorganic" (Lowie 1937:206 on Durkheim). More positively, Melville Herskovits, early in his career, argued that acculturation studies not only could bridge the gap between historical and functional studies, but also could address the issue of the individual and culture (1937a). I leave a discussion of the culture-history texts produced by these Boasians in the middle to the conclusion of this paper.

At either end were Boasians who wanted to close off the question of individual creativity and cultural constitution. Radin represented the particularistic, or individualistic, extreme. He taxed other Boasians with ignoring the constructive role of individuals, and he envisioned a culture history that was the story almost entirely of such individual constructions (Radin 1933:42–43 ff.). Not at all by chance, Radin gave anthropology a distinctive text in which a single life-course was the central story, namely, the (auto)biography of the Other, Crashing Thunder. Kroeber was at the opposite, cultural determinist, end. He asserted "the principle of civilizational determinism as against individualistic randomness" (Kroeber 1919: 261). His concept of the superorganic powerfully argued that "the concrete effect of each individual upon civilization is determined by civilization itself" (Kroeber 1917). Kroeber's text was the story of cultural configuration over time: the pulsation of cultural creativity, the cycles of bodices and hems, the spread of salt, dogs, and tobacco. Kroeber's text was therefore superorganic.

The squabbles among the early Boasians over the individual and culture are well known, but it is not so often recognized that this crucial contest over ideas was also played out in texts. When it was a matter of educating laymen, rather than convincing scholars, the early Boasians cooperated on other texts. They could write, for example, factual but fictional (here meaning "fabricated") chapters based on individual lives for a semipopular text like *American Indian Life* (Parsons 1925). Even Kroeber set aside the superorganic to write an introduction to the collection; in it, he extolled such "psychological" studies—for a popular audience.

The early Boasians never really resolved this contest because in the meantime they lost the bigger game for control over the discipline. Their culture history gave way to Mead's and Benedict's cultural psychology, which depended on a synchronic integration of culture: now, texts told of basic personality structure or about the configuration that culture had chosen from the great arc of human potential. They closely duplicated the grand encounter with the Other inscribed in Malinowskian ethnography.[8] The individual was still an important focus, but not in terms of creativity or even creative acculturation; rather, individual enculturation became the issue.

As this shift came about, a powerful cultural determinism came to condition anthropology. Mead and Benedict, for example, allowed individuals to be deviant, not creative—and therefore, they only allowed them to be culturally ineffective (cf. Fox 1989). Subsequent anthropologies did not press the question of the individual and culture. A muscular cultural determinism and an ahistorical functionalism exercised culturology, cultural ecology, the New Ethnography, structuralism, symbolic anthropology, and cultural materialism. In their sameness, I wish to argue, they came to constitute an anthropology with an affiliated text, the ethnography. Another regimen began to develop only with the anthropology of cultural practice, in the inclusive way Sherry Ortner (1984) defines it, in the 1960s and 1970s. Even the purported anthropology of practice at times works out to consist of cultural-determinist closures, as when Sahlins (1985) speaks of a "structure of the conjuncture" and Bourdieu (1977) subsumes the individual in class trajectories.

THE NEARLY NEW CULTURE HISTORY

How then can we pluralize and lower-case anthropology to allow a culture history and its affiliated textual form? One way is to remember an anterior agonistic field, as I have just tried to do. Another way is to show that past contentions can become future courses of action. At the very center of the controversy among the early Boasians was the question of individual creativity and cultural constitution. Kroeber and Radin proceeded as if this controversy could be resolved by scholarly fiat. I want to argue that we can use the question itself to plot a future culture history.

The philosopher Paul Ricoeur and the Mahatma Mohandas Gandhi show the way to transform the Boasian agitation into *an* anthropological agenda.[9]

Ricoeur (1965:38) contrasts two sorts of history, one whose object is to find structure and system, and another that speaks of individuals and the way they may remake the world. He argues that history is only history when it is shown as a combination of the structural and the singular. If the presentation moves to the extreme of structure, there is "a false objectivity" (Ricoeur 1965:40); there is system but no history (Ricoeur 1965: 76). An account that deals only with singularities has equivalent problems, because history also must include forces and systems. Historians, and I suppose Ricoeur would include culture historians too, have to "tackle an event-filled history and a structural history at the same time," a history "between the great personages who make their appearance and the slowly progressing forces" (Ricoeur 1965:39). The central question becomes the relationship of individual creativity to cultural constitution, much as it was for the early Boasians.

Ricoeur is especially critical of structural accounts of the production of ideologies—which I read to include accounts of the production of cultural meanings. In such accounts, Ricoeur says, "ideology is *anonymous*" because it is treated as "typical" of a group or class rather than as singular, the production of a particular thinker. Such accounts do not acknowledge that before an ideology becomes a generalized "answer" (that is, a public cultural meaning), it is first of all an individual "problematic" or question, a philosophy posed by an individual thinker. An individual problematic, to be sure, has a relationship to its sociocultural milieu, but it also defines that milieu by being posed—any philosophy has a "situation" in Ricoeur's terminology. We have to look at the philosophy to see the "situation" that it in some measure reflects, but also we must see the "situation" as being defined by the philosophy's very existence and by what it "brought to the surface and exhibited" (Ricoeur 1965:60–61, 70).[10]

How does an individual problematic become a collective answer that leads to cultural innovation? To ask this question is to probe the connection between the singular and the structural. At issue is the relationship of individual creativity to existing cultural forms and prospective culture change. About this, Ricoeur says little, whereas Gandhi is forthright. In his moral philosophy and political practice, Gandhi understood that any cultural innovation was first of all an individual problematic, an experiment based on a utopian vision of the future, and only afterward, as it gained devotees who struggled against their current world, might it lead to new revolutionary realities. Utopian "dreams," to use Gandhi's language, motivate continuous human struggles—enduring "experiments with truth"—to achieve those dreams; the struggles in turn require a confrontation with existing systems of authority and their legitimizing ideologies.

Gandhi thereby provides the text for Ricoeur's history of the singular and structural. Such a text narrates the singularities of human intentions as they confront or experiment with the existing cultural structure and the inequalities it encodes. This text also records the cultural forms that result from such experiments.[11]

Ricoeur reminds us that an anthropology can be a historical science, not a physics. Gandhi shows us how this history can make the issue of individual creativity and cultural change central again. This culture history would chronicle how new sets of cultural meanings and forms develop (or do not).[12] It would trace how human actors originate ideas about their society out of cultural meanings already constituted, and then how they experiment with these ideas. Such experiments may contest the present and may conceive a revolutionized future, or they may fail to do so and confirm the present. That is, once made into public answers, a set of cultural meanings compels but also enables future cultural experimentation. It stipulates the form that new utopian experiments, attacking present conditions—or that ideologies, defending them—will take.

And so on: the human endeavor to build more nearly perfect cultures within existing material conditions and out of existing cultural meanings or ideologies is the agency behind this progression. Experiments, however they progress, are not, then, anonymous; they are authored by individual dreams, authorized by group struggle, and deauthorized by the opposition they meet—until the next time. This progression in turn authorizes a culture history that is at once structural and singular; it validates texts that tell the story of experiments with truth.

If I am right that this culture history is only nearly new, then I should be able to show that it is also somewhat old. Up to now, I have only given instances of Boasian texts that narrated a history of the singular (Radin) or the structural (Kroeber). The texts by Radin and Kroeber took extreme positions. A true anticipation, Alexander Lesser's study of Pawnee hand games, occupied the middle ground.

PAWNEE EXPERIMENTS

Lesser chronicled the culture history of Pawnee hand games as they changed from entertainments to ritual performances and back again to mere games. In an article critical of functionalist anthropology, Lesser made clear his commitment to culture history: "Institutions, customs, beliefs, artifacts have careers in time, and . . . their form and character are molded more by what has happened to them in the course of that history than by what particular things they occur associated with at any one time" (1935: 393; see also Lesser 1933: 335–336).

By "career in time," Lesser meant something quite different from Kroeber's periodization of formal-dress patterns and other studies of cultural commodities, even more recent ones. The Pawnee hand game advanced from gambling game to ritual performance because new structural forces but also new individual problematics mobilized it. Lesser told of how the hand game became a ritual as Pawnee life became "barren" under American domination. The old rituals of warfare, agriculture, and the hunt were no longer possible. New hope for the Pawnees came from a cultural experiment, the Ghost Dance, which incorporated the hand games into its ceremonialism. By promising the Indians resurrection, the Ghost Dance led the Pawnees and other Indians to resurrect or reinvent distinctive cultural practices.

Lesser traced the development of the Ghost Dance among the Pawnees in terms of singularities, namely, the individuals who introduced and developed aspects of it. He documented the accretions of innovations in the hand games that transformed them into nativist rituals and then later into Christian rites and finally into social entertainments. He also showed the singularities directing Pawnee consciousness to change: winning the hand game, which originally signified legerdemain, later represented spiritual talent. Lesser also gave a history of structure, in particular, the fact that the Ghost Dance found fertile ground because of the American government's policy of assimilation, which had left the Pawnees at "a cultural impasse" (Lesser 1933: 105). In the end, the Pawnee experiment failed: the Ghost Dance vision weakened, Christianity assimilated the reinvented hand-game rituals, and finally, the hand games turned back into entertainments. This failure, however, makes Lesser's narrative no less the story of an "experiment with truth": "This [central] theme is the story of the development among the Pawnee of an institution which in part filled their intellectual and social needs in the midst of cultural barrenness— a cultural barrenness produced by uncontrolled assimilation (Lesser 1933: 337).

From his culture history, Lesser tells a story not easily narrated in ethnography: he finds a middle ground between the singular and the structural. From this vantage, he can see the construction of the Pawnees (including their near destruction and attempted reconstruction). He can also chronicle the changing character of a cultural trait (the hand game) in relation to both the wider context of (American) domination and the individual (Pawnee) context of intention.

CONCLUSION: CULTURED LIVES
AND LIVED CULTURES

I have proposed the study of individual creativity in relation to cultural constitution over time as one possible anthropology. It would lead to texts narrating "experiments with truth" over time, that is, culture histories acknowledging the role of individual creativity without denying the formative character of culture. I have argued that this endeavor is presaged in the agonistic intellectual field fought over by the Boasian culture historians.

Two different methods of telling such culture histories come readily to my mind, although they would ultimately overlap. One way would be to study "cultured lives," that is, to deal with the actual cultural construction of a real individual or individuals, and then with how or to what extent those individuals constructed or reconstructed their cultures. The emphasis would be on how new cultural meanings may (or may not) grow out of the experiences of these individuals in their cultures. The obvious precedent for this approach in anthropology is the study of "life history," but often such studies have emphasized the individual as a carrier of culture rather than as an (attempted) innovator. This "leveling" (as Joan Vincent labeled it during the seminar), so typical of anthropology's approach to life history, need not be duplicated in culture history.

Neither must the study of "cultured lives" be a "life and times" exercise, as conventionally done in historical biography, because it is informed by an anthropological view of culture. For example, it need not start with the birth of the individual, as conventional biographies do, nor need it stop with the individual's death. "Cultural reputation" and "individual contribution" have to be constructed during a lifetime and can continue (and be reconsidered and "hijacked") after a person's death. A person becomes a cultural subject and object at points during a lifetime and after death. Studying cultured lives means recognizing how individuals construct reputation in their own cultures and how their innovations and reputations fare after their deaths (see Fox 1989 for a treatment of Gandhi in relation to Gandhian utopia). A culture history based on cultured lives insists that even innovative lives are culturally lived, and that they are innovative for precisely that reason.

The other way to do culture history would be to deal with "lived culture." This is akin to (but not equivalent with) what was once called the history of institutions, and it should be easily recognized by anthropologists. Lesser's work on Pawnee hand games is exemplary. Rather than beginning with the individual, this text starts with a cultural practice or belief and traces its history—with emphasis on its creation by specific authors, its diffusion by actual individuals or institutions, and its acceptance, rejection, or modification in particular new environments. Nonviolent resistance (*satyagraha*), for example, once discovered or invented by Gandhi, became a cultural form that was lived out in new circumstances by Martin Luther King, Jr., César Chávez, and even members of the Pro-Life movement in the 1980s (this culture history is the subject of my current research).

If ethnography is truly morbid and maybe moribund, as the postmodern critics say, we must discover or recover other anthropologies and related texts that promise us liveliness and livelihood. The culture history that enlivened Boasian anthropology in the past—and which today could tell the story of how individual lives are culturally lived or how cultural forms are individually cultured—might be worthy of reincarnation.

———— *Notes* ————

I want to thank the participants in the School of American Research advanced seminar for their helpful comments. I also want to thank Sidney Mintz for useful comments and information on Alexander Lesser's influence in the field. I also thank the John Simon Guggenheim Memorial Foundation and the National Endowment for the Humanities for their material support.

1. Anthropologists are trained to disentangle what cultures entangle: for example, genitorship and paternity, sex and marriage, lineals and collaterals. It should be relatively easy, therefore, to disentangle our own disciplinary assumptions. Yet we often treat ethnography, a field method, and ethnography, a text form, as being inseparable. A negative instance best reflects our entanglement: Radcliffe-Brown wrote up his Andaman culture-historical research as if he had done Trobriand-style ethnography (see Radcliffe-Brown 1964:vii, and Appendix A and its line drawings of material-culture items). Text form and field method were quite distinct in this case. Another example might be Boasian accounts of reservationized Native Americans. Here the anthropologist did ethnographic fieldwork but wrote of remembered cultures (cf. Thornton 1983). Ethnography as a text and ethnography as a field method, therefore, are not necessarily any more companionate than sex and marriage.

2. I think here not only of Geertz, but before him, of Margaret Mead—both of whom have greater (and well-deserved) stature as individual scholars than as students of the particular others they studied. Malinowski represents the opposite, I believe: he is respected more as the Trobriand ethnographer than independently.

3. My view of this period differs considerably from George Stocking's (1976:42–44). He argues for a gradual evolution in American anthropology rather than a revolution. He makes a strong case for professional and organizational continuity, which we might expect given that most anthropologists were

students of Boas's, or students of Boas's students, and that the American Anthropological Association remained the central professional institution. There was a "live and let live" attitude among many early Boasians, as when even Kroeber (1936b) allowed that his historical approach and Radcliffe-Brown's functional method were just two ways of attacking the same question. That Boas could interpret the new anthropology of the 1930s as developing from ideas he had as early as 1910 also probably minimized or masked major changes. Furthermore, he tried to pass on his professional position to Benedict. Professionally, then, there was not the vivid confrontation between historical science and ethnography that Ian Langham (1981) chronicles in the U.K.

Stocking does show major changes in the discipline of anthropology, however. And although Kroeber may have been willing to live with Radcliffe-Brown and some of the later Boasians, it is not at all clear that they reciprocated. I think Stocking may underplay the revolutionary character of these changes by portraying them as a simple shift in perspective from "diachronic" to "synchronic" (Stocking 1976:15), rather than as the more fundamental change from a historical science to a social ("physics") science and from a culture-historical to an ethnographic text—which is the way I see them.

4. In general, Boas's first students and affiliates—Kroeber, Lowie, Radin, Sapir, Wissler, Goldenweiser—did culture history, but there is no neat generational or temporal separation, and there are transitional figures, such as Lesser, Benedict (the last culture historian?) and Herskovits. "Preethnographic Boasians" is perhaps a better phrase, but it is cumbersome—and misleading if not understood to refer to text rather than necessarily to field technique. "Early," as I use it, is more of a typological than a temporal label.

5. Stocking (1976:6) notes the paradox that the Boasians stressed their "scientific" anthropology against the evolutionists, in spite of "the anti-scientific current in their thinking."

6. The term "realism," as I use it here, is not the same "realism" that many reflexive anthropologists find deficient in "realist ethnography."

7. Handler (1983:219) asserts that Sapir departed from the Boasian tradition by his continuing interest in the role of the individual, whereas I am arguing that this question was their central problematic.

8. There is another parallel between American and British developments: many pre-Malinowskian British anthropologists were deeply interested in individual creativity, as Joan Vincent (1986b:337) argues for Marett and Rivers, but it was also true of diffusionists like Smith and Perry, who were Malinowski's archrivals. Malinowski claimed his "pure" or unhyphenated functionalism differed from Radcliffe-Brown's structural-functionalism precisely because it took cognizance of the individual. However, Malinowski mainly recognized the individual as a bundle of biological wants rather than as an intentional actor, and even in terms of these wants, he emphasized the way they were defined by culture.

9. Elsewhere (Fox 1989: chapter 2) I discuss these issues at much greater length.

10. Ricoeur continues this discussion in a later work (1986) in which he contrasts "utopia" and "ideology." Although this distinction is important to my culture history, I do not have the space to discuss it here (but see Fox 1989).

11. Jean-Paul Sartre (1963) suggested many of these themes as the basis for a "historical anthropology" and illustrated them by a study of Flaubert and his production of *Madame Bovary*. Sartre's approach is limited, however, by a relatively untheorized understanding of individual lives and culture (see the last section of this paper; also see Burke [1980: 103]).

12. These new cultural forms may range from sets of meanings underlying mass protest, as in Gandhi's *satyagraha*, to new items of material culture, as in Gandhi's program of *khadi*.

Chapter 7

REPRESENTATION, ETHNICITY, AND THE PRECURSORY ETHNOGRAPHY

Notes of a Native Anthropologist

José E. Limón

*I*N this essay, I want to speak of a place—a spatial place, but also a temporal, structural, and cultural one. All of these senses of place and perhaps others have generated an ideologically accented culture among the people who live there. The place is southern Texas, and the people are its predominantly Mexican-American, largely working-class population. There are also among them those who are thought of as "Anglo," as well as a small but powerful Mexican-American upper class. A comprehensive assessment should speak to all of these groups, but this essay is historically chosen to speak chiefly only to one, at least in a conscious, foregrounded manner: the working-class Mexican-Americans, or *mexicanos,* as they still prefer to call themselves.[1]

In writing about this place and these people, I want to enter into recent conceptual discussions concerning the closely interrelated issues of ethnographic construction, authority, and representation (Clifford 1988c; Clifford and Marcus 1986; Marcus and Fischer 1986). My particular interest is in addressing two subjects that have generally been absent from these discussions: first, the problematics of ethnicity and "native" anthropology, and second, the question of what I shall call the precursory ethnography. These two subjects can themselves become closely interrelated issues, as they shall in this paper. The first refers to the particular challenges posed to the "native" anthropologist in his or her attempt ethnographically to represent ethnic worlds riven with cultural contradiction in this postmodern moment, while responding critically to a history of flattening stereotypical representations of these worlds. The second issue has to do with the ways in which prior and "master" ethnographic texts about such worlds deeply influence the construction of later ethnographies. My essay offers no salient, linear, clarifying thesis on these issues, but a processual illustration of them for the enlightenment it may shed.

SOCIAL DOMINATION, ETHNOGRAPHIC PRECURSORS

Like any other anthropologist or ethnographer with her or his place, I have spent a considerable portion of my professional career, twelve years now, trying to make sense of mine—of its people and, of course, of what I have called its ideologically accented culture. Unlike most anthropologists, however, it happens that I am born and bred of the place I study. Over the years, I have also become simultaneously of another place as well, a child of the Enlightenment, of high literary modernism, of classical anthropology. This combination of birthrights has produced an interesting complexity that the less observant might mistake for a dilemma. It is this complexity that I would also address in my remarks, if only implicitly. For the moment, let me note that I am not the first of my other tribe, the tribe of anthropology, to visit among these, my people.

As with most peoples under social domination, south Texas *mexicanos* have hosted their share of anthropologists.[2] Further, the social domination and the anthropology have not been distinct endeavors. To use Fredric Jameson's phrase, the "political unconscious" of the latter has been implicated in the ideological ratification of the former (Jameson 1981). In a chapter in a book in progress called *Dancing with the Devil*—the present essay is an anticipatory statement—I trace this relationship in the work of three major anthropologists, my predecessors. I argue that at its beginning, anthropology, to paraphrase Clausewitz (1968), is the continuation of social warfare against the *mexicanos* of south Texas—a quite literal warfare waged periodically against these people ever since the U.S. army invaded the area in 1845 on its way into the Republic of Mexico.

Indeed, in the figure of John Gregory Bourke, we find the exact conjuncture of warfare and anthropology. Captain Bourke was the first professional anthropologist to study this area. As a U.S. cavalry officer, he was assigned to the area in the 1890s to suppress the anti-American guerrilla operations of the *mexicano* Catarino Garza. However, when not in combat against the Garza forces, Captain Bourke, as a representative of the Bureau of American Ethnology in Washington, D.C., found time to conduct ethnographic fieldwork among his enemy other, although almost exclusively among the local *mexicanas*—the women—who, frankly, were not as likely to put a bullet into the good captain (Porter 1986). Possibly displacing his own ambivalence toward his Irish identity at that historical moment, Bourke's writings issue forth a recurrent, often virulent, anti-Mexican racism and stereotyping, a practice abetted by the then-reigning Victorian evolutionary anthropology (Stocking 1987).

In my own work, I find myself in open warfare with this first of my precursors, given our contemporary understandings of culture. However, I have a more immediate precursor who also happens to be my mentor: Américo Paredes, who wrote the now-classic *With His Pistol in His Hand* (1958).[3] This was a book that momentarily reversed the tide of ideological battle over south Texas and elsewhere through its critique of domination in two distinct realms of discourse.

With His Pistol in His Hand is an ethnography of a period in greater Mexican history characterized by the emergence of an epic, heroic form of balladry known as the *corrido*, a key symbol of this period's culture. Specifically, the book focuses on the anti-American resistance of one *mexicano*, Gregorio Cortez, and the corpus of ballads celebrating his exploits. It is a historical ethnography in at least two senses: first, Cortez's story occurred between the years 1901 and 1907, and second, the balladry represents a specific period of heroic resistance that had diminished by the 1930s, but which Américo Paredes was historically close to as a child growing up in south Texas. Thus, it is a historical recounting, an oral history, from the perspective of the 1950s, when the book was written.

As I have argued in another place, this book had two critical effects. First, it fundamentally questioned the flattening effect of all other anthropology in this area by demonstrating a historical, resistive *mexicano* culture. In showing us this model of culture, Paredes's book and Paredes himself as a charismatic figure also became models for the genesis of an emergent political and literary culture in the 1960s—the Chicano movement. Second, I argue that in addition to its critical "content," the book was able to take on this significance because of its modernist "ideology of form," to use another of Jameson's concepts (1981 : 98–102). In this formal respect, as well as in others, Paredes's work anticipated, by example, current discussions concerning the "experimental moment" in anthropology (Limón 1990).

The compelling critical content and form of Paredes's masterpiece argue for recasting it as an "intellectual poem," Lukacs's fine phrase for a master essay, as well as a "sociological poem," Miller's praise phrase for the work of C. Wright Mills (Lukacs 1910; Miller 1986). If permitted such recasting, I can then take further license by comparing *With His Pistol in His Hand* to a master poem, a mighty precursor—to use Harold Bloom's terms—exerting its strong influence over all those who would write after it.[4] Those who write in the long shadow or strong light of great precursory "poems" necessarily must experience what Bloom (1973, 1975) also calls "the anxiety of influence." This anxiety is generated in the contradiction between the sense of deep indebtedness to the strong precursor and the sharp Romantic injunction to originality. Yet, for Bloom, all those who would truly write their own strong poems *must* experience this anxiety of influence, must feel the weight of indebtedness to their strong precursor, even while feeling the urge to "independent" poetic flight.

Yet to strike out on one's own is a fiction, for the precursor's influence has been deeply internalized and must be worked out, as it were, to achieve any measure of poetic distance. For Bloom, not only is this working out not independent of poetry itself, it actually constitutes it. In the subsequent strong poetry, its constitutive imagery and form are fundamentally a series of revisionary rhetorical strategies for absorbing and controlling the precursor's influence. The degree of their manifest success for the reader is a function of this struggle and of the relative ability of each poetic son to come to terms with his precursory poetic father.

When I began the fieldwork and ethnographic construction for *Dancing with the Devil*, I decided to focus on the ubiquitous, polka-centered, popular dancing culture among the *mexicanos*. As my charter for this focus, I took Sherry Ortner's (1973) concept of key symbols in a culture, which, by their redundancy, pervasiveness, and importance can be seen as capturing and expressing a society's focal cultural concerns. But even then, and certainly now with the benefit of Bloom's reflections on deep precursory influence, I became increasingly aware of other, perhaps more latent and impulsive, motivations for our ethnographic constructions. As we write about our peoples, do we not also write against our master precursory ethnographers? I am not speaking of surface theoretical or methodological issues, but of the very constitution of our writing. I cannot, at this time, propose this as a way of understanding the entire historical development of ethnography, as Bloom has done for the whole of Anglo-American strong poetry. I can only offer the possibility, while sharing my sense of my own relationship to *With His Pistol in His Hand*. Let me partially illustrate the point by tracing the flow of my ethnographic work out of *With His Pistol in His Hand*, as illustrated by a selection from *Dancing with the Devil*. This tracing will then lead me back to the question of representation and ethnicity as experienced by one "native" anthropologist.

THE NATIVE DANCES

Early in *With His Pistol in His Hand*, Paredes gives voice to a collective cultural perspective on the historical period of the *corrido* and men like Gregorio Cortez. In modernist fashion, he creates this retrospective voice by amalgamating the Cortez legends he collected into a single narrative told by a fictive, elderly, collective persona. Let me quote the beginning of this story (Paredes 1958:33–39) from which I take my revisionary stance.

> They still sing of him—in the *cantinas* and the country stores, in the ranches when men gather at night to talk in the cool dark, sitting in a circle, smoking and listening to the old songs and the tales of other days. Then the *guitarreros* [guitarists] sing of the border raids and the skirmishes, of the men who lived by the phrase, "I will break before I bend."
>
> . . . After the song is sung there is a lull. Then the old men, who have lived long and seen almost everything, tell their stories. And when they tell about Gregorio Cortez, the telling goes like this:
>
> . . . That was good singing, and a good song; give the man a drink. Not like these pachucos nowadays, mumbling damn-foolishness into a microphone; it is not done that way. Men should sing with their heads thrown back, with their mouths wide open and their eyes shut. Fill your lungs, so they can hear you at the pasture's farther end. And when you sing, sing songs like *El Corrido de Gregorio Cortez*.

Américo Paredes's collective legend and his fictive persona tell us of past and present, probably from a post–World War II vantage point. As the elders comment favorably on the *corrido* singing of earlier days, they cannot avoid a disparaging commentary on the present. That heroic *corrido* singing and, by implication, men like Gregorio Cortez were "not like these pachucos nowadays," nor, we can assume, were they like those who dance to this "mumbling damn-foolishness."

Paredes's persona is critically commenting upon a post-war popular music and dancing scene. It was and continues to be a scene centered on

the accordion-led *conjunto* for its nineteenth-century-derived polka music
and dance; a scene set in commercial dance halls; a scene that becomes a
major expressive signification of a lower-working-class sector that our
persona negatively and too easily signifies through the figure of the pachuco, the *mexicano* street-gang adolescent (Peña 1985). In what I have
called the imbedded, tragic poetics of culture in Américo Paredes's entire
corpus of work, this popular music and dancing express the decline of
mexicano culture in south Texas from its heroic state to a modern one of
degradation (Limón n.d.).

But here is precisely where I shall begin: with those who mumble
"damn-foolishness" into microphones, and particularly with those who
dance to it. For if the heroic ballad was at the center of Américo Paredes's
youth and enabled his scholarly poetics of culture, then popular music
and dancing might do the same for me.

As a *mexicano* working-class native of south Texas, growing up in the
late fifties and the early sixties, I never knew a time of small ranches and
country stores; I knew only the asphalt-concrete pachuco mean streets of
cities. I knew no pastures, only federal housing projects, where, if you
walked to the project's farther end, you could still hear the radio music—the polka music—from a hundred open windows on hot summer
nights. For hot it was, and everyone would sit outside in the common
yards, polkas in the background, while women talked quietly, men drank,
and children played. Then sirens would cut through the night and an
elderly woman might say, "Por hay anda el diablo" ("the devil is about"),
as the police cruisers would come up the narrow alleys and all of us might
imagine the devil and wage the continuing war.

Been doing it since junior high in Corpus Christi, Texas, in the late fifties.
But I'm really not very good at it. Never really have been.

She knows it too.

I awkwardly push my body towards hers; she holds me, tightly, and I
think she thinks, Well, he'll be better next time.

I know I won't.

I'll never really be good at it. Not like the other guys—Lencho, Tony,
la rata. All of us drift back to our table after it's over. They with their
women; me, with "mine."

Pretty good polka, huh? says Tony. Yeah, well, I think to myself, if
you're good at it. I'm not.

Consolation: I'm not here to dance, really. I'm an anthropologist. Forget consolation: maybe I won't be any good at that either. But that is why

I am here. Reenter consolation: maybe I can get to be a better dancer, here at El Cielo Azul—The Blue Heaven—Dance Hall.

As she expects me to, I help Beatrice to her chair as the rest of our friends sit down, except for la rata, who stands by the table. Beatrice, or *la* Beatrice, as she is called in Ruperto's Lounge, where I met her, smiles a thank you. She'll help me, I think, in dancing and anthropology, although I've been having a devil of a time explaining the latter to her. Once I do, however, I think she'll help me. I think she likes me. Took her to dinner at Las Brisas. That ought to count for something. Yeah, maybe she'll help me. What textbooks call a key informant.

La rata is asking who wants another round. It's his turn to go to the beer concession. (I have to remember: la rata, then me, then Lencho, then Tony. The women never go.) *Cinco* Lone Stars? *Dos* Schlitz? (I have to remember: I had one at Las Brisas, one a while ago, maybe one more and that's it. Fieldwork, *compa.*[5] More observation, less participation.)

What about you? la rata asks Lencho's date, la Rosemary with the big almond-shaped eyes. She uses mostly an accented English and doesn't say much in Spanish.

I want a white wine.

¿Cómo que un white wine? (What do you mean, a white wine?) In a heavy voice la rata reverts to Spanish, and then her own Spanish suddenly emerges, such as it is.

Chingao, you asked me what I wanted! I want a *chingao* white wine!

Lencho rolls his eyes and pretends to be talking seriously to Tony. Rosemary, you see, lived a number of years in southern California before moving back to San Antonio after her divorce. Worked in a clothing factory in L.A., but now she's a waitress at Las Brisas. Temporarily, she says. Until they call her from the blue-jean place in San Antonio. She and Lencho met during his morning coffee stop as a truck driver for Zarsky's Lumber. The almond eyes—and the rest—proved irresistible, but Lencho's wife would probably want a second opinion. Not to blame L.A. or anything, but Rosemary's not quite like the others, not like Delia, Amalia, la Beatrice—or Lencho's wife. *Más* classy, according to Lencho. The other women don't like her much. *Muy agabachada* (very Anglicized). *Se cree mucho* (thinks she's better). Perhaps it's the well-dyed blond hair, the extra baubles hanging all over her neck and arms. It's not education. They're all dropouts. La rata doesn't like her either, perhaps for the same reasons. She also calls him "rat" in English, which really pisses him off. Lencho's wife agrees with all this—and more. *La voy a matar a la puta* (I'm going to kill the whore). Lencho likes to repeat the line. Tony likes Rosemary, mostly because she's *bien buenota* (has a really good body), but Lencho's got her, and for tonight anyway, la Delia, a laundry worker, is with Tony. For tonight anyway.

Rosemary wants white wine and will not be budged. Tony, Lencho, and I are snickering, and la rata is up on the fence looking at shit on one side and piss on the other. He leans hard across the table, stares at Rosemary and tells her, *Aquí no hay* white wine (there's no white wine here).

She stares back: Go see, she says, drawing only a bit from what are obviously giant reserves of "cool."

Rata looks hard at Lencho, turns abruptly, and goes off to get our stuff. They're tight, these two guys. Dropped out of high school together—*de la brack*. Been drinking buddies at Ruperto's for seven, eight years when Beatrice introduced them to me. Tight. Even if Lencho did go airborne and not into the marines. The story at Ruperto's is that the night before rata shipped out to Pendleton, he got drunk, stood on top of the bar, stripped off his shirt, and yelled, *¿Watchan este cuerpo? ¡Se lo voy a dar a los marines!* (See this body? I'm going to give it to the marines!)

As the band kicks off another polka, we are left to imagine la rata at the bar at the opposite end of El Cielo Azul, this large, Quonset-hut dance hall on the outer, *mexicano* west side of San Antonio. Rata will carefully insert his dark, wiry frame into the seams of a huge mass of Mexican man-flesh clumped around the bar. Big guys, many of them. These days, it seems, *mexicanos* are neither really short nor really tall; they grow simultaneously in all directions. Rata will be careful to avoid pushing hard on anybody. The *vato* might shove back and then rata, as he says, "would have to call in an airstrike," but right now he doesn't want trouble. He'll squeeze and squirm his way up to the bar, trying to keep his new J. C. Penney *guayabera* from getting wrinkled. Didn't buy it at J. C. Penney exactly. First, a friend got it from a friend who lifted it at *el centavo*. Then la rata got it. J. C. Penney sticker still on it. Marked down. Special. Stuff from Macy's costs more. Tighter security. *Más* classy. Rata, currently unemployed, can't afford to shop there.

At the bar, surrounded by part-time construction workers, part-time truck drivers, part-time busboys, an occasional full-time drug dealer—all of them still pretty much in native dress—la rata, himself a little of each of these, will say—will have to yell—to the fat bartender: *Quiero cinco* Lone Stars, *dos* Schlitz, *y un* white wine. Only to be told: *No hay* white wine. Everyone will look at him. White wine? Though nobody will say anything. Just smiles. Tight smiles.

Threading his way through the folding tables, chairs, and people— all *mexicanos*—gathered around the large central dance floor, la rata then cuts across a corner of the floor to reach our table as couples glide by to the rhythm of the polka. He puts down the beer and spits the bartender's message into Rosemary's once high-school-beautiful, now thickly made-up face: *No hay* white wine! The rest of us snicker quietly again. Very quietly. Rata, I have been told, killed a North Vietnamese soldier with his bare hands and two others with his knife at Khe Sanh in 1968. I'm certainly not going to fuck with him *or* with Rosemary, who is now deciding whether the world will end in fire or ice. Everybody else, including Lencho, is also staying out of this one.

But a truce is declared for now. One of the bartenders has followed la rata back to the table to inform us that the management is sending out for white wine. *Aquí nomas al 7-11 ahorita vienen* (just right next door at the 7-11, they'll be right back). Thank heaven for 7-11. The manager thinks he's onto a new trend, as he will verify later: warm summer nights in the barely air-conditioned Cielo Azul, hot polka music, and cold white wine. A gallon at $8.95, twenty cups at $2.50 a cup. Keeps the *rucas* happy. *A toda madre.* And if they don't drink it, *se lo llevo a mi vieja* (I'll take it to my old lady). A real cultural innovator, this one.

Except for Beatrice and me, everyone goes out to dance again, as the band puts down another throbbing, wailing polka. Neither the traditional accordion *conjunto* nor the traditional *orquesta* with wind and brass instruments, this six-man group combines a few elements of both—trumpet, alto sax, rhythm, and guitar, with an electric keyboard carrying the staccato lead part of the traditional accordion. In the 1970s, more and more of these hybrid small groups are popping up as young kids, high-school dropouts with band training, try to make it big. They carry names like this group's—Magia Negra (Black Magic). And they start here in places like El Cielo Azul—cheaply constructed halls at the margins of town catering to the *mexicanos* at the margins of society. And though they play rock'n'roll, country-western, and Latin American *cumbias*, the polka is the music of choice, the battle hymn of this republic.

I want to sit this one out because I want to think and mentally record all that has happened thus far. I actually write a note or two while Bea watches me with amusement until, her tolerance exhausted, she gives me the look: I want to dance. So, I'm off to try again.

Better, this time, I think. Beatrice seems to be getting into what I laughingly call my rhythm. She has me somewhat outweighed and she's about half a head shorter, but again, she hangs on tight and, with me feeling in pretty good control, we're off, moving fast and slow, fast and slow, counter-clockwise around the large floor, as we ourselves slowly rotate counter-clockwise as a couple, like the other forty or so all around us. Hey, pretty good! I think to myself.

At one time I wasn't that bad. Really. Did a lot of dancing growing up in Corpus. Started at age twelve, as I remember, at the summer night dances on the basketball court in the Wiggins Federal Housing Project where I was raised, protected always by our very own gang, los wolves de la Wiggins, who lurked in the shadows, holding their women. Later in my life, Domingo Peña, the famous (or infamous) south Texas dance promoter, had dances every weekend at Memorial Coliseum. Come on, Mrs. Gutierrez, hurry up! all of us sackboys would say to ourselves at eight P.M., as the last customer in Biel's Grocery Store on Leopard Street slowly made her way to the check-out stand. Then she was gone. A fast mop and we were off as a group walking down Leopard to the dance. Still wearing our jeans, black ties, and sweaty white shirts (we'd steal a bottle of Mennen After-Shave at the store and pass it around), we'd get to the coliseum and hit the floor for a good time. Getting home was tougher. Gang territories all the way. But the cops were more dangerous. Always the cops. Always. All Anglo then. Stopping. Searching. How come you Meskin kids cause so much trouble? Spread-eagled on the hood of a police car at age fifteen, I once declared war, I now do anthropology, and I've almost forgotten how to dance.

I'm remembering all this as Beatrice and I come out of a fast turn and I'm trying also to "observe." Then it happens. I have my left hand up a little too high holding Beatrice's right, and as we turn I hit him in the face. I turn to say *perdón*, excuse me, but he has already abandoned his partner, who is screaming something like, Don't kill him, Chente! while she grabs him with both arms around a very ample torso. He looks to be on the verge of doing just that when Tony and Delia whirl by. Turns out he knows Tony; they work at the cement plant. Tony mediates; I mumble an apology and endure a very hard stare, a monstrous calloused forefinger two inches from my nose, and a ¡La siguiente vez, watchate, pendejo! (Next time, watch it, stupid!) At 150 pounds, with ten years of college education and no Marine Corps training, I can only agree. Beatrice takes me in her arms and dances me away. This time, her wiry-stiff, sprayed hair in my face, her thick perfume, the faint popping of her chewing gum are all oddly comforting.

That was close, bro! says Tony, when we're all sitting down again. Rata wants to go talk to the *puto*. The marines never leave their dead behind, *ese*, and always retaliate, he says. Rata is so comforting. We talk him out of it. Lencho and Rosemary have not rejoined us, and we see them by the wall. Lencho is working his hands all over her. At a distance she does look beautiful. A few moments later they're gone, probably out to Lencho's car. They'll be back to dance again. After the dance, they'll go to her place. He'll go home at three or four, have a fight with his wife. Get up late the next day. Watch the NFL game, make *fajitas* for the family and have a few. So will Tony. La rata is not married; divorced. Maybe he and I will drop by Lencho's tomorrow for *fajitas*. Then maybe Ruperto's. Maybe tomorrow I should write, though.

We dance a few more without sitting down. This time I watch my swings and look out for *him*. I think he's gone, says Beatrice with a giggle. Am I getting any better, Beatrice? I ask her. Yeah, a little bit, she says. You need to practice. I'll teach you.

When we return, rata and Lencho are on their feet on opposite sides of the table. It looks as if at any moment, the 1st Marine Division is about to go head-to-head with the 82d Airborne. Rosemary is sitting smugly, half-smile on her face, sipping white wine. Smart money says this is about her again, this time with more beer for fuel. Tony talks to la rata; I talk to Lencho. Over the last year I've become somehow oddly closer to him. Don't know why exactly. Maybe because, like me, he grew up in a housing project. Casiano Projects. Maybe it's his lumberyard work. I used to do that when I was working my way through Del Mar junior college. I know about one-by-eight, two-by-four, Douglas fir, yellow pine, sheetrock, and tossing 96-pound bags of cement from the back of a truck under a south Texas summer sun. While the always-Anglo foremen watch. Another declaration of war. Maybe it's just our age. We're both thirty-two. The other guys are younger.

Things calm down, for the moment anyway. As I said, these guys are tight, so I think it'll be all right. Everybody goes off to dance again, except for Bea and me. I need a bathroom break.

The bathroom reeks of everything in this world that reeks. As I am finishing up at the urinals, I become aware of three or four guys watching me intently as they pass a joint among themselves. Tough. Sullen. Long scraggly black hair. Dark glasses. One really big guy, the others lean and gaunt but tough. They all look like they've vacationed in Huntsville, the state prison. The Wiggins Wolves twenty years later. I feel cold all over, and I know it's not the air conditioner at the Cielo Azul. I zip up, turn slowly, and, with a distant approximation of nonchalance, walk by them to the door. As I go by, their eyes follow—even with dark glasses, I can tell—and one of them lifts his head up ever so slightly and softly says, ¿Qu'uvo? (What's goin' on?) I look him carefully in the dark glasses and say just as softly, Aquí nomás (everything's cool). Then, I am out into the welcome public scene of the dance floor area. Peace. To celebrate the occasion, I decide to get another round for the group even though it's not my turn. I'll have one also. Is this the third or fourth?

When I return, Beatrice informs me that two or three guys asked her to dance and she said no. More dancing; getting better all the time. I even try some of the fancy stuff. Holding only your partner's hand with one of your own, and using the other to give her a slight spin at the waist, you turn her round and round, pass her behind you, swing her in front, take her in your arms again, and pick up the forward motion of the polka on the beat (a move borrowed and adapted from American swing in the thirties). Without hitting anybody. Forty or so moving, swinging couples on the dance floor of El Cielo Azul constitute an expressive, well-armed truce, but perhaps this is a definition of art. Or so it occurs to me as, over Beatrice's head, I watch la rata and Amalia, a single body in two not-always-discernible parts, smoothly gliding with rhythmic dipping—like the good Mexican cotton pickers that I watched as a boy working Saturdays in the cotton fields outside Corpus Christi before the machine pickers came—all the while slowly turning on a firm axis. La rata even seems to have his eyes closed, no doubt imagining Amalia later, after the dance, but the dancing flows effortlessly. They slip in and out of traffic, sleek and quick, like a lovely black Jaguar that I remember seeing once on the San Diego freeway, a moving form always at the point of violent contact but deftly avoiding it at the last second. Meanwhile, I putt along in my little Honda, watching, with Beatrice along for a rather uneventful ride.

We are gliding by the bandstand when a fight breaks out in the second row of tables near the wall. The truce has broken down. I start spinning Beatrice round and round because I want to see. She soon gets dizzy and has the good sense to say, let's just stop. There's a lot to hear but not much to see since a crowd has quickly built up. Lots of screaming and cursing, and what is visible gives you a pretty good sense of what is going on. With a regular rhythm, a hand holding a beer bottle by the neck appears and disappears, appears and disappears, above the heads of the crowd. Two overweight, older *mexicano* security cops, probably long retired from the San Antonio police department, are making their way into the crowd, but not at great speed. Even though everyone was frisked at the door, you never know what might be waiting in there. No sense in spoiling a nice retirement, what with the grandchildren and all and your eldest boy slowly getting his pharmacy degree in Austin. I feel a little tug from Beatrice. I turn, she smiles, and we dance away, for the band has not missed a beat.

It's getting late, one A.M. Amalia wants *menudo* and Beatrice wants to hear the mariachi at Mario's Restaurant. The guys look at each other. Mario's is "classy," so they're thinking money, since they'll have to pay, and wives, since it is a key public scene in San Antonio *mexicano* life. I'm not worried about money. Tony and Delia have only a couple of hours, so they're not coming. We make it a foursome, but la rata, after seven or eight beers and a joint, is fading fast even after the hot, spicy menudo. The marines always retrieve their dead and wounded, so Amalia drives him home. As they teeter-totter out, she keeps taking his hand off her rump. She won't stay with him tonight. It's too late; she lives at home and it's not worth the fight with her father the next day. She'll take him as far as her house, and then *que Dios lo bendiga* (may God bless him). She also wants to sleep. She'll serve the lunch and dinner shift at Luby's Cafeteria tomorrow, on her feet all day.

Through soft slurps of menudo, I ask Beatrice more about herself. This will be the first time I've really talked to her at length, although I've known her now two years since I started going to Ruperto's, where she tends bar part-time. Usually she's too busy to talk much, or, in time-honored fashion, I spend more time talking to the men. A mother at sixteen, now twenty-six, divorced. Her boy is living in Arizona with his father. She doesn't explain. I don't ask. Worked at a paper factory running some sort of machine that makes paper cups. Laid off. A cousin has a part-interest in Ruperto's, so he got her a part-time job. Would like to get married again. Why work? But, she says, not many good guys around.

We attempt more conversation. You must read a lot of books, she says. She doesn't. Popular fashion magazines, mostly to look at the pictures. Watches TV. *Telenovelas* and also the American kind. The Price is Right. Come on down! she cries gleefully, causing the other restaurant patrons to look at us, and embarrassing me. (Why am I embarrassed?) I ask her about the dances. Does she go often? That reminds her of the dance floor incident, and she laughs, repeating Tony's line—That was close!—and adds, what if you had been killed! What would your professor friends at the university think? And your wife? I tell her, I don't know what they would think, and I'm not married. Not exactly single, though I don't tell her that. There is supposed to be a someone. So what am I doing here? I ponder myself dead on the dance floor and envision a headline in one of the yellow-journalist San Antonio newspapers: Professor Zapped. Said to Be Doing "Fieldwork." Had It Coming. *¿Quién le manda?* (Who said he should be there?)

So what about the dance, Beatrice? She doesn't say much. It's something to do. Guys ask her out now and then and this is where they usually take her. To dances. Like me. We were at Ruperto's on a Saturday afternoon. Lencho and Tony wanted to go. Said they knew some *rucas*. Beatrice was off for the night, they said. Why don't you ask her? Why not? We seemed friendly enough. So here we are. Getting to know you.

Does she enjoy dances? A seemingly stupid question until she says, no, not really. Like I said, it's something to do, she says. It's about the only place to meet guys. But usually those that ask her out or that she meets there when she goes with girlfriends, *pues nomas no* (well, thank you, but no thank you). Maybe it's different in the "better" dance halls, but she doesn't get asked there and she can't afford it. Nonetheless, she thanks me for taking her out and for dinner. Usually she doesn't even get dinner, and they all want something. I don't mean you, you understand. You're not even my type anyway. She laughs: you can't even dance good! That was close, José!

Anyway, she continues, I like to dance but I don't always like the dances, *¿me entiendes?* (You know what I mean?) There's too much *borlote* (trouble) all the time. *Y los guys, pues nomás no.* They really are bad places sometimes. You shouldn't be going, really, José. My mother says that's why the devil has been coming. *El diablo chulo* (the cute devil).

Yeah, I think to myself, I've heard about the devil, but I think nothing more of it then.

Time to go home. We leave Mario's, turn on Commerce and drive into the deep west side, past run-down or boarded-up stores and shops, lots of cantinas, and, on the side-streets, small houses with the predictable profusion of flowers and bric-a-brac in front. I drop her off at one of these houses, which she shares with two other women. She invites me in. I thank her, say no, and lie, it's getting late. But I am thinking, this is enough. No more. Can't do it. Besides, I'm not her type anyway. Can't even dance good . . . I mean, well . . . but I am learning, again.

ETHNIC ANXIETIES AND INFLUENCE

It is now somewhat clear to me, as I work on *Dancing with the Devil,* that my ethnographic rendering of a lower-class *mexicano* world of popular dancing responds to the influence of Américo Paredes's heroic world. And this influence provocatively accentuates the host of problems and possibilities presented by "insider" ethnic research and writing (Aguilar 1981; Fahim 1982; Jones 1970; Jules-Rosette 1978; Maruyama 1974; Ohnuki-Tierney 1984). For me the chief issue here is the relationship of this influence to the legacy of warfare over the question of social domination and ethnic stereotyping.

I think I can see that, along with other subjective and "objective" motivations, my choice of this decidedly unheroic culture as an object of study may be the kind of rhetorical revising move that Bloom (1973) calls a *clinamen.*[6] This reaction to the precursor represents an initial and drastic swerve away from his influence, as the younger poet attempts to stake out his own original ground for creativity (Bloom 1973:19–45). Yet this move in the direction of the unheroic immediately plunges me into a serious contradiction: as I stake out this ground, I am obligated to speak fully about the *mexicano* world, to articulate not only its concern with dancing but also its violence, its exaggerated masculinity, and its toll on women—all of which representations potentially place me in an uncomfortable relationship with a history of denigrative "Mexican" stereotypes often used to validate the mistreatment of these, my people. Beyond the purely personal level, this potential relationship is also discomforting in political-intellectual terms, and it poses a contradiction within my work. First, I myself have written critically about such stereotyping (1973), and second, such a position runs counter to a deeper indebtedness to my precursor. That is, while I do not think it possible now, in the seventies and eighties, to render "heroic" worlds, nonetheless I wish to speak of the critical politics possible in the world of El Cielo Azul, just as Paredes did for the world of Gregorio Cortez.

In an effort to overcome this contradiction, I take a next step in my writing about the polka-dancing scene at El Cielo Azul, a step that acknowledges rather than denies the precursor's influence and begins its more serious and possibly creative internalization.[7] For reasons that, frankly, I do not fully understand, this next revisionary step leads me into debates on modernism and postmodernism as these make sense in south Texas. It is through these discourses that I both respond to *With His Pistol in His Hand* and continue to write my interpretive ethnography, which amount to the same thing.

MODERNISM AND POSTMODERNISM AMONG THE *MEXICANOS*

Whatever their political stance on the "postmodern"—critical, celebratory, or ambivalent— almost all critics identify it as an inherently valorized movement within arts and letters and/or mass-mediated popular culture (Berman 1982; Foster 1983; Gitlin 1989; Jameson 1984; Lyotard 1984). Few, if any, seem to take into account other, more socially pervasive and imbedded, usually negating articulations of postmodernity, especially as postmodernity may be experienced daily within racial, class, and ethnic subaltern sectors.[8] James Clifford at least senses this negative possibility when he speaks of one facet of the Caribbean postmodern condition as "a history of degradation, mimicry, violence and blocked possibilities" (1988c:15), although the general tendency of his work is toward the "creative" postmodern.

What I initially identified as the "unheroic" character of the world that

I chose against that of the precursor, I would now reidentify as this kind of negative postmodernity, which increasingly constitutes *mexicano* life in the cities of south Texas and elsewhere. But, as Clifford notes, such worlds of degradation and violence can also be "rebellious, syncretic and creative" (1988c:15). It is in this formulation, or a version of it, that in my ongoing writing about this world I return, in a different stance, to the precursor's influence.

If the *corrido* was the major signifier of the critical politics of Américo Paredes's heroic world, then I take the polka as that of my own world—the polka not so much as a musical form, but as dance. I opt for the dancing rather than the music because, as Peña has clearly suggested (1985:157–161), the music is increasingly more open to late capitalist and postmodern commodification, while, in my view, the dancing stands at some critical distance from the postmodern effect. Amid a world of degrading postmodernity, the polka is something else. At the same time, I do not think of it as the "rebellious, syncretic and creative" side of postmodernism that Clifford clearly values. While creative, it is not so in the made-anew-in-the-historical-instant manner that Clifford seems to imply, and it is not particularly rebellious, at least in any manifest sense. Neither is it a pure local narrative of "cultural continuity and recovery" (Clifford 1988c:15), nor a pure pastoral tradition. Let me propose another option. Let me speak of dancing at El Cielo Azul as an enactment of modernism at the level of the subordinated.

> The modern, according to Spender, finds its character by confronting the past and including this confrontation within itself as part of a single total experience. It is more than a cultivation of immediacy, of free or fragmented awareness; it is the embodiment in current imagery of a situation always larger than the present, and as such it is also a containment of the resources and perils of the present by rediscovery of a relevant past. In this sense, modernism is synthetic in its very indeterminacy. Modern writers, working often without established models and bent on originality, have at the same time been classicists, custodians of language, communicators, traditionalists in their fashion. (Ellman and Feidelson 1965: vii)

Written in the early sixties, this passage from Ellman and Feidelson conceives of a modernism of arts and letters as a paradoxical synthesis of tradition and innovation, one socially critical in its character and intent. While a number of influential critics have lost confidence in high modernism's critical capacity—always, of course, for the elite audiences of such modernist texts—they also seem to maintain some skepticism toward that which has presumably supplanted it, namely, postmodernism (Foster 1983). I believe Ellman and Feidelson were already implicitly and negatively identifying postmodernism when they spoke approvingly of modernism as "more than a cultivation of immediacy, of free or fragmented awareness." Sharing this skeptical stance toward the postmodern in thought, literature, the arts, and social practice, Marshall Berman, above all others, seems intent on restoring modernism's muted critical voice (1982).

This is not the place to enter fully into this large debate, but let me attempt a contribution by proposing that whatever the fate of modernism in other circles, the nineteenth-century-derived, pure formal dancing at El Cielo Azul is very akin to a modernist critical performance. By its very modernist emphasis on form, the dancing becomes something like "the embodiment in current imagery of a situation always larger than the present, and as such . . . also a containment of the resources and perils of the present by rediscovery of a relevant past"—that is, a political form. But how is this specific cultural practice political?

Randy Martin (1985:55) offers us a way to see dance form as a "decidedly non-symbolic and non-signifying politics." He analogizes the human bodies in dancing to the body politic, proposing that dance acts as the artful and deeply satisfying production of a desire that he says is present but usually not acted upon in society, "the desire to act politically." In the absence of such periodic action there can only result an attenuation of consciousness. Dancing can act as an organized resurgence of such desire, in which art and collective will are marshalled to a transcendent end—transcendent, that is, beyond the "normal," dominated character of society (1985:56).

But how is a dance enactment—a moment seemingly free from politics—an analogy of thwarted desire expressed in collective art, rather than an escape into art *from* all these social repressions? In a particularly insightful move, Martin (1985:57) reminds us of the role of the choreographer to show us the politics of dance:

> The dance company, while poised for the production of desire in performance, could stand for any community or totalized agent bound by some means of authority or regulation. At the onset of the rehearsal process, choreographer and company exist as state and people, capital and labor, patriarch and gender, as a totality which finds its representation and as such identity or consciousness of itself through an external authority. In this sense, authority can be said to symbolize totality without the means to realize

it. Initially, the company looks to the choreographer for dancing as people look to the state for government. What is obscured in this signifying gaze is exactly who wields practical power over social action.

We need not qualify Martin's dynamic model much to appropriate it to our purpose. At their "best," when couples at El Cielo Azul glide across the floor in seemingly synchronized fashion, all their turning moves well executed, the dancing approaches the artistically articulated desire that Martin would have us valorize as a physical politics, a pure form that speaks, nondiscursively, of people's desire artfully to assert their presence. One can detect an emic awareness of this desire expressed in a different pure form in the *gritos*, long cries of celebratory approval, coming from the men sitting or standing at the bar, as they watch a particularly artful execution on the floor.

But, to continue with Martin, this is not the articulation of collective desire expressed against a repressive domination from beyond the dance hall. Rather, as with all modernism, the site of contestation, of the formation of the adversarial culture, is within the dance hall, at the point of dance production. To understand this local struggle and to see why pure dancing is political, we need critically to identify our own version of Martin's authoritarian, totalizing choreographer—our own representative of the state political economy. In El Cielo Azul, such dominating power appears, paradoxically, from two unlikely places, both seeking to control and subvert desire.

In a study of such dances in Fresno, California, Peña (1980) describes the role of the dance band and its leader in stage-managing the dance. Such groups obviously generate the dancing, even as they attempt to impose their externalized sense of order upon it. They do so, for example, by deciding when a too-stimulating, energetic polka will *not* be played, substituting instead a slow, saccharine, romantic song that does not require great dancing art. Further, as a professional group, the band to some degree embodies the profitable political economy of the dance, with its marked tendency to treat the dancers as commodities and consumers. The disjuncture between art and commodity occasions the disputes that sometimes mark the end of the dance: the crowd wants more music, while the band and the dance-hall promoter are thinking about their labor and profit (Peña 1980:62–64).

But there is another kind of paradoxical choreographer at the dance, one located in the human body itself. The inseparable triad of hard, working-class labor, alcohol, and sexual desire may initially motivate the dancing—a desire to relax tired muscles; a desire physically to hold the sexual other in the ultimate interests of sex in a cheap hotel or a car seat; and alcohol as a desire that drives the other two. This triad choreographs the dance even as it can also produce a fourth desire: to take the race and class war within oneself, perniciously transform it into "manhood," and sometimes inflict it upon other men—perhaps on the slight pretext of a bump on the dance floor or a prolonged stare at one's woman. In the sudden violence of a fight, we see the ultimate disarray, the sometimes too-final fragmentation, in the continually fragmented lives of these people.

Yet amid incipient violence, to watch a Cielo Azul couple on the floor at its best, to hear the sharp, well-formed class-consciousness of the *grito*, is to realize that, for a moment, some measure of artful control against these forces—some measure of victory—has been achieved in the never-ending struggle against the choreography of race, class, and, one has to say, gender. For transcending sexual intention on both sides, or, better still, sublimating it, the dance, in its best moment, even with the male in ostensible control, makes the couple look *como si fueran uno* (as if they were one).

For Randy Martin (1985), dancing is the artful management of the human body in the sentient and ultimately political articulation of form, critically transcending the domination that initially creates it and tries to control it. I suggest that this artful control over the effects of a negating, postmodernist climate is what *mexicanos* achieve in their dancing. There are, of course, great differences between these dancers and the ones Martin writes about; the *mexicanos* are working-class ethnics, not innovative "art" dancers on the New York stage. They draw on what Raymond Williams might have identified as a "residual tradition," formed in the past but made politically serviceable in the present (Williams 1977:121–127). Williams's identification of the creative, critical unifications of past and present seems wholly consistent with Ellman and Feidelson's sense of a critical modernism.

What I presume to have identified is a kind of working-class modernism through which a socially negating postmodernism is itself negated whenever la rata takes Amalia out on the floor. At the physical point of dance production, modernism struggles for control of the Mexican-American body politic against the forces of late capitalism that are so obviously present in the dance hall and inflicted on the body. I see the dancing as a modernist performance, keyed as it is on the persistence of a historical tradition yet adapted to the present, rather than as a wholly emergent contemporary phenomenon in the manner of the postmodern. This reliance on the past frees the dancing from a total dependent linkage to an absorbing postmodern present. While it is now fashionable to disparage modernism in avant-garde circles, I believe it remains the crucible in which the critical temper of the sixties was forged, whose like we have yet to see emerging from a fundamentally quiescent postmodernist culture (Gitlin 1989; Jameson 1984).[9] Linking a working-class practice with this now-repressed tradition of modernism may be, in a small way, a contribution toward modernism's reevaluation.

At the same time, it is my desire rhetorically to appropriate the force of modernism toward addressing the two principal concerns that motivated my ethnographic writing. If the identification of a subaltern practice can in any way enhance our thinking about "high" modernism, then thinking about such practices as modernist may, in turn, enhance the reader's appraisal of a culture historically disparaged through stereotypes. Yet paradoxically, as noted earlier, I myself have now played the dangerous game of stereotyping in the interest of distancing myself from my precursor.

I close this genealogy of my ethnographic writing with questions. Is my turn to modernism as an interpretive resource a useful, resolving, revisionary strategy for creatively absorbing the influential imperative from my precursor's heroic world? Given my sense that such precursors may lie behind our ethnographic constructions and representations, have I forged a creative relationship with mine in my representation of the world of El Cielo Azul? That is, does my revisionary effort to render the world I have experienced as a "native" anthropologist respond critically enough to a generally negating history of ethnographic representations? Finally, and subsuming all of these, to paraphrase Yeats, is knowing the dance knowing the dancers?

––––––– *Notes* –––––––

1. The question of appropriate ethnic nomenclature for this population is always with us. For my extended views on the "name" issue, see Limón (1981).

2. For wholly persuasive accounts of this historical and contemporaneous process of social domination, see Paredes (1958), Foley (1978), de Leon (1982; 1983), and Montejano (1987).

3. For a biographical account of Paredes, see Limón (1980).

4. I also take license from Bloom himself, who insists on thinking of cultural criticism (his, at least) as a form of poetry (Bloom 1973:12–13).

5. See glossary.

6. For Bloom, many great Western poems—largely in the Anglo-American tradition—tend to pursue a sequence of six revisionary rhetorical strategies (clinamen, tessera, kenosis, daemonization, askesis, and apophrades), each demonstrating an increasing acceptance but creative transformation of the precursor's influence (Bloom 1973:14–15).

7. I can take this initial step in this kind of auto-analysis of my work, but I do not think it possible to carry it off completely. I offer here only an illustration of a possible way to read ethnographies.

8. Here, I cannot help comparing the world I have worked in in the 1970s with the world of my childhood, the latter perhaps even more economically deprived, yet not beset by the overwhelming problems today commonly associated with the "underclass": increasing divorce rates, continuous substance abuse, wife battering, the feminization of poverty, random street violence, etc. It is this sharply enhanced complex of negating effects that I identify as the postmodernization of the working class.

9. Indeed, in my current Bloomian moment, I toy with the idea of postmodernism as a kind of giant social swerve away from the too-strong influence of modernism, to which, gradually, we may be returning with distance, respect, maturity, and insight.

──────── *Glossary* ────────

a toda madre Fine, terrific, great. *Madre* (mother) is a near-sacred role and symbol in *mexicano* culture, so that it has great potency for use as an expression of extreme approval, as in *a toda madre* (literally, "it's very mother"), or as an ultimate curse, as in *chinga tu madre* (fuck your mother).

agabachada From *gabacho,* one of several *mexicano* slur words for Anglos. Used here in the feminine, an *agabachada* is an Anglicized woman.

bro Short for "brother." As with so much *mexicano* English slang, this one is borrowed from blacks, with whom *mexicanos* often have contiguous neighborhoods and shared occupations.

centavo Literally, a cent or penny. Hence, in south Texas, J. C. Penney is sometimes called *el centavo.*

chingao Local pronunciation of *chingado,* from *chingar* (to sexually violate). Can be used as an all-purpose curse, the way "fuck" is in English.

conjunto A musical ensemble consisting of a lead accordion, guitars, rhythm section, and vocalization.

compa Short either for *compañero* (companion) or *compadre* (coparent). Something like "good buddy" in English.

ese Guy, dude.

la brack Slang *mexicano* expression for Brackenridge High School in San Antonio.

menudo Mexican beef tripe soup. Consumed ritually after a night out on the town or on Saturday or Sunday mornings.

puta (o) A promiscuous individual, but also used as a general all-purpose curse.

ruca Literally, an old hag, but used more often as a slang term for woman, perhaps something like "broad" or "chick."

telenovelas Latin American soap operas.

vato Guy, dude.

watchate A Hispanicized version of "Watch it!"

Chapter 8

WRITING AGAINST CULTURE

Lila Abu-Lughod

W*RITING CULTURE* (Clifford and Marcus 1986), the collection that marked a major new form of critique of cultural anthropology's premises, more or less excluded two critical groups whose situations neatly expose and challenge the most basic of those premises: feminists and "halfies"—people whose national or cultural identity is mixed by virtue of migration, overseas education, or parentage.[1] In his introduction, Clifford (1986a) apologizes for the feminist absence; no one mentions halfies or the indigenous anthropologists to whom they are related. Perhaps they are not yet numerous enough or sufficiently self-defined as a group.[2] The importance of these two groups lies not in any superior moral claim or advantage they might have in doing anthropology, but in the special dilemmas they face, dilemmas that reveal starkly the problems with cultural anthropology's assumption of a fundamental distinction between self and other.

In this essay I explore how feminists and halfies, by the way their anthropological practice unsettles the boundary between self and other, enable us to reflect on the conventional nature and political effects of this distinction and ultimately to reconsider the value of the concept of culture on which it depends. I will argue that "culture" operates in anthropological discourse to enforce separations that inevitably carry a sense of hierarchy. Therefore, anthropologists should now pursue, without exaggerated hopes for the power of their texts to change the world, a variety of strategies for writing *against* culture. For those interested in textual strategies, I explore the advantages of what I call "ethnographies of the particular" as instruments of a tactical humanism.

SELVES AND OTHERS

The notion of culture (especially as it functions to distinguish "cultures"), despite a long usefulness, may now have become something anthropologists would want to work against in their theories, their ethnographic practice, and their ethnographic writing. A helpful way to begin to grasp why is to consider what the shared elements of feminist and halfie anthropology clarify about the self/other distinction central to the paradigm of anthropology. Marilyn Strathern (1985, 1987a) raises some of the issues regarding feminism in essays that both Clifford and Rabinow cited in *Writing Culture*. Her thesis is that the relationship between anthropology and feminism is awkward. This thesis leads her to try to understand why feminist scholarship, in spite of its rhetoric of radicalism, has failed to fundamentally alter anthropology, and why feminism has gained even less from anthropology than vice versa.

The awkwardness, she argues, arises from the fact that despite a common interest in differences, the scholarly practices of feminists and anthropologists are "differently structured in the way they organize knowledge and draw boundaries" (Strathern 1987a: 289) and especially in "the nature of the investigators' *relationship to* their subject matter" (1987a: 284). Feminist scholars, united by their common opposition to men or to patriarchy, produce a discourse composed of many voices; they "discover the self by becoming conscious of oppression from the Other" (1987a: 289). Anthropologists, whose goal is "to make sense of differences" (1987a: 286), also constitute their "selves" in relation to an other, but do not view this other as "under attack" (1987a: 289).

In highlighting the self/other relationship, Strathern takes us to the heart of the problem. Yet she retreats from the problematic of power (granted as formative in feminism) in her strangely uncritical depiction of anthropology. When she defines anthropology as a discipline that "continues to know itself as the study of social behavior or society in terms of systems and collective representations" (1987a: 281), she underplays the self/other distinction. In characterizing the relationship between anthropological self and other as nonadversarial, she ignores its most fundamen-

tal aspect. Anthropology's avowed goal may be "the study of man [sic],"
but it is a discipline built on the historically constructed divide between
the West and the non-West. It has been and continues to be primarily the
study of the non-Western other by the Western self, even if in its new
guise it seeks explicitly to give voice to the Other or to present a dialogue
between the self and other, either textually or through an explication of
the fieldwork encounter (as in such works as Crapanzano 1980, Dumont
1978, Dwyer 1982, Rabinow 1977, Riesman 1977, Tedlock 1983, and
Tyler 1986). And the relationship between the West and the non-West, at
least since the birth of anthropology, has been constituted by Western
domination. This suggests that the awkwardness Strathern senses in the
relationship between feminism and anthropology might better be understood as the result of diametrically opposed processes of self-construction
through opposition to others—processes that begin from different sides
of a power divide.

The enduring strength of what Morsy (1988:70) has called "the hegemony of the distinctive-other tradition" in anthropology is betrayed by
the defensiveness of partial exceptions. Anthropologists (like Ortner, this
volume) conducting fieldwork in the United States or Europe wonder
whether they have not blurred the disciplinary boundaries between anthropology and other fields such as sociology or history. One way to retain their identities as anthropologists is to make the communities they
study seem "other." Studying ethnic communities and the powerless as-
sures this.[3] So does concentrating on "culture" (or on the method of holism based on it, as Appadurai [1988] has argued), for reasons I will
discuss later. There are two issues here. One is the conviction that one
cannot be objective about one's own society, something that affects indigenous anthropologists (Western or non-Western). The second is a tacit
understanding that anthropologists study the non-West; halfies who study
their own or related non-Western communities are still more easily recognizable as anthropologists than Americans who study Americans.

If anthropology continues to be practiced as the study by an unproblematic and unmarked Western self of found "others" out there, feminist
theory, an academic practice that also traffics in selves and others, has in
its relatively short history come to realize the danger of treating selves and
others as givens. It is instructive for the development of a critique of
anthropology to consider the trajectory that has led, within two decades,
to what some might call a crisis in feminist theory, and others, the development of postfeminism.

From Simone de Beauvoir on, it has been accepted that, at least in the
modern West, women have been the other to men's self. Feminism has

been a movement devoted to helping women become selves and subjects rather than objects and men's others.[4] The crisis in feminist theory (related to a crisis in the women's movement) that followed on the heels of feminist attempts to turn those who had been constituted as other into selves—or, to use the popular metaphor, to let women speak—was the problem of "difference." For whom did feminists speak? Within the women's movement, the objections of lesbians, African-American women, and other "women of color" that their experiences as women were different from those of white, middle-class, heterosexual women problematized the identity of women as selves. Cross-cultural work on women also made it clear that masculine and feminine did not have, as we say, the same meanings in other cultures, nor did Third World women's lives resemble Western women's lives. As Harding (1986:246) puts it, the problem is that "once 'woman' is deconstructed into 'women' and 'gender' is recognized to have no fixed referents, feminism itself dissolves as a theory that can reflect the voice of a naturalized or essentialized speaker."[5]

From its experience with this crisis of selfhood or subjecthood, feminist theory can offer anthropology two useful reminders. First, the self is always a construction, never a natural or found entity, even if it has that appearance. Second, the process of creating a self through opposition to an other always entails the violence of repressing or ignoring other forms of difference. Feminist theorists have been forced to explore the implications for the formation of identity and the possibilities for political action of the ways in which gender as a system of difference is intersected by other systems of difference, including, in the modern capitalist world, race and class.

Where does this leave the feminist anthropologist? Strathern (1987a: 286) characterizes her as experiencing a tension—"caught between structures . . . faced with two different ways of relating to her or his subject matter." The more interesting aspect of the feminist's situation, though, is what she shares with the halfie: a blocked ability to comfortably assume the self of anthropology. For both, although in different ways, the self is split, caught at the intersection of systems of difference. I am less concerned with the existential consequences of this split (these have been eloquently explored elsewhere [e.g., Joseph 1988, Kondo 1986, Narayan 1989]) than with the awareness such splits generate about three crucial issues: positionality, audience, and the power inherent in distinctions of self and other. What happens when the "other" that the anthropologist is studying is simultaneously constructed as, at least partially, a self?

Feminists and halfie anthropologists cannot easily avoid the issue of positionality. Standing on shifting ground makes it clear that every view is a view from somewhere and every act of speaking a speaking from somewhere. Cultural anthropologists have never been fully convinced of the ideology of science and have long questioned the value, possibility, and definition of objectivity.[6] But they still seem reluctant to examine the implications of the actual situatedness of their knowledge.[7]

Two common, intertwined objections to the work of feminist or native or semi-native anthropologists, both related to partiality, betray the persistence of ideals of objectivity. The first has to do with the partiality (as bias or position) of the observer. The second has to do with the partial (incomplete) nature of the picture presented. Halfies are more associated with the first problem, feminists the second. The problem with studying one's own society is alleged to be the problem of gaining enough distance. Since for halfies, the Other is in certain ways the self, there is said to be the danger shared with indigenous anthropologists of identification and the easy slide into subjectivity.[8] These worries suggest that the anthropologist is still defined as a being who must stand apart from the Other, even when he or she seeks explicitly to bridge the gap. Even Bourdieu (1977: 1–2), who perceptively analyzed the effects this outsider stance has on the anthropologist's (mis)understanding of social life, fails to break with this doxa. The obvious point he misses is that the outsider self never simply stands outside. He or she stands in a definite relation with the Other of the study, not just as a Westerner, but as a Frenchman in Algeria during the war of independence, an American in Morocco during the 1967 Arab-Israeli war, or an Englishwoman in postcolonial India. What we call the outside is a position *within* a larger political-historical complex. No less than the halfie, the "wholie" is in a specific position vis-à-vis the community being studied.

The debates about feminist anthropologists suggest a second source of uneasiness about positionality. Even when they present themselves as studying gender, feminist anthropologists are dismissed as presenting only a partial picture of the societies they study because they are assumed to be studying only women. Anthropologists study society, the unmarked form. The study of women is the marked form, too readily sectioned off, as Strathern (1985) notes.[9] Yet it could easily be argued that most studies of society have been equally partial. As restudies like Weiner's (1976) of Malinowski's Trobriand Islanders or Bell's (1983) of the well-studied Australian aborigines indicate, they have been the study of men.[10] This does not make such studies any less valuable; it merely reminds us that we must constantly attend to the positionality of the anthropological self and its representations of others. James Clifford (1986a: 6), among others, has convincingly argued that ethnographic representations are always "partial truths." What is needed is a recognition that they are also positioned truths.

Split selfhood creates for the two groups being discussed a second problem that is illuminating for anthropology generally: multiple audiences. Although all anthropologists are beginning to feel what might be called the Rushdie effect—the effects of living in a global age when the subjects of their studies begin to read their works and the governments of the countries they work in ban books and deny visas—feminist and halfie anthropologists struggle in poignant ways with multiple accountability. Rather than having one primary audience, that of other anthropologists, feminist anthropologists write for anthropologists and for feminists, two groups whose relationship to their subject matter is at odds and who hold ethnographers accountable in different ways.[11] Furthermore, feminist circles include non-Western feminists, often from the societies feminist anthropologists have studied, who call them to account in new ways.[12]

Halfies' dilemmas are even more extreme. As anthropologists, they write for other anthropologists, mostly Western. Identified also with communities outside the West, or subcultures within it, they are called to account by educated members of those communities. More importantly, not just because they position themselves with reference to two communities but because when they present the Other they are presenting themselves, they speak with a complex awareness of and investment in reception. Both halfie and feminist anthropologists are forced to confront squarely the politics and ethics of their representations. There are no easy solutions to their dilemmas.

The third issue that feminist and halfie anthropologists, unlike anthropologists who work in Western societies (another group for whom self and other are somewhat tangled), force us to confront is the dubiousness of maintaining that relationships between self and other are innocent of power. Because of sexism and racial or ethnic discrimination, they may have experienced—as women, as individuals of mixed parentage, or as foreigners—being other to a dominant self, whether in everyday life in the U.S., Britain, or France, or in the Western academy. This is not simply an experience of difference, but of inequality. My argument, however, is structural, not experiential. Women, blacks, and people of most of the non-West have been historically constituted as others in the major political systems of difference on which the unequal world of modern capitalism has depended. Feminist studies and black studies have made sufficient progress within the academy to have exposed the way that being studied by "white men" (to use a shorthand for a complex and historically constituted subject-position) turns into being spoken for by them. It becomes a sign and instrument of their power.

Within anthropology, despite a long history of self-conscious opposition to racism, a fast-growing, self-critical literature on anthropology's links to colonialism (for example, Asad 1973, Clifford 1983a, Fabian 1983, Hymes 1969, Kuper 1988), and experimentation with techniques of ethnography to relieve a discomfort with the power of anthropologist over anthropological subject, the fundamental issues of domination keep being skirted. Even attempts to refigure informants as consultants and to "let the other speak" in dialogic (Tedlock 1987) or polyvocal texts—decolonizations on the level of the text—leave intact the basic configuration of global power on which anthropology, as linked to other institutions of the world, is based. To see the strangeness of this enterprise, all that is needed is to consider an analogous case. What would our reaction be if male scholars stated their desire to "let women speak" in their texts while they continued to dominate all knowledge about them by controlling writing and other academic practices, supported in their positions by a particular organization of economic, social, and political life?

Because of their split selves, feminist and halfie anthropologists travel uneasily between speaking "for" and speaking "from." Their situation enables us to see more clearly that dividing practices, whether they naturalize differences, as in gender or race, or simply elaborate them, as I will argue the concept of culture does, are fundamental methods of enforcing inequality.

CULTURE AND DIFFERENCE

The concept of culture is the hidden term in all that has just been said about anthropology. Most American anthropologists believe or act as if "culture," notoriously resistant to definition and ambiguous of referent, is nevertheless the true object of anthropological inquiry. Yet it could also be argued that culture is important to anthropology because the anthropological distinction between self and other rests on it. Culture is the essential tool for making other. As a professional discourse that elaborates on the meaning of culture in order to account for, explain, and understand cultural difference, anthropology also helps construct, produce, and maintain it. Anthropological discourse gives cultural difference (and the separation between groups of people it implies) the air of the self-evident.

In this regard, the concept of culture operates much like its predecessor—race—even though in its twentieth-century form it has some important political advantages. Unlike race, and unlike even the nine-teenth-century sense of culture as a synonym for civilization (contrasted to barbarism), the current concept allows for multiple rather than binary differences. This immediately checks the eay move to hierarchizing; the shift to "culture" ("lower case *c* with the possibility of a final *s*," as Clifford [1988a: 234] puts it) has a relativizing effect. The most important of cul-ture's advantages, however, is that it removes difference from the realm of the natural and the innate. Whether conceived of as a set of behaviors, customs, traditions, rules, plans, recipes, instructions, or programs (to list the range of definitions Geertz [1973a: 44] furnishes), culture is learned and can change.

Despite its anti-essentialist intent, however, the culture concept retains some of the tendencies to freeze difference possessed by concepts like race. This is easier to see if we consider a field in which there has been a shift from one to the other. Orientalism as a scholarly discourse (among other things) is, according to Said (1978: 2), "a style of thought based upon an ontological and epistemological distinction made between 'the Orient' and (most of the time) 'the Occident'." What he shows is that in mapping geography, race, and culture onto one another, Orientalism fixes differences between people of "the West" and people of "the East" in ways so rigid that they might as well be considered innate. In the twentieth century, cultural difference, not race, has been the basic subject of Ori-entalist scholarship devoted now to interpreting the "culture" phenomena (primarily religion and language) to which basic differences in develop-ment, economic performance, government, character, and so forth are attributed.

Some anticolonial movements and present-day struggles have worked by what could be labelled reverse Orientalism, where attempts to reverse the power relationship proceed by seeking to valorize for the self what in the former system had been devalued as other. A Gandhian appeal to the greater spirituality of a Hindu India, compared with the materialism and violence of the West, and an Islamicist appeal to a greater faith in God, compared with the immorality and corruption of the West, both accept the essentialist terms of Orientalist constructions. While turning them on their heads, they preserve the rigid sense of difference based on culture.

A parallel can be drawn with feminism. It is a basic tenet of feminism that "women are made, not born." It has been important for most femi-nists to locate sex differences in culture, not biology or nature. While this has inspired some feminist theorists to attend to the social and personal effects of gender as a system of difference, for many others it has led to explorations of and strategies built on the notion of a women's culture. Cultural feminism (cf. Echols 1984) takes many forms, but it has many of the qualities of reverse Orientalism just discussed. For French feminists like Irigaray (1985a, 1985b), Cixous (1983), and Kristeva (1981), masculine and feminine, if not actually male and female, represent essentially different modes of being. Anglo-American feminists take a different tack. Some attempt to "describe" the cultural differences between men and women—Gilligan (1982) and her followers (e.g., Belenky et al. 1986) who elaborate the notion of "a different voice" are popular examples. Others try to "explain" the differences, whether through a socially informed psychoanalytic theory (e.g., Chodorow 1978), a Marxist-derived theory of the effects of the division of labor and women's role in social reproduction (Hartsock 1985), an analysis of maternal practice (Ruddick 1980), or even a theory of sexual exploitation (MacKinnon 1982). Much feminist theorizing and practice seeks to build or reform social life in line with this "women's culture."[13] There have been proposals for a woman-centered university (Rich 1979), a feminist science (Rose 1983, 1986), a feminist methodology in the sciences and social sciences (Meis 1983; Reinharz 1983; Smith 1987; Stanley and Wise 1983; see Harding 1987 for a sensible critique), and even a feminist spirituality and ecology. These proposals nearly always build on values traditionally associated in the West with women—a sense of care and connectedness, maternal nurturing, immediacy of experience, involvement in the bodily (versus the abstract), and so forth.

This valorization by cultural feminists, like reverse Orientalists, of the previously devalued qualities attributed to them may be provisionally useful in forging a sense of unity and in waging struggles of empowerment. Yet because it leaves in place the divide that structured the experiences of selfhood and oppression on which it builds, it perpetuates some dangerous tendencies. First, cultural feminists overlook the connections between those on each side of the divide, and the ways in which they define each other. Second, they overlook differences within each category constructed by the dividing practices, differences like those of class, race, and sexuality (to repeat the feminist litany of problematically abstract categories), but also ethnic origin, personal experience, age, mode of livelihood, health, living situation (rural or urban), and historical experience. Third, and perhaps most important, they ignore the ways in which experiences have been constructed historically and have changed over time. Both cultural feminism and revivalist movements tend to rely on notions of authenticity and the return to positive values not represented by the dominant other. As becomes obvious in the most extreme cases, these moves erase history. Invocations of Cretan goddesses in some cultural-feminist circles and, in a more complex and serious way, the powerful invocation of the seventh-century community of the Prophet in some Islamic movements are good examples.

The point is that the notion of culture which both types of movements use does not seem to guarantee an escape from the tendency toward essentialism. It could be argued that anthropologists use "culture" in more sophisticated and consistent ways and that their commitment to it as an analytical tool is firmer. Yet even many of them are now concerned about the ways it tends to freeze differences. Appadurai (1988), for example, in his compelling argument that "natives" are a figment of the anthropological imagination, shows the complicity of the anthropological concept of culture in a continuing "incarceration" of non-Western peoples in time and place. Denied the same capacity for movement, travel, and geographical interaction that Westerners take for granted, the cultures studied by anthropologists have tended to be denied history as well.

Others, including myself (1990b), have argued that cultural theories also tend to overemphasize coherence. Clifford notes both that "the discipline of fieldwork-based anthropology, in constituting its authority, constructs and reconstructs coherent cultural others and interpreting selves" (Clifford 1988b: 112) and that ethnography is a form of culture collecting (like art collecting) in which "diverse experiences and facts are selected, gathered, detached from their original temporal occasions, and given enduring value in a new arrangement" (Clifford 1988a: 231). Organic metaphors of wholeness and the methodology of holism that characterizes anthropology both favor coherence, which in turn contributes to the perception of communities as bounded and discrete.

Certainly discreteness does not have to imply value; the hallmark of twentieth-century anthropology has been its promotion of cultural relativism over evaluation and judgment. If anthropology has always to some extent been a form of cultural (self-) critique (Marcus and Fischer, 1986), that too was an aspect of a refusal to hierarchize difference. Yet neither position would be possible without difference. It would be worth thinking about the implications of the high stakes anthropology has in sustaining and perpetuating a belief in the existence of cultures that are identifiable as discrete, different, and separate from our own.[14] Does difference always smuggle in hierarchy?

In *Orientalism*, Said (1978: 28) argues for the elimination of "the Orient" and "the Occident" altogether. By this he means not the erasure of all differences but the recognition of more of them and of the complex ways in which they crosscut. More important, his analysis of one field seeks to show how and when certain differences, in this case of places and the people attached to them, become implicated in the domination of one by the other. Should anthropologists treat with similar suspicion "culture" and "cultures" as the key terms in a discourse in which otherness and difference have come to have, as Said (1989:213) points out, "talismanic qualities"?

THREE MODES OF WRITING AGAINST CULTURE

If "culture," shadowed by coherence, timelessness, and discreteness, is the prime anthropological tool for making "other," and difference, as feminists and halfies reveal, tends to be a relationship of power, then perhaps anthropologists should consider strategies for writing against culture. I will discuss three that I find promising. Although they by no means exhaust the possibilities, the sorts of projects I will describe—theoretical, substantive, and textual—make sense for anthropologists sensitive to issues of positionality and accountability and interested in making anthropological practice something that does not simply shore up global inequalities. I will conclude, however, by considering the limitations of all anthropological reform.

DISCOURSE AND PRACTICE

Theoretical discussion, because it is one of the modes in which anthropologists engage each other, provides an important site for contesting "culture." It seems to me that current discussions and deployments of two increasingly popular terms—practice and discourse—do signal a shift away from culture. Although there is always the danger that these terms will come to be used simply as synonyms for culture, they were intended to enable us to analyze social life without presuming the degree of coherence that the culture concept has come to carry.

Practice is associated, in anthropology, with Bourdieu (1977; also see Ortner 1984), whose theoretical approach is built around problems of contradiction, misunderstanding, and misrecognition, and favors strategies, interests, and improvisations over the more static and homogenizing cultural tropes of rules, models, and texts. Discourse (whose uses I discuss in L. Abu-Lughod 1989 and Abu-Lughod and Lutz 1990) has more diverse sources and meanings in anthropology. In its Foucauldian derivation, as it relates to notions of discursive formations, apparatuses, and technologies, it is meant to refuse the distinction between ideas and practices or text and world that the culture concept too readily encourages. In its more sociolinguistic sense, it draws attention to the social uses by individuals of verbal resources. In either case, it allows for the possibility of recognizing within a social group the play of multiple, shifting, and competing statements with practical effects. Both practice and discourse are useful because they work against the assumption of boundedness, not to mention the idealism (Asad 1983), of the culture concept.[15]

CONNECTIONS

Another strategy of writing against culture is to reorient the problems or subject matter anthropologists address. An important focus should be the various connections and interconnections, historical and contemporary, between a community and the anthropologist working there and writing about it, not to mention the world to which he or she belongs and which enables him or her to be in that particular place studying that group. This is more of a political project than an existential one, although the reflexive anthropologists who have taught us to focus on the fieldwork encounter as a site for the construction of the ethnographic "facts" have alerted us to one important dimension of the connection. Other significant sorts of connections have received less attention. Pratt (1986:42) notes a regular mystification in ethnographic writing of "the larger agenda of European expansion in which the ethnographer, regardless of his or her own attitudes to it, is caught up, and that determines the ethnographer's own material relationship to the group under study." We need to ask questions about the historical processes by which it came to pass that people like ourselves could be engaged in anthropological studies of people like those, about the current world situation that enables us to engage in this sort of work in this particular place, and about who has preceded us and is even now there with us (tourists, travelers, missionaries, AID consultants, Peace Corps workers). We need to ask what this "will to knowledge" about the Other is connected to in the world.

These questions cannot be asked in general; they should be asked about and answered by tracing through specific situations, configurations, and histories. Even though they do not address directly the place of the ethnographer, and even though they engage in an oversystemization that threatens to erase local interactions, studies like those of Wolf (1982) on the long history of interaction between particular Western societies and communities in what is now called the Third World represent important means of answering such questions. So do studies like Mintz's (1985b) that trace the complex processes of transformation and exploitation in which, in Europe and other parts of the world, sugar was involved. The anthropological turn to history, tracing connections between the present and the past of particular communities, is also an important development.

Not all projects about connections need be historical. Anthropologists are increasingly concerned with national and transnational connections of people, cultural forms, media, techniques, and commodities (for example, see Appadurai, this volume).[16] They study the articulation of world capitalism and international politics with the situations of people living in particular communities. All these projects, which involve a shift in gaze to include phenomena of connection, expose the inadequacies of the concept of culture and the elusiveness of the entities designated by the term *cultures*. Although there may be a tendency in the new work merely to widen the object, shifting from culture to nation as locus, ideally there would be attention to the shifting groupings, identities, and interactions within and across such borders as well. If there was ever a time when anthropologists could consider without too much violence at least some communities as isolated units, certainly the nature of global interactions in the present makes that now impossible.[17]

ETHNOGRAPHIES OF THE PARTICULAR

The third strategy for writing against culture depends on accepting the one insight of Geertz's about anthropology that has been built upon by everyone in this "experimental moment" (Marcus and Fischer 1986) who takes textuality seriously. Geertz (1975a, 1988) has argued that one of the main things anthropologists do is write, and what they write are fictions (which does not mean they are fictitious).[18] Certainly the practice of ethnographic writing has received an inordinate amount of attention from those involved in *Writing Culture* and an increasing number of others who were not involved. Much of the hostility toward their project arises from the suspicion that in their literary leanings they have too readily collapsed the politics of ethnography into its poetics. And yet they have raised an issue that cannot be ignored. Insofar as anthropologists are in the business of representing others through their ethnographic writing, then surely the degree to which people in the communities they study appear "other" must also be partly a function of how anthropologists write about them. Are there ways to write about lives so as to constitute others as less other?

I would argue that one powerful tool for unsettling the culture concept and subverting the process of "othering" it entails is to write "ethnographies of the particular." Generalization, the characteristic mode of operation and style of writing of the social sciences, can no longer be regarded as neutral description (Foucault 1978; Said 1978; Smith 1987). It has two unfortunate effects in anthropology that make it worth eschewing. I will explore these before presenting some examples from my own work of what one could hope to accomplish through ethnographies of the particular.

I will not be concerned with several issues frequently raised about generalization. For example, it has often been pointed out that the generalizing mode of social scientific discourse facilitates abstraction and reification. Feminist sociologist Dorothy Smith (1987: 130) put the problem vividly in her critique of sociological discourse by noting that

> the complex organization of activities of actual individuals and their actual relations is entered into the discourse through concepts such as class, modernization, formal organization. A realm of theoretically constituted objects is created, freeing the discursive realm from its ground in the lives and work of actual individuals and liberating sociological inquiry to graze on a field of conceptual entities.

Other critics have fixed on different flaws. Interpretive anthropology, for example, in its critique of the search for general laws in positivistic social science, notes a failure to take account of the centrality of meaning to human experience. Yet the result has been to substitute generalization about meanings for generalizations about behavior.

I also want to make clear what the argument for particularity is not: it is not to be mistaken for arguments for privileging micro over macro processes. Ethnomethodologists (discussed by Watson, this volume) and other students of everyday life seek ways to generalize about microinteractions, while historians might be said to be tracing the particulars of macroprocesses. Nor need a concern with the particulars of individuals' lives imply disregard for forces and dynamics that are not locally based. On the contrary, the effects of extralocal and long-term processes are only manifested locally and specifically, produced in the actions of individuals living their particular lives, inscribed in their bodies and their words. What I am arguing for is a form of writing that might better convey that.

There are two reasons for anthropologists to be wary of generalization. The first is that, as part of a professional discourse of "objectivity" and expertise, it is inevitably a language of power. On the one hand, it is the language of those who seem to stand apart from and outside of what they are describing. Again, Smith's critique of sociological discourse is relevant. She has argued (1987: 62) that this seemingly detached mode of reflecting on social life is actually located: it represents the perspective of those involved in professional, managerial, and administrative structures and is thus part of "the ruling apparatus of this society." This critique applies as well to anthropology with its inter- rather than intrasocietal perspective and its origins in the exploration and colonization of the non-European world rather than the management of internal social groups like workers, women, blacks, the poor, or prisoners.

On the other hand, even if we withhold judgment on how closely the social sciences can be associated with the apparatuses of management, we have to recognize how all professionalized discourses by nature assert hierarchy. The very gap between the professional and authoritative discourses of generalization and the languages of everyday life (our own and others') establishes a fundamental separation between the anthropologist and the people being written about that facilitates the construction of anthropological objects as simultaneously different and inferior.

Thus, to the degree that anthropologists can bring closer the language of everyday life and the language of the text, this mode of making other is reversed. The problem is, as a reflection on the situation of feminist anthropologists suggest, that there may be professional risks for ethnographers who want to pursue this strategy. I have argued elsewhere (1990a) that Rabinow's refreshingly sensible observation about the politics of ethnographic writing—that they are to be found closer to home, in academia, than in the colonial and neocolonial world—helps us understand a few things about feminist anthropology and the uneasiness about it that even someone like Clifford betrays in his introductory essay for *Writing Culture*.[19] His excuse for excluding feminist anthropologists was that they were not involved in textual innovation. If we were to grant the dubious distinction he presumes between textual innovation and transformations of content and theory, we might concede that feminist anthropologists have contributed little to the new wave of experimentation in form.

But then a moment's thought would provide us with clues about why. Without even asking the basic questions about individuals, institutions, patrons, and tenure, we can turn to the politics of the feminist project itself. Dedicated to making sure that women's lives are represented in descriptions of societies and women's experiences and gender itself theorized in accounts of how societies work, feminist scholars have been interested in the old political sense of representation. Conservatism of form may have been helpful because the goal was to persuade colleagues that an anthropology taking gender into account was not just good anthropology but better anthropology.

The second pressure on feminist anthropology is the need to assert professionalism. Contrary to what Clifford writes (1986a:21), women *have* produced "unconventional forms of writing." He just ignored them, neglecting a few professional anthropologists like Bowen (Bohannon) (1954), Briggs (1970), and Cesara (Poewe) (1982) who have experimented with form.[20] More significantly, there is also what might be considered a separate "woman's tradition" within ethnographic writing. Because it is not professional, however, it might only reluctantly be claimed and explored by feminist anthropologists uncertain of their standing. I am referring to the often excellent and popular ethnographies written by the "untrained" wives of anthropologists, books like Elizabeth Fernea's *Guests of the Sheik* (1965), Marjorie Shostak's *Nisa* (1981), Edith Turner's *The Spirit of the Drum* (1987), and Margery Wolf's *The House of Lim* (1968). Directing their works to audiences slightly different from those of the professional writers of standard ethnographies, they have also followed different conventions: they are more open about their positionality, less assertive of their scientific authority, and more focused on particular individuals and families.

Why does this other tradition not qualify as a form of textual innovation? A partial answer can be found in *Writing Culture* itself. The proponents of the current experiments and critiques of ethnographic writing tend to break with humdrum anthropology by borrowing from elite disciplines like philosophy and literary theory rather than looking to more prosaic sources like ordinary experience or the terms in which their anthropological subjects operate.[21] They reject the rhetoric of social science not for ordinary language but for a rarefied discourse so packed with jargon that a press editor was provoked to compose a mocking jargon poem playing with their vocabulary of tropes, thaumasmus, metonymy, pathopoeia, phenomenology, ecphonesis, epistemology, deictics, and hypotyposis—a poem ironically included as an invocation in the preface to the book (Clifford and Marcus 1986:ix). Whatever the merits of their contributions, the message of hyperprofessionalism is hard to miss. Despite a sensitivity to questions of otherness and power and the relevance of textuality to these issues, they use a discourse even more exclusive, and thus more reinforcing of hierarchical distinctions between themselves and anthropological others, than that of the ordinary anthropology they criticize.

The second problem with generalization derives not from its participation in the authoritative discourses of professionalism but from the effects of homogeneity, coherence, and timelessness it tends to produce. When one generalizes from experiences and conversations with a number of specific people in a community, one tends to flatten out differences among them and to homogenize them. The appearance of an absence of internal differentiation makes it easier to conceive of a group of people as a discrete, bounded entity, like the "the Nuer," "the Balinese," and "the Awlad 'Ali Bedouin" who do this or that and believe such-and-such. The effort to produce general ethnographic descriptions of people's beliefs or actions tends to smooth over contradictions, conflicts of interest, and doubts and arguments, not to mention changing motivations and circumstances. The erasure of time and conflict make what is inside the boundary set up by homogenization something essential and fixed. These effects are of special moment to anthropologists because they contribute to the fiction of essentially different and discrete others who can be separated from some sort of equally essential self. Insofar as difference is, as I have argued, hierarchical, and assertions of separation a way of denying responsibility, generalization itself must be treated with suspicion.

For these reasons I propose that we experiment with narrative ethnographies of the particular in a continuing tradition of fieldwork-based writing.[22] In telling stories about particular individuals in time and place, such ethnographies would share elements with the alternative "women's tradition" discussed above. I would expect them to complement rather than replace a range of other types of anthropological projects, from theoretical discussions to the exploration of new topics within anthropology, a range well represented by the contributors to this volume. I will take up in the final section the reason ethnographies are still important to write. Before that I want to give some sense of the potential value of such ethnographies.

Anthropologists commonly generalize about communities by saying that they are characterized by certain institutions, rules, or ways of doing things. For example, we can and often do say things like "The Bongo-Bongo are polygynous." Yet one could refuse to generalize in this way, instead asking how a particular set of individuals—for instance, a man and his three wives in a Bedouin community in Egypt whom I have known for a decade—live the "institution" that we call polygyny. Stressing the particularity of this marriage and building a picture of it through the participants' discussions, recollections, disagreements, and actions would make several theoretical points.

First, refusing to generalize would highlight the constructed quality of that typicality so regularly produced in conventional social scientific accounts. Second, showing the actual circumstances and detailed histories of individuals and their relationships would suggest that such particulars, which are always present (as we know from our own personal experiences), are also always crucial to the constitution of experience. Third, reconstructing people's arguments about, justifications for, and interpretations of what they and others are doing would explain how social life proceeds. It would show that although the terms of their discourses may be set (and, as in any society, include several sometimes contradictory and often historically changing discourses), within these limits, people contest interpretations of what is happening, strategize, feel pain, and live their lives. In one sense this is not so new. Bourdieu (1977), for example, theorizes about social practice in a similar way. But the difference here would be that one would be seeking textual means of representing how this happens rather than simply making theoretical assertions that it does.

By focusing closely on particular individuals and their changing relationships, one would necessarily subvert the most problematic connotations of culture: homogeneity, coherence, and timelessness. Individuals are confronted with choices, struggle with others, make conflicting statements, argue about points of view on the same events, undergo ups and downs in various relationships and changes in their circumstances and desires, face new pressures, and fail to predict what will happen to them or those around them. So, for example, it becomes difficult to think that the term "Bedouin culture" makes sense when one tries to piece together and convey what life is like for one old Bedouin matriarch.

When you ask her to tell the story of her life, she responds that one should only think about God. Yet she tells vivid stories, fixed in memory in particular ways, about her resistances to arranged marriages, her deliveries of children, her worries about sick daughters. She also tells about weddings she has attended, dirty songs sung by certain young men as they sheared the elders' sheep herds, and trips in crowded taxis where she pinched a man's bottom to get him off her lap.

The most regular aspect of her daily life is her wait for prayer times. Is it noon yet? Not yet. Is it afternoon yet? Not yet. Is it sunset yet? Grandmother, you haven't prayed yet? It's already past sunset. She spreads her prayer rug in front of her and prays out loud. At the end, as she folds up her prayer rug, she beseeches God to protect all Muslims. She recites God's names as she goes through her string of prayer beads. The only decoration in her room is a photograph on the wall of herself and her son as pilgrims in Mecca.

Her back so hunched she can hardly stand, she spends her days sitting or lying down on her mattress. She is practically blind and she complains about her many pains. People come and go, her sons, her nephews, her daughter, her nieces, her granddaughters, her great-grandson. They chat, they confer with her about connections between people, marriages, kinship. She gives advice; she scolds them for not doing things properly. And she plays with her great grandson, who is three, by teasing, "Hey, I've run out of snuff. Come here so I can sniff your little tuber."

Being pious and fiercely preserving protocol in the hosting of guests and the exchanging of visits and greetings does not seem to stop her from relishing the outrageous story and the immoral tale. A new favorite when I saw her in 1987 was one she had just picked up from her daughter, herself a married mother of five living near Alamein. It was a tale about an old husband and wife who decide to go visit their daughters, and it was funny for the upside-down world it evoked.

This tale depicted a world where people did the unthinkable. Instead of the usual candy and biscuits, the couple brought their daughters sacks of dung for gifts. When the first daughter they stayed with went off to draw water from the well, they started dumping out all the large containers of honey and oil in her merchant husband's house. She returned to find them spilling everything and threw them out. So they headed off to visit the second daughter. When she left them minding her baby for a while, the old man killed it just to stop if from crying. She came back, discovered this and threw them out. Next they came across a house with a slaughtered sheep in it. They made belts out of the intestines and caps out of the stomachs and tried them on, admiring each other in their new finery. But when the old woman asked her husband if she didn't look pretty in her new belt he answered, "You'd be really pretty, except for that fly sitting on your nose." With that he smacked the fly, killing his wife. As he wailed in grief he began to fart. Furious at his anus for farting over his dead wife, he heated up a stake and shoved it in, killing himself.

The old woman chuckles as she tells this story, just as she laughs hard over stories about the excessive sexuality of old women. How does this sense of humor, this appreciation of the bawdy, go with devotion to prayer and protocols of honor? How does her nostalgia for the past— when the area was empty and she could see for miles around; when she used to play as a little girl digging up the occasional potsherd or glass bottle in the area now fenced and guarded by the government Antiquities Organization; when her family migrated with the sheep herds and milked and made butter in desert pastures—go with her fierce defense of her favorite grandson, whose father was furious with him because the young man was rumored to have drunk liquor at a local wedding? People do not drink in the community, and drinking is, of course, religiously proscribed. What can "culture" mean, given this old woman's complex responses?

Time is the other important dimension that gets built in if one takes seriously the narrative of people's everyday lives. When the young man's father hits him, the son who has been accused of drinking at the wedding sells his cassette player to a neighbor to raise cash and then disappears. His grandmother cries over him, his aunts discuss it. His father says nothing. It is days before a distant in-law comes to reassure his grandmother that the young man is fine and to indicate that they know his whereabouts (he is working at a construction site about 100 kilometers away). No one knows what the consequences of this event will be. Will he return? What will his father do? Family honor is at stake, reputations for piety, paternal authority. When the young man returns several weeks later, accompanied by a maternal uncle from 50 kilometers west who intervenes to forestall any further punishments, his grandmother weeps in relief. It could easily have turned out differently. Since his disappearance, her days had been taken up with worrying, discussing, waiting, and not knowing what would happen next. That beating and that running away, events that happened in time, become part of the history of that family, the individuals involved, and their relationships. In this sequence of events in a particular family in 1987, we can read what we call the "larger forces" that made it possible, things like growing opportunities for wage labor, the commercialization of Bedouin weddings, and the influx of goods from the cities. Yet because these "forces" are only embodied in the actions of individuals living in time and place, ethnographies of the particular capture them best.

Even ritual, that communal practice for which time seems to have such a different, perhaps cyclical, meaning, that kind of practice which in anthropological discourse so perfectly marks the (exotic, primitive) cultural other as different, turns out to be particular and anything but timeless. If looked at closely in terms of the actual participants and ritual event, it involves unpredictability. Even in ritual the unfolding of what cannot be known beforehand generates great drama and tension. Let me give an example, again from my work. Within the first week of my arrival in the Bedouin community in Egypt where I was to spend years, the young girls in my household outlined for me the exact sequence of events every bride went through in a Bedouin wedding. Over the years, I attended many weddings, all of which followed this outline, yet each of which was distinct. For each bride and groom, not to mention their families, the wedding would mark a moment of major life transformation, not just of status but of associations, daily life, experience, and the future. Each wedding was different in the kinds of families being brought together, the network of relations created and the goods exchanged, spent, and displayed.

More important, the elements of unpredictability were many. Would the bride stay? Would the couple get along? Would there be children?

How soon? Even the central rite of the wedding celebration itself—the defloration or public virginity test—was an event of great dramatic tension whose outcome was unknowable in advance. The pattern of the defloration, as I have written elsewhere (1988), is standard: in the daytime when the wedding guests are gathered, the groom, accompanied by his friends, penetrates the women's sphere and enters the room in which his bride, surrounded and supported by several old women, waits. Yet every defloration involves a specific set of people and takes place in a particular way. The narratives of the women who stay with the bride as the groom takes her virginity underscore this specificity. They describe the bride's reactions, her words, the extent of her struggle, their own specific locations in the room and role in the event, the groom's reactions, their advice to him, the problems encountered, the tension of getting that blood out. They compare brides they have known and the blood stains on the white cloth. They evaluate the skills and qualities of the various old women who stay in with the brides. Their narratives, as well as the responses of all participants at weddings, reveal the central question that provides the drama of weddings: Will there be blood? Events take different courses. That is the nature of "life as lived" (Riesman 1977), everywhere. Generalizations, by producing effects of timelessness and coherence to support the essentialized notion of "cultures" different from ours and peoples separate from us, make us forget this.

CONCLUSION: TACTICAL HUMANISM?

The critiques of anthropology that have emerged recently from various quarters have encouraged us to question what we work on, how we write, and for whom we write. I have been arguing that cultural difference, which has been both the ground and product of anthropological discourse, is a problematic construction and have proposed a number of strategies, most already taken up by others, for "writing against culture." I gave examples from my own work of the way in which one strategy—ethnography of the particular—might be an especially useful way to disturb the culture concept.

The special value of this strategy is that it brings out similarities in all our lives. To say that we all live in the particular is not to say that for any of us the particulars are the same. It could well be that even in looking at the everyday we might discover fundamental differences, such as those between everyday experience in a world set up to produce the effect of structures, institutions, or other abstractions (as Mitchell [1988] argues the modern West has been), and in worlds that have not. But the dailiness, in breaking coherence and introducing time, keeps us fixed on flux and contradiction. And the particulars suggest that others live as we perceive ourselves living, not as robots programmed with "cultural" rules, but as people going through life agonizing over decisions, making mistakes, trying to make themselves look good, enduring tragedies and personal losses, enjoying others, and finding moments of happiness.

The language of generalization cannot convey these sorts of experiences and activities. In our own lives, we balance the accounts of ourselves that social science purveys with the ordinary language we use in personal conversations to discuss and understand our lives, our friends and family, and our world. For those who live "outside" our world, however, we have no discourse of familiarity to counteract the distancing discourses of anthropology and other social sciences, discourses that also serve development experts, governments, journalists, and others who deal with the Third World.

Ethnographies of the particular could provide this discourse of familiarity, a familiarity that the humanist conventions favored by the unprofessional and devalued women ethnographers always encouraged. Why invoke humanism when it has become so discredited in poststructural and postmodernist circles?[23] There are certainly good reasons to be suspicious of a philosophy that has continually masked the persistence of systematic social differences by appealing to an allegedly universal individual as hero and autonomous subject; a philosophy that has allowed us to assume that the domination and exploitation of nature by man was justified by his place at the center of the universe; a philosophy that has failed to see that its essential human has culturally and socially specific characteristics and in fact excludes most humans; and a philosophy that refuses to understand how we as subjects are constructed in discourses attached to power.

Because humanism continues to be, in the West, the language of human equality with the most moral force, we cannot abandon it yet, if only as a convention of writing. In advocating new forms of writing—pastiche, dialogue, collage, and so forth—that break up narrative, subject identities, and identifications, antihumanists ask their readers to adopt sophisticated reading strategies along with social critique. Can anthropologists ask this? Already, complaints about boredom and resistance to being jarred have been leveled against experimental ethnographies. Humanism is a language with more speakers (and readers), even if it, too, is a local language rather than the universal one it pretends to be. To have an effect on people, perhaps we still need to speak this language, but to speak it knowing its limitations.

This might be called a tactical humanism, made both politically necessary and limited in its effects by anthropology's location on the side of
domination in the context of a world organized by global inequality along
lines of "cultural" difference. We should not have illusions that tactical
humanism, whether in the form of ethnographies of the particular or
other modes of writing against culture, contributes to some universal language or universal good. From our positions as anthropologists, however
tenuous our identifications if we are feminists or "halfies," we work as
Westerners, and what we contribute to is a Western discourse. As Mudimbe (1988: 19) writes in *The Invention of Africa*, "it seems impossible to
imagine any anthropology without a Western epistemological link." I argued earlier that positionality could not be escaped. Nor can the fact, as
Riesman (1982) bluntly puts it in his critical response to proposals for
dialogic anthropology, "that we are using other people for our own purposes all the time" and "using the knowledge they give us for goals they
would never imagine themselves." That does not mean that the goals are
not worth pursuing or that working with Western discourse is not crucial.
As Said (1989: 224) notes, "anthropological representations bear as much
on the representer's world as on who or what is represented." The West
still has tremendous discursive, military, and economic power. Our writing can either sustain it or work against its grain.

We must also be prepared, despite efforts directed at the West, to be
confronted with the problems posed when even our most enlightened
humanistic endeavors reach those in other contexts where the conventions may not be recognized and the power issues are read differently.
Again I can illustrate from my work. Writing in the context of widespread
Western antipathy towards the people of the Middle East has been in part
a project to convey a sense of the common everyday humanity of an Arab
community.[24] Yet although I can try to explain this context to the members of that community, the work cannot be received by them in the same
way. My revelation of Bedouin individuals' attachments and vulnerabili-
ties through their poetry, to create for Westerners a sense of recognition,
not distance, has provoked several other responses in Egypt. When one
woman heard someone read from the book a few of the poems she had
recited years earlier, she exclaimed, half joking, "You've scandalized us!"
For her, a book about particular people and everyday life in her community might seem only a public display of family secrets.

My presentation of the way ideals of personal autonomy and independence were manifested in men's lives also took on complex and different
meanings in Egypt. A copy of a long review (in Arabic) of my book came
to the attention of an Awlad ʿAli Bedouin who was a civil servant and

aspiring official in the Egyptian government. He confronted my host with the article, angry that I had reported that they liked to carry guns, evade taxes, and guard their rights to settle their own disputes rather than let the government interfere. As my host told me, the man accusingly argued, "This is your girl who wrote this!" What happened then I will never know, since I was not there and heard only my host's version. He was, as usual, defiant, retorting that he had taught me everything I knew. And wasn't it true? Didn't this man have unlicensed guns? Did he report all his sheep for tax purposes? My host had often told me he wanted my book translated into Arabic so that Egyptians would come to understand and appreciate the superior moral standards of his community—of which many Egyptians were contemptuous. Yet this incident showed that he was only one voice in the Bedouin community and his ideas about what would gain him respect were different from those of someone loyal to the government. My work, intended for a different audience, had entered a local political field where the relationship between Awlad ʿAli Bedouins and the Egyptian state was a contested issue.

Like all anthropological works these days, my writings will no doubt enter into a range of other debates. That is not cause for despair. Rather, in forcing us to reflect on dilemmas about anthropological practice that we can no longer ignore—because we live in times when the boundaries of "culture" are harder to keep in place and global politics less certain—such problems enable us to choose provisional strategies in line with our hopes but without self-righteous illusions about the larger value of our contributions.

──────── *Notes* ────────

None of the many people to whom I am indebted for conversations on which I have built over the years should be held liable for what I made of them. As a Mellon Fellow at the University of Pennsylvania, I benefitted from discussions with Arjun Appadurai, Carol Breckenridge, and various participants in the South Asia Program's seminar on "Orientalism and Beyond." I am grateful also to the members of the 1987–88 Gender Seminar at the Institute for Advanced Study (in which I was able to participate through generous support from the National Endowment for the Humanities) for intense and helpful discussions about feminist theory. Dan Rosenberg first started me thinking critically about the parallels between "culture" and "race." Tim Mitchell helped me clarify many aspects of my argument, as did the participants in the enormously stimulating advanced seminar at the School of American Research, where I first presented this paper. Ultimately, however, it has been the generosity of the Awlad ʿAli families in Egypt with whom I have lived that has made me seek ways to undermine notions of otherness. My most recent extended stay with them, in 1987, was made possible by a Fulbright Islamic Civilization Award.

1. *Halfies* is a term I borrowed from Kirin Narayan (personal communication).

2. Likewise, Marcus and Clifford (1985) and Marcus and Fischer (1986) gesture toward feminists as important sources of cultural and anthropological critique but do not discuss their work. Fischer (1984, 1986, 1988), however, has long been interested in the phenomenon of biculturality.

3. It is still rare for anthropologists in this society or others to do what Laura Nader (1969) advocated many years ago—to "study up."

4. Its various strategies are based on this division and the series of oppositions (culture/nature, public/private, work/home, transcendence/immediacies, abstract/particular, objectivity/subjectivity, autonomy/connectedness, etc.) associated with it: (a) women should be allowed to join the valued men's world, to become like men or have their privileges, (b) women's values and work, even if different, should be as valued as men's, or (c) women and men should both change and enter each other's spheres so that gender differences are erased.

5. It does not, Harding adds, dissolve feminism as a political identity, but the most pressing issue in feminist circles now is how to develop a politics of solidarity, coalition, or affinity built on the recognition of difference rather than the solidarity of a unitary self defined by its opposition to an other which had formerly defined it as other. The most interesting thinking on this subject has been Haraway's (1985).

6. For a discussion of the convergence of anthropological and feminist critiques of objectivity, see Abu-Lughod (1990a).

7. In his 1988 address to the American Anthropological Association, Edward Said's central point was that anthropologists had to attend not just to "the anthropological site" but to the "cultural situation in which anthropological work is in fact done" (1989:212).

8. Much of the literature on indigenous anthropology is taken up with the advantages and disadvantages of this identification. See Fahim (1982) and Altorki and El-Solh (1988).

9. See also my discussion of the study of gender in Middle East anthropology (L. Abu-Lughod 1989).

10. In parallel fashion, those who study the black experience are thought of as studying a marked form of experience. It could be pointed out, and has been by such figures as Adrienne Rich, that the universal unmarked form of experience from which it differs is itself partial. It is the experience of whiteness.

11. Crapanzano (1977) has written insightfully about the regular process of distancing from the fieldwork experience and building identifications with the anthropological audience that all anthropologists go through when they return from the field.

12. This is happening, for example, in heated debates in the field of Middle East women's studies about who has the right to speak for Middle Eastern women.

13. Some would like to make distinctions between "womanism" and "feminism," but in much of literature they blur together.

14. Arens (1979), for example, has asked the provocative question of why anthropologists cling so tenaciously to the belief that in some cultures cannibalism is an accepted ritual practice, when the evidence (in the form of eye witness accounts) is so meager (if not, as he argues, absent).

15. In my own work on an Egyptian Bedouin community I began to think in terms of discourses rather than culture simply because I had to find ways to make sense of the fact that there seemed to be two contradictory discourses on interpersonal relations—the discourse of honor and modesty and the poetic discourse of vulnerability and attachment—which informed and were used by the same individuals in differing contexts (Abu-Lughod 1986). In a recent reflection on Bedouin responses to death (Abu-Lughod n.d.), I also had to make sense of the fact that there were multiple discourses on death in this community. Not only did people play with contradictory explanations of particular deaths (invoking, in one case of an accidental killing, stupidity, certain actions on the part of family members, the [evil] eye, fate, and God's will), but the two primary discourses—ritual funerary laments and the Islamic discourse of God's will—were attached to different social groups, men and women, and worked to sustain and justify the power differences between them.

16. Two new journals, *Public Culture: Bulletin of the Center for Transnational Cultural Studies* and *Diaspora: A Journal of Transnational Studies*, provide forums for discussion of these transnational issues.

17. For evidence of a "world system" in the thirteenth century, see J. Abu-Lughod (1989).

18. Dumont (1986) has recently reiterated this, declaring changes in social theory to be merely methodological changes.

19. For a more detailed and interesting discussion of Clifford's unease with feminism, see Gordon (1988).

20. To this list could be added many others, including most recently Friedl (1989).

21. This may also explain their neglect of Paul Riesman, whose experiment in ethnographic writing was published in French in 1974 and in English in 1977, making it one of the earliest.

22. My own experiment in this sort of narrative ethnography is forthcoming (Abu-Lughod, in press).

23. So damning is an association with humanism that Said's lapse into it is the crux of Clifford's (1980) critique of *Orientalism*.

24. The strength of anti-Arab racism in the West has sometimes seemed to make this a discouraging project. A recent article called "The Importance of Hugging" used a misrepresentation of my work as evidence for its argument that the natural violence and bloodthirstiness of Arabs are caused by their supposed failure to hug their children (Bloom 1989).

Chapter 9

READING AMERICA

Preliminary Notes on Class and Culture

Sherry B. Ortner

ANTHROPOLOGISTS are turning in increasing numbers to the study of modern American society. When I was in graduate school in the sixties, it was virtually unheard of to get the blessings of the department (not to mention a grant) to do American fieldwork. The only project in my era to get such backing was a study of American drag queens (Newton 1972), and one could argue that this was only because drag queens were seen as so exotic and "other" that they might as well have been Australian aborigines.

The growth of anthropological studies of the U.S. began in the seventies (I will discuss some of these studies below). The turn to such work may be taken in part as a response to the sixties' call for "relevance," for bringin' it all back home. Insofar as I would argue that we are still in the process of playing out many of the changes set in motion in the sixties, the point still applies. At the same time, quite a few things have happened since then, both out in the world and in the pages of academia. Sticking to the academic front, there has been an extraordinary growth of concern about the question of how we produce and authorize the claims we as scholars make about the world. Part of this concern has focused on the discursive constraints within which we unreflexively operate (and thus unintentionally reproduce), as in Said's arguments about the controlling discourse of Orientalism (Said 1978). Part of it has focused on the ways in which we construct our texts so as to silence some voices and heighten the authority of our own (Clifford 1986a). Both of these lines of argument have been powerful and productive. There is, however, a third strand to this problematic, most broadly laid out perhaps in Marcus and Fischer's *Anthropology as Cultural Critique* (1986), that has received somewhat less attention: the question of what produces *us*? If "working in the present" (the subtitle of this book) has any meaning at all, it seems to be the emphasis not (only) on how we produce what we produce (in terms of discursive constraints, genre constraints, and so forth), but on the conditions of that production. I read most of the papers of this volume as addressing this question, and that is how I situate the project to be discussed in this paper.

I am currently at the very beginning of a project for which the short title is something like "class and culture in America," and for which the long title is something like this: the study of American culture as a capitalist system, and the study of American capitalism as a cultural system. I begin by observing the absence of any strong cultural category of "class" in American discourse. As I will argue in this paper, class is central to American social life, but it is rarely spoken in its own right. Rather, it is represented through other categories of social difference: gender, ethnicity, race, and so forth. At the broadest level, I am concerned with what such discursive patterns—silences, displacements, exaggerations—mean in relation to a range of questions: what they mean for "capitalism" as a mode of society and culture (how far can we go with the notion that capitalism is culturally constructed?), for the lives of people in an ordinary sense, and for the shape of academic discourse.

I have written elsewhere about some of the issues involved in constructing the ethnographic entity for this project (Ortner 1989b). Here I will simply say that I am planning to do the project in the general vicinity of Newark, New Jersey, where I grew up. I am planning to use the members of my high school class (class of '58 from Weequahic High School), along with their parents and children, as the core ethnographic group of study. In quite a literal sense, this is one of the sites in which I was produced (and against which I have seen much of my adult self as reacting). Much more generally, however, such sites of largely (but not entirely) white, largely (but not entirely) middle-class reproduction can be seen as the breeding grounds of much of dominant American culture, as well as of the people who go off to universities and eventually forge the academic discourses within which we talk about the world.

The theoretical space within which I locate the project is defined by a cluster of varied but overlapping work. Clifford Geertz's work (and behind that, Max Weber's) still informs a good part of what I do, though it has been modified over time by Marxist, feminist, and—broadly speaking—Foucauldian interests.[1] The writings of Raymond Williams (e.g., 1977), for me as for many others, capture at least part of these culture-critical transformations on a basically interpretive perspective. Williams's insights in turn have been further developed in the work of the so-called Birmingham school, or "cultural studies" group, associated with the writings of Stuart Hall (e.g., 1988), Dick Hebdige (1979), Paul Willis (1977), and others. These writers focus particularly on the relationship between class and culture, and are central (as both inspirations and foils) to my current project. Bourdieu's *Distinction* (1984) plays a similar role. Proceeding as it were on a parallel track, there is a major body of feminist cultural theory on which I also draw (e.g., de Lauretis 1986, Mohanty 1988). And finally, as discussed a moment ago, there is the reflexive critique within anthropology, as embodied most powerfully in *Writing Culture* (Clifford and Marcus 1986). While I have specific agreements and disagreements with all of these works, individually and in terms of "schools," I am in broad agreement with the kinds of questions they are asking, and the ways in which, in a general sense, they are trying to go about answering those questions. I invoke them here not to engage them theoretically, however, but simply to define the theoretical landscape within which I will be operating.[2]

POINT OF ENTRY: CLASS AND CULTURE IN AMERICA

One dimension of the project on the culture of capitalism involves a consideration of the ways in which class as a problem has and has not appeared in social science discourse in the United States. My first effort to enter this dimension of the project was to get a general grasp on the "class" literature, notable for its overwhelming volume and sometimes for the acrimony of its debates. Starting small, I tried to look at the presence of class in ethnographies (rather than in survey studies), because—for me, still—the ethnography provides the "thickest" form of information. The first thing that strikes an anthropologist reading the ethnographic literature on America, written by both sociologists and anthropologists, is the centrality of "class" in sociological research and its marginality in anthropological studies. Sociologists may argue intensely over the meanings and implications of class, but there is no doubt that it is a meaningful category of discussion for them. Given that, until recently, the sociologists virtually "owned" America as a research domain, even for ethnographic research, most of the ethnographic work was, in one form or another, concerned with class.[3] The sociologists' concern with class also extended into the work of the one anthropologist to do a major ethnographic study in America before World War II, W. Lloyd Warner. In the monumental Yankee City project (beginning with Warner and Lunt 1941), Warner both accepted the sociological emphasis on class and transformed it with his "emic," anthropological perspective. I will say a bit more about Warner later; he merits a paper himself but cannot be discussed in any detail here.

Other than the Yankee City project, there were scattered anthropological forays into American community studies before the 1970s (Hortense Powdermaker's work [1939, 1950] is the main example), but anthropologists do not come into the ethnography of America in a major way until that decade. The difference of focus between the sociologists and the anthropologists is breathtaking. The anthropologists study the marginal areas of society: street gangs (Keiser 1969), retirement communities (Jacobs 1974), and ethnic groups (mostly Jews [e.g., Myerhoff 1978; Kugelmass 1987]). They seek out "classic" anthropological topics like kinship (Schneider 1980; Neville 1987), ritual (Errington 1987), "coming of age" (Moffatt 1989). They do general community studies focusing on "friendship" and "individualism" (Varenne 1977). All of the works just mentioned are excellent studies, and we learn a great deal from them about the workings of many parts of American society. But with a few exceptions before the eighties—*Rockdale* (Wallace 1972) is really the only one that comes to mind—they do not bring class into analytic focus at all.[4] The entire section on "social structure" in a 1975 reader on the anthropology of American culture—*The Nacirema* (Spradley and Rynkiewich 1975)—consists of entries concerning "totemism," "caste," "social race," ethnic relations, social identity formation in high schools, and urban networks. A second reader (Arens and Montague 1976) similarly has a section called "Social Strategies and Institutional Arrangements"; it includes entries on coffee-drinking, friendship, moonshining, poker, astrology, volunteer firemen, and health-care seeking behavior. I do not mean to ridicule these concerns; the ethnography of the minutiae of everyday life can be very revealing. Nonetheless, there is a tendency to avoid almost any kind of macrosociological analysis, let alone making class a central category of research.

Besides for the most part ignoring class, anthropological studies of the United States have had a chronic tendency to "ethnicize" the groups under study, to treat them as so many isolated and exotic tribes. This is true even for studies of what are clearly class-defined groups—longshoremen

(Pilcher 1972) or construction workers (Applebaum 1981). The major exception to this tendency, in the period before the eighties, is to be found in ethnographies of black communities (e.g., Hannerz 1969; Stack 1974). These studies attempt to work out various compromises between, on the one hand, the classic anthropological desire to see the cultures of these communities as having a certain authenticity in their own terms (i.e., the "ethnicizing" move) and, on the other, the recognition that African-Americans are not simply another colorful ethnic group, but rather operate within a larger structure of racial inequality and a larger cultural hegemony.[5] In this sense these studies come closer to what I am trying to sort out here as the contemporary shift in the anthropology of America: they focus not only on a segment of our own society, but also on the conditions of inequality under which we are all produced. Yet while seeking to understand the cultures of these groups as shaped by conditions of inequality, they do not go to the other extreme of denying the genuine meaningfulness and subjectively felt authenticity of the (sub)culture for those who live within it.

Yet studies of black communities implicitly continue the tradition of working around the (class-) edges of American society. It is only in the past few years that we have seen anthropologists—who are, after all, overwhelmingly white and middle class—take the bull by the horns and tackle both the American white middle class as such, and the complex dynamics that reproduce the American class structure. I would mention only two such studies here. One is Katherine Newman's study of the experience of middle-class families whose primary wage earners lose their jobs (1988). Newman explores the sudden and novel experience of powerlessness undergone by middle-class people in these circumstances, and the ways in which they are forced to deal with themselves and the social universe under these conditions. Another is Penelope Eckert's ethnography of a suburban high school near Detroit (1989). Eckert studied the social groups of high school—"jocks" and "burnouts." She is particularly conscious of, and effective in, treading the line alluded to a moment ago: attending to the cultures of these groups as being "authentic" (in the sense of providing both meaning and order for their members—the traditional "functions" of culture), while at the same time being both constituted by, and contributing to the reproduction of, enduring structures of class in the larger society. Her book most closely resembles Paul Willis's landmark work, *Learning to Labor* (1977), and although it is rather less powerfully written, it nonetheless has the real advantage of looking at both the (largely middle-class) jocks and the (largely working-class) burnouts as mutually constituting one another within a single social universe.

So what is class? There is, to say the least, no single answer. The sociological debates (joined as well by some economists, political scientists, historians, and others) take place along several major axes. There is first of all a split between the so-called bourgeois theorists and the Marxists. Broadly speaking, bourgeois theorists in one form or another treat class as "stratification"—as a set of differential positions on a scale of social advantage—rather than as a set of fundamentally conflictual relations. Marxists, by contrast, work from a theoretical model in which classes are not merely sets of differentially successful people, but are derived from the specifically exploitative form of production that is capitalism, and are inherently antagonistic.

Further debates are visible within each camp. The bourgeois theorists tend to split among themselves between those who think class should be defined by objective indicators (income, occupation, education, etc.), and those who think class should be defined in terms of how the natives themselves create social rankings, that is, in terms of something like "status." A good example of the first is Lipset and Bendix's classic study, *Social Mobility in Industrial Society* (1957), which treats class as almost entirely equivalent to occupation. A good example of the second is Coleman and Rainwater's *Social Standing in America* (1978), which is entirely concerned with how people define and rank "status."[6] There are further divisions within these ranks, and also certain mixings and matchings: the objectivists tend to ask in their last chapter how their objective indicators line up with native categories; those who emphasize native categories or "statuses" tend to ask in their last chapter how these line up with objective indicators like income or education.

The Marxists have their own splits. As Erik Olin Wright puts it, there are people who are interested in "class structure," as against the people who are interested in "class formation" (1985: 9–10). Wright himself falls largely on the "class structure" side, concerned with the ways in which capitalism is or is not functioning the way Marx thought it did or should, and the implications thereof. Some of the major issues here include the implications for capitalism (as well as for Marxist theory and for social transformation) of the growth of the salaried middle class, of different forms of the state, and of different modes of relationship between state and economy. The "class formation" thinkers, for their part, are primarily concerned with the problem of how and why classes (normally, the working class) do or do not come to be self-conscious political actors. This camp in turn seems to be undergoing further splits: on the one hand, we have a kind of austere structural approach to the question of class formation, as seen in Anthony Giddens's *The Class Structure of the Advanced*

Societies (1973). Giddens is concerned with the "variables," in a socio-logical sense, that do or do not facilitate such coming to awareness. On the other hand, there is the historical sociology camp, deriving much of its inspiration from E. P. Thompson's *The Making of the English Working Class* (1968). Here the argument is that we should stop looking at what the working class has only infrequently done, which is become conscious of itself as the vehicle for revolutionary social change. Instead, we should look at the extraordinary range of ways in which it has formulated and expressed a distinct identity and a distinct relationship to the rest of so-ciety (Katznelson and Zolberg 1986; Somers 1989).

Let me approach this range of theoretical and methodological perspec-tives obliquely, by restating the problem for the present paper. It is well known that American natives almost never speak of themselves or their society in class terms. In other words, class is not a central category of cultural discourse in America, and the anthropological literature that ig-nores class in favor of almost any other set of social idioms—ethnicity, race, kinship—is in some ways merely reflecting this fact. Paul Fussell speaks of the discourse of class in America as being under a "taboo" (1983). And in an ethnographic study of a chemical plant in Elizabeth, New Jersey, the British sociologist David Halle found that the plant work-ers defined themselves as "working men" and "working women," but did not see themselves as members of a "working class" (1984: chapter 10). Indeed, in those rare instances in which they used class terms at all, they described themselves—as the vast majority of Americans do—as "middle class."[7]

At the same time, it is clear that class is a "real" structure in American society, whether it is recognized in native discourse or not. Part of this reality is what is described in the classic Marxist account of differential relations to the means of production: some people own most of the major systems of the production of wealth in America, while others produce that wealth yet garner for themselves only a small part of its value. An-other part of the reality of class is one that is increasingly talked about in neo-Marxist discussions about the salaried middle class: power (admin-istrative, regulatory, etc.) over other people's lives, whether one owns a piece of the means of production or not (Poulantzas 1974; Vanneman and Cannon 1987). And part of it, discussed most directly in studies of blacks and other poor minorities, has to do with discrimination, prejudice, stig-matization, and pain. Indeed, if one asks which aspects of the reality of class are displaced into the discourses of ethnicity, race, and gender, they are really largely the second two dimensions just noted. That is, if Ameri-cans can be said to have a discourse of class at all, it is, like that of *both*

Marx and the bourgeois theorists, an economistic one: Americans have a discourse of money. What are not represented by the folk, and only fragmentarily represented by the class theorists, are both the power and the pain of class relations.

It is important to note here that I take the position that class is not the only such "objective" structure of domination, that it is no more or less real than a number of others, and that it should not be construed as more fundamental.[8] Further it is not distinguished from other such structures as being somehow more "material"; all structures of domination are simultaneously material and cultural. Nonetheless, it is real in the sense that one can speak of its existence and its constraints even when it is not directly articulated in native discourse. In fact, as I shall argue in this paper, it does appear in native discourse (no "reality" could fail to do so), but not in terms that we would immediately recognize as a discourse "about class."

But if the constraints of class are real, so too, apparently, are the high rates of social mobility in the American system. There are literally hundreds of studies of mobility, done at different times and with different assumptions over the course of the twentieth century, but the statistical findings seem to be relatively consistent with one another, and I will use the one provided in Lipset and Bendix's *Social Mobility in Industrial Society* (1957). The authors do an exhaustive survey of mobility studies and come up with the following figures: The average for upward mobility (narrowly defined as a shift from manual to nonmanual labor), drawn from studies done with different assumptions, and at different historical moments, runs around 33 percent, with a range from 20 percent to 40 percent. The average for downward mobility runs around 26 percent, with a range from 15 percent to 35 percent (Lipset and Bendix 1957: 25, and chapter 2 passim). These rates are quite high. On average, one out of three male Americans (only males were studied) will personally experience upward mobility in his lifetime; on average, one out of four will personally experience downward mobility. (The rate of upward mobility always seems to be slightly ahead of the rate for downward mobility. Much has been written about this, but the general, though not uncontested, point is that the middle class has been gradually expanding over time.) Even if the specific figures are disputed, no one seems to disagree with the general statement that there are high rates of social mobility in America.

According to Lipset and Bendix, the United States is not unique in having these high rates of mobility. The central point of this book is that such rates are characteristic of all the class societies, including Europe as well as the United States. What is unique about the American system is its ideology. Where European cultures have tended to emphasize traditional ranks and statuses, and to present themselves as more rigid in class terms than they really are, the United States has glorified opportunity and mobility, and has presented itself as more open to individual achievement than it really is. There is nothing terribly new about this point, but it is, I think, one of many strands feeding into what is probably a massively overdetermined phenomenon: the absence of class discourse in American culture. The deeply individualistic grounding of American social thought no doubt also plays a role in generating this absence, in that classes are social categories that cannot be understood in terms of individual motives and desires. Anyone who has taught an introductory social science course to American undergraduates knows the extent to which society is culturally conceived by them as the sum of empirical, skin-bound individuals, and social institutions are conceived as the products of individual motives, desires, and wills. These two points in turn may be combined to suggest a reason for the patterns of displacement (and not just absence) that we see. Because hegemonic American culture takes both the ideology of mobility and the ideology of individualism seriously, explanations for nonmobility not only focus on the failure of individuals (because they are said to be inherently lazy or stupid or whatever), but shift the domain of discourse to arenas that are taken to be "locked into" individuals—gender, race, ethnic origin, and so forth.

Whatever the explanation (and again, this is a highly overdetermined phenomenon), one of the effects of jamming the cultural airwaves with respect to class is to be seen in what Richard Sennett and Jonathan Cobb have called "the hidden injuries of class" (1972). Poorer and less successful Americans tend to blame themselves for their failures, and not to recognize the ways in which their chances for success were circumscribed from the outset. Another of the effects, I suggest, is the one to be documented in this paper: a displacement of class strain and friction into other arenas of life, a displacement not without its costs for experience in those other arenas.

CLASS AND THE SOCIAL GEOGRAPHY OF GENDER AND SEXUAL PRACTICES

The particular pattern I want to focus on here is the displacement of class frictions into the discourse and practices of gender and sexual relations. The basic point, which emerged for me more or less accidentally as I read a set of American community studies with, initially, no particular agenda, is this: gender relations for both middle-class and working-class Americans (I have only glanced at elites at this point) carry an enormous burden of quite antagonistic class meaning. To turn the point around, class discourse is submerged within, and spoken through, sexual discourse, taking "sex" here in the double English sense of pertaining to both gender and the erotic (see Ortner and Whitehead 1981). And while the general point of displacement holds for both middle-class and working-class discourse, it works differently in each case. I start with the working class.

(I should note here that I will use the present tense throughout this paper, though the examples to be discussed run from the early fifties through the early eighties. The patterns in question seem to have been, with only minor variations, impressively durable.)

WORKING CLASS DISCOURSES OF SEX AND CLASS

I begin with the assumption that the classes are relationally constituted, that they define themselves always in implicit reference to the other(s). Thus, while we normally think of class relations as taking place *between* classes, in fact each class contains the other(s) within itself, though in distorted and ambivalent forms. This is particularly visible in the working class, where the class structure of the society is introjected into the culture of the working class itself, appearing as a problematic choice of "life-styles" for working-class men and women—a choice between a life-style modeled essentially on middle-class values and practices and one modeled on more distinctively working- or lower-class values and practices.[9] This split, which is given different names by different ethnographers and different ethnographees, shows up in virtually every study of both white and black working-class communities. One example may be seen in Herbert Gans's classic study (1962) of an urban working-class community in Boston. Gans sees two major styles of working-class life, which he labels the styles of the "routine seekers" and the "action seekers" (1962:28). To this basic split he adds two more extreme types, the "maladapteds" at the very bottom of the working class, and the "middle-class mobiles" at the top of the class. The general pattern of these styles will be intuitively comprehensible to any American native. Routine seekers follow a relatively settled life-style centered on family and work. Action seekers, on the other hand, live the "fast" life, centered importantly on relations with "the boys," the male peer group; family and work are avoided or minimized as much as possible. Of the two more extreme versions of this basic split, middle-class mobiles are similar to routine seekers except that they are more oriented, as the label suggests, toward actual upward mobility. Maladaptives are similar to action seekers, but generally have a problem such as alcoholism or drug abuse that renders them more irredeemable.

To characterize the split within working-class culture in terms of activity (as in "action seekers") and passivity (as in "routine seekers") is reminiscent of Paul Willis's account of the culture of British working-class high school students (1977). Willis focused on the "lads," or the non-conformists, who divided the school between themselves and what they called the "ear'oles": "The term 'ear'ole' itself connotes the passivity and absurdity of the school conformists for 'the lads.' It seems that they are always listening, never *doing*; never animated with their own internal life, but formless in rigid reception" (1977:14; see also Sennett and Cobb 1972:82).

The same pattern of life-style split, between a "middle-class" life-style (whether oriented toward actual upward mobility or not) and a working- or lower-class lifestyle, shows up in the black ghetto neighborhood studied by the Swedish anthropologist Ulf Hannerz:

> The people of Winston Street often describe themselves and their neighbors in the community as comprising two categories distinguished according to way of life. . . . Some refer to one category—in which they usually include themselves—as "respectable," "good people," or, more rarely and somewhat facetiously, as "model citizens." More seldom do they refer to this category as "middle class." . . . They use these labels to distinguish themselves from what they conceive of as their opposites, people they describe as "undesirables," "no good," "the rowdy bunch," "bums," or "trash." (1969:34–35)

In sum, there is a general tendency for working- or lower-class culture to embody *within* itself the split in society *between* the working and the middle class. This split appears as a subcultural typology of "styles": the action-seekers versus the routine-seekers, the lads versus the ear'oles, the respectables versus the undesirables.

From the actor's point of view, the split in turn appears as a set of choices, a set of life possibilities between which a young man growing up within the working class will consciously or unconsciously choose. Here is where class, now translated as "life-style," intersects with the discourses and practices of gender and sexuality. For it appears overwhelmingly the case in working-class culture that women are symbolically aligned, from both the male point of view and, apparently, their own, with the "respectable," "middle-class" side of those oppositions and choices. Thus every sexual choice is symbolically also a class choice, for better or worse.

This pattern is again seen in virtually every ethnography of working-class culture. Gans describes it for the neighborhood he studied in Boston: "Marriage is a crucial turning point in the life of the West End boy. It is then that he must decide whether he is going to give up the boys on the corner for the new peer group of related siblings and in-laws—a decision related to and reflected in his choice of a mate" (1962:70). In the extreme instance, which is to say the instance of (would-be) mobility, the couple will move to the suburbs. Such a move is generally blamed (by "the boys") on the wife's ambitions (Gans 1962:53), and this may indeed be the case. Gans goes on to say that these kinds of pulls create a great deal of strain between husband and wife (1962:70).

David Halle, in his ethnography of chemical workers in Elizabeth, New Jersey (1984), reports much the same patterns and explores them with great insight. His fine-grained ethnography shows that the perception of women as more "middle class" than men, and as aligned with middle-class values and practices, extends into (or emerges from) the workplace as well as the domestic situation. Within the single plant studied, the men normally work in the production areas, while the women normally work in the office. The men's jobs are dirty and physical, while the women's jobs both allow and require them to be more dressed up and to remain clean throughout the day. Further, women in the office work more closely and directly with management. For all these reasons, they are apparently symbolically associated with management (Halle 1984:61).

As Halle explored with male workers their own cultural category of "working man," he found that the term contained several meanings: it meant quite literally working, as opposed to not working (the very rich and the "welfare bums" are similar in not working at all); it meant hard, physical labor as opposed to soft, easy work; and it meant productive labor as opposed to purposeless paper pushing. To the male workers, even women with paid employment, including the clerical and office workers in the men's own plant, were not seen as "working" (Halle 1984:206):

> Researcher: How about secretaries? [i.e., are they "working persons"?]
> Worker: No! They often spend half the afternoon reading magazines. I've seen them through the window.

And in another interview (Halle 1984:207):

> Researcher: How about secretaries?
> Worker: No, they work in an office . . . They just answer the phone and type letters.

Let me return to the issue of women as not merely displaying middle-class patterns (as in the cleanly dressed secretary) but of actually seeming to enforce such patterns on men. While it is the perception of "the boys" that it is women, as wives, who exert a middle-class pull on their husbands, this perception may have some basis in women's actual practice. Although Halle's information comes mostly from male informants, their claims are specific enough to have the ring of true reporting. Thus, many men say that their wives complain about their social status being too low and exert pressure on them to change their kinds of work, or at least their behavioral styles, in a more "middle-class" direction (Halle 1984: 59). Husbands found this irritating, to say the least. Issues of behavioral style—how a man eats or speaks, for example—connect to (or are perceived as being connected to) lack of education, and are "particularly explosive since the overwhelming majority of workers are very sensitive about their lack of formal education" (Halle 1984:60).

The pattern is essentially identical in the black neighborhood studied by Ulf Hannerz, who did talk to women as well as men. He found that while women recognized variation among men in terms of life-style, there was a general tendency to lump all men in the "nonrespectable" pool, and themselves implicitly in the respectable group (Hannerz 1969:97, 99).

Nor are these symbolic alignments simply matters of "discourse" abstracted from lived experience. Both Halle and Hannerz discuss at some length the ways in which men's and women's perceptions of each other articulate with a pattern of often highly conflictful and unhappy gender relations. Although some of Halle's male informants (one suspects that Gans would have classified them as "routine seekers") felt that their wives' (real or imagined) middle-class inclinations "rescued them from the wild life-style of the male culture, a life-style they believe would in the end have been their downfall" (Halle 1984:64), this feeling was less common than its opposite—that women's real or supposed identification with middle-class ideals placed their husbands under a great deal of strain.

At this point, class no longer appears as a choice of lifestyle, but as an imposed pressure and constraint. Yet the imposition appears to come not from class "enemies"—the rich, the politicians, the pampered sons of the middle class—but from the men's own girlfriends and wives. I will return to this point below.

MIDDLE-CLASS DISCOURSES OF CLASS AND SEX

Given both the high rates of social mobility in America and the strong cultural emphasis on its possibility and desirability, each class has a characteristic stance on the question. Moreover, each class views the others not only, or even primarily, as antagonistic groups but as images of their hopes and fears for their own lives and futures. For the white working class, it is the black working class (which is poorer and less secure than the white) that represents their worst fears for themselves; this, as much as any putative threat of economic competition, underlies much of white working-class racism. The middle class, in contrast, is a source of tremendous ambivalence from a working-class perspective. Middle-class status is highly desirable for its greater material affluence and security, but undesirable for all the ways in which its patterns are culturally "other," and for the ways in which upward mobility would pull one away from kin, friends, or neighborhood.

For the middle class, the pattern of fears and desires is different. There is much less ambivalence about upward social mobility, since much of it would not involve significant changes of "culture." The "fear of falling," however (to borrow a phrase from Barbara Ehrenreich's recent study of middle-class culture [1989]), is intense. This may be true particularly at the lower edge of the class, and particularly for new arrivals, but it seems to be a general and pervasive substrate of middle-class thought. If much of working-class culture can be understood as a set of discourses and practices embodying the ambivalence of upward mobility, much of middle-class culture can be seen as a set of discourses and practices embodying the terror of downward mobility.

In both cases the complex attitudes held about adjacent classes derive from the classes' functioning as mirrors of these possibilities. Although the middle class and the working class may be inherently antagonistic as a result of their positioning within the capitalist productive order, in the phenomenology of class cultures the frictions between them seem largely to derive from this mirroring function. And for each class, the frictions are introjected into, and endlessly replayed through, social relations internal to the class itself.

My sense is that it is parent-child relations in the middle class that carry much of the burden of introjected "class struggle" and even class "war," comparable to the ways in which gender carries this burden in the working class. There is no doubt that gender carries a lot of this for the middle class as well, and I will come back to that in a moment. But it seems to me—and at this point I speak more from my experience as a native than from anything I have seen yet in ethnographies—that there is the kind of both chronic friction and explosive potential in middle-class parent-child relations that one sees in working-class gender relations (see especially Ehrenreich 1989: ch.2).

At a practical level, there is always the question of whether middle-class children will successfully retain the class standing the parents have provided them. As a result of this practical question, which revolves around issues of education, occupation, and (here is the intersection with gender) marriage choice, there are tremendous parental attempts to control their children's behavior, over a much longer span of time and to a much later age than in the working class. (Both Willis [1977: 21–22] and Gans [1962: 56–57] indicate that working-class parents do not attempt to impose, and especially to extend, these kinds of controls.) But if middle-class parents see their children as embodying the threat of a working-class future (for the children if not for themselves), and attempt to control them accordingly, adolescent children respond in kind. They criticize their parents' values, which is to say essentially class values, and they resist their parents' controls precisely through representations of lower-class affiliation—language, hairstyle, clothing, music, and sometimes cross-class friendships and cross-class dating or sexual relationships. It is hardly a novel observation that much of middle-class adolescent culture is drawn both from "real" lower-class culture (e.g., by way of the lower-class origins of many rock groups) and from marketing fantasies of what lower-class culture looks like. In any event, it is clear that the discourse of parent-child relations (specifically parent-child conflict) in the middle class, like the discourse of gender in the working class, is simultaneously a class discourse. It draws on and feeds the fears and anxieties that make sense if we assume that the classes view each other as their own pasts and possible futures.

But although parent-child relations carry a good bit of the burden of class antagonism or fear in the middle class, discourses on gender and sexuality are not without their own significant freight of class meanings. Here, however, the pattern is quite different from that seen in the working class. Where for the working class, class is, in effect, pulled into the subculture and mapped onto internal relations of gender and sexuality, for the middle class, gender and sexuality are projected out onto the world of class relations.[10] Specifically, the working class is cast as the bearer of an exaggerated sexuality, against which middle-class respectability is defined.

One of the best places to see these patterns is in predominantly middle-class high schools. They almost always contain at least some kids from working-class backgrounds, and the high-school ethnosociology tends to build distinctions around these differences, reproducing the split between respectable and nonrespectable that is so central to working-class culture. This split is called by endlessly different names in different schools. In my high school in the fifties, the terminology was inconsistent—the respectables were largely merged with the dominant ethnic category (Jews), while the nonrespectables were usually called "hoods," a term that was apparently of near-national scope at that time. In the school studied by Gary Schwartz and Don Merten in the early seventies, the terms were "socies" and hoods (1975). In the school studied by Eckert in the early eighties, the terms were jocks and burnouts (1989). Whatever the labels, the social category split marked by these terms is almost never recognized by the students as a class split, and the terms used for it almost never refer to class or even money differences—a good example of the taboo on class discourse in America. Nonetheless, the split tends to map rather accurately onto differences that adults or parents or social scientists would recognize as class differences.

The distinctions between the two groups are marked in a whole range of ways—clothing; language; haircuts; attitudes toward teachers, school work, and school citizenship; and all the rest. But for the middle-class adolescents, one of the key dimensions of difference is a supposed difference in attitudes toward and practices of sexual behavior. Middle-class kids, both male and female, define working-class kids as promiscuous, highly experienced, and sexually unconstrained. I give one ethnographic example; the pattern is so well known that it does not require extensive illustration. Schwartz and Merten studied sorority initiation rites in a middle-class American high school (1975). The high-school social system was divided by the sorority girls (who were at the top of it) into "socialites," or "socies," and "hoods" or "greasers." (The authors identify a middle category that is neither really "hoody" nor cool enough to be among the "socies," but which is said generally to approve of "socie" values.) [11]

While the bulk of Schwartz and Merten's article focuses on interpreting the sorority hazings as initiation rites that facilitate identity transformations of various kinds (which is doubtless true), the authors move into a discussion of the class dimensions of the categories toward the end. Here we see the ways in which class differences are largely represented as sexual differences:

> For socie girls, those who subscribe to the adolescent version of a middle-class way of life are morally acceptable; girls who follow the adolescent variant of a working-class way of life are morally contemptible. All of our socie informants felt that hoody girls tended to be promiscuous, sloppy, stupid, and unfriendly. (Schwartz and Merten 1975: 207)

Clothing and cosmetic differences are taken to be indexes of the differences in sexual morals between the girls of the two classes:

The act of smearing [socie sorority] pledges with lipsticks on hell night [of the initiation rites] is a veiled reference to what socies believe is a most salient feature of the hoody cosmetic style, the use of makeup in ways that resemble the appearance of a slut. . . . Socies interpret hoody hairstyles, in which the hair is worn massed on top of the head and is held together by a liberal application of hair spray, as a sign of a lack of sexual restraint. (Schwartz and Merten 1975:210)[12]

It is painfully ironic that the same girls who are taken to be "sluts" by middle-class sorority girls will be taken by their own men to be agents of middle-class values and resented as such. Here truly is a "hidden injury of class."[13]

As in the case of the working class, this kind of sexual mapping of classes will also appear, at least to some middle-class actors, as a set of choices or possibilities for their own lives. There is both a similarity with and a difference from working-class patterns. For both groups, there is a sense that different women will pull men in different directions in class terms. For the working class, the pattern, or at least the threat, tends to be generalized to all women, and men do not represent themselves as having a great deal of agency in the matter. For middle-class men, however, there seems to be more of a notion of choice. Women of various class positions appear as kind of smorgasbord of sexual-cum-class possibilities, most of which are not likely to be realized, but all of which are apparently "good to think."[14] Although there might be some ethnographic work on this that I have not yet come across, the pattern is most clearly seen in certain American novels. This brings me to the final section of my discussion.

FICTION AS ETHNOGRAPHY

Is ethnography fiction? If by that we mean that ethnography is always partial, always inadequate to the fullness of its object, and always colored by the author's interests in the broadest sense, then the answer is certainly yes. But if the question is meant to imply that in most ethnographies any resemblance to cultures living or dead is purely coincidental, then the answer, as even James Clifford would agree (1986a:7), is certainly no, and the question is simply mischievous. Interestingly, while anthropologists increasingly ponder the fictionality of ethnography, a number of major American novelists (and some minor ones as well) seek to cast their fictions as ethnographies.[15] Saul Bellow sprinkles his novels with references to cultural and physical anthropology. The paragraph on Bellow at the front of *Humboldt's Gift* (1975) informs us—out of all the myriad personal and professional details it might have mentioned—that Bellow was an anthropology major as an undergraduate. And in Philip Roth's latest novel, *The Counterlife*, he essentially accuses himself of being an ethnographer.

In *The Counterlife*, Nathan Zuckerman, the character who stands in for Roth in many of his novels, sort of dies (I say "sort of dies" because it is something more complex than that, but I do not want to give away the plot), and his editor delivers a eulogy for him. Zuckerman had written a novel called *Carnovsky*, a fairly clear stand-in for Roth's famous (or infamous) novel, *Portnoy's Complaint*. The editor says of Zuckerman,

> On the evidence of *Carnovsky*, he would have made a good anthropologist; perhaps that's what he was. He lets the experience of the little tribe [the Jews of the Weequahic section of Newark], the suffering, isolated, primitive but warmhearted savages that he is studying, emerge in the description of their rituals and their artifacts and their conversations, and he manages, at the same time, to put his own "civilization," his own bias as a reporter—and his readers'—into relief against them. (Roth 1988a: 239)

In fact, Zuckerman/Roth has precisely the inverse problem of today's ethnographers (as represented in Clifford and Marcus 1986): pretending to write fiction, he is accused of *telling the truth*. As the editor continues in the eulogy, "Why, reading *Carnovsky*, did so many people keep wanting to know, 'Is it fiction?'"—implying that Roth was simply writing the most thinly disguised autobiography. In his autobiography, wonderfully called *The Facts* (1988b), Roth feels compelled to deny this.

Philip Roth grew up in a self-described "lower middle-class" family, in my neighborhood of Newark, New Jersey. He graduated from my high school, Weequahic High School, in 1951. He is clearly a figure of great interest for my project, at a whole range of levels. I do think he is a brilliant ethnographer (indeed, I think a good part of the great ethnography of America is in novels), but he is also, for purposes of the present paper, a great informant. In order to conclude my discussion of the ways in which class is spoken through images of gender and sexuality, I will look at Roth's two great Newark novels, *Goodbye, Columbus* and *Portnoy's Complaint*.

Roth's first book, *Goodbye, Columbus and Five Short Stories*, won the

1960 National Book Award for fiction. In the title story, the narrator is a young Jewish man named Neil Klugman who works in the Newark public library and lives with his aunt and uncle in Newark. The aunt and uncle are clearly working class: among other indicators, they are described as going to Workman's Circle meetings.[16] Neil falls in love with Brenda Patimkin who, though also Jewish, has clearly moved far up the ladder of money and status in the middle class. Both the money and the status are signalled by the fact that her family lives in Short Hills (an expensive suburb to which Jews from Newark aspired to move if they could afford to do so). Brenda's parents disapprove of Neil, whose lower status is signalled largely through disparaging references to Newark. As the story progresses, Brenda worries about whether Neil will turn into the kind of person of whom her parents will approve, while Neil is ambivalent about whether he can or wants to do so. Nonetheless, Neil and Brenda begin sleeping together, and Neil insists that she get a diaphragm. When Brenda goes back to Radcliffe in the fall, she leaves the diaphragm in her drawer and her mother finds it. Her parents are very upset, and Brenda feels she can no longer bring Neil into her house. The relationship is over.

The main story line is paralleled by the story of a little black boy who comes to the library where Neil works, to look again and again at a book of Gauguin paintings. For the boy these paintings are paradisiacal, and he looks at them with great longing: "These people, man, they sure does look cool. They ain't no yelling or shouting here, you could just see it . . . that's the fuckin life" (Roth 1960: 37). Neil finds that he cares about the boy's interest in the pictures, and when another borrower tries to check out the book, Neil lies in order to keep it available in the stacks for the boy. But then Neil takes a vacation from the library to spend a week at the Patimkins' before Brenda goes back to school. When he returns, the book is checked out and the little boy never comes back. He assumes that the boy was disappointed about the book's being checked out, but he tries to tell himself that it is all for the best: "He was better off, I thought. No sense carrying dreams of Tahiti in your head, if you can't afford the fare" (1960: 120).

That the story is explicitly about dreams and fears of mobility could not be much clearer. Yet it is a peculiarity of the narrative that Neil has, quite late in the story, what can only be described as a revelation, in which it comes to him as a great shock that he might have been engaged in social climbing. While waiting in New York City for Brenda to come back from her diaphragm fitting, Neil goes into St. Patrick's Cathedral and has a conversation with God about what he's been doing (Roth 1960: 100).

What is it I love, Lord? Why have I chosen? Who is Brenda? The race is to the swift. Should I have stopped to think?

I was getting no answers but I went on. . . . Where do we meet [Lord]? Which prize is you?

. . . I got up and walked outside, and the noise of Fifth Avenue met me with an answer:

Which prize do you think, *schmuck*? Gold dinnerware, sporting-goods trees, nectarines, garbage disposals, bumpless noses, Patimkin Sink, Bonwit Teller—

The revelation is necessary, I would argue, because Roth has done what our cultural discourse always does—displaced the class meanings of his story, conscious though they are at one level—into domains of gender, race, and sex.

Roth's other major Newark novel, *Portnoy's Complaint*, was published in 1967. Although it was a huge best seller and made Roth a great deal of money, it did not win any awards. On the contrary, it was actually banned from some libraries in the United States (and apparently in some places still is) for obscenity. The story takes the form of the narrator, Alexander Portnoy, talking to his psychiatrist about his psychological and sexual problems. There is little in the way of plot. At the time of the novel, Portnoy is the assistant commissioner for the New York City "Commission on Human Opportunities" and, as he signals throughout the book, a kind of generalized liberal working on various poverty programs and the like. In speaking to his psychiatrist, Portnoy rambles over his life till then—his relationships with his parents and with women.

A class framework is invoked at the beginning, through a language of ethnicity. Portnoy's father works for a large insurance company, which he holds in a certain awe but which he also loathes for its anti-Semitism. These feelings come together around the image of the president, an upper-class WASP named N. Everett Lindabury: "'Mr. Lindabury,' 'The Home Office' . . . my father made it sound to me like Roosevelt in the White House in Washington . . . and all the while how he hated their guts, Lindabury's particularly, with his corn-silk hair and his crisp New England speech, the sons in Harvard College and the daughters in finishing school, oh the whole pack of them up there in Massachusetts" (Roth 1967:8). Moreover, although his father is very good at selling insurance, it is clear that the company will never promote him because he is Jewish. Both the WASPness of N. Everett Lindabury and the Jewishness of Portnoy's father (and himself) have, in the context, clear class meanings. Whereas in *Goodbye, Columbus*, class signals were set up in part *between* Jews, in terms of where they lived and how much money they had, here the class structure is projected entirely onto other groups, and entirely in terms of ethnicity. The upper class is represented by WASPs, the middle class by Jews, and the lower class by other ethnics—Italians, Poles, Irish, blacks.

The various classes/ethnicities in turn are, for Portnoy, personified most directly in terms of the women with whom he has sex. He is fascinated with non-Jewish women, at first with the working-class girls who live around his neighborhood and who are, not surprisingly, assumed to be—and sometimes are—sexually available. Later, when he leaves Newark and goes to college, and later still when he works in Washington on behalf of various good social causes, he becomes involved with upper-class WASP women, but he also continues to be involved with lower-class/non-Jewish women. At the actual time of the story, he is just ending an affair with a woman whose father was, we are told in the first lines of her introduction, an illiterate coal miner in West Virginia.

He never has sex with a Jewish woman, or in the code of the story, with a woman of his own class. Since class appears as a matter of either discrimination, from above to below, or climbing, from below to above, but never as a matter of simply being where one is, and since sex for Roth is the idiom of these forms of class orientations, there can be no sex with Jewish—which is to say middle-class—women. This point may provide some insight into what is perhaps the most foregrounded aspect of Portnoy's sexuality in the book: his luxuriant masturbation. The masturbation that threads its way through the story, and that more than anything else generated the obscenity charges when the book first came out, seems to occupy the space created by the missing sex with women of Portnoy's own class.

Returning to women, we can see that they form a kind of landscape of class/ethnic sexual possibilities. But there is more. Not only are the classes displaced onto different ethnicities, the class/ethnicities in turn are projected through a geography of sexual practices: working-class girls are willing to do anything sexually, while WASPs apparently have problems with all but the most conventional forms of sex. In Portnoy's high school, there was Bubbles Girardi, whose brother was a boxer and whose father drove a cab by day and a car for the mob by night. Bubbles performed various sex acts for Portnoy and his friends when no other girl they knew was available for sex at all. And now there is the Monkey, the daughter of the illiterate West Virginia coal miner. The Monkey, we are told several times, will do absolutely anything at all, including at one point hiring a prostitute to join them for a three-way sexual engagement.[17] The Monkey, though now a highly paid fashion model, is herself barely literate, bearing the scars of her own class origins. Alex finds himself falling in love with her, but cannot imagine marrying this lower-class person. This is one of the things that has driven him to the psychiatrist.

The class/ethnicity of the WASP women, by contrast, is represented through repressed and conventional sexuality. Portnoy acquires his first WASP girlfriend, Kay ("Pumpkin") Campbell, in college. At first they do not have sexual intercourse at all; she is "the girl who has let me undo her brassiere and dry-hump her at the dormitory door" (Roth 1967:220). Later they evidently have sex and there is a pregnancy scare, but eventually the relationship breaks up because Kay will not convert to Judaism. With the other WASP woman in the book, Sarah Abbot Maulsby, nick-named "the Pilgrim," sex is again completely conventional: "In bed? Nothing fancy, no acrobatics or feats of daring and skill"(1967:234). In particular, Sarah Abbot Maulsby is unable or unwilling to practice oral sex on Alex, which upsets him in a way that is more than simple sexual frustration, as we shall see in a moment (1967:238).

Class is thus spoken through a language of sexual practices, as well as through languages of gender and ethnicity. As in the case of *Goodbye, Columbus*, an initial awareness of class as a major source of Portnoy's pain is systematically displaced and dispersed over several hundred pages of characters and activities that embody class but do not articulate it. But again, as in *Goodbye, Columbus*, there is a kind of waking up at the end, a kind of revelation about the underlying politics of his sexuality. It begins as Portnoy is talking to his psychiatrist about Sarah Abbott Maulsby: "What I'm saying, Doctor, is that I don't seem to stick my dick up these girls, as much as I stick it up their backgrounds" (Roth 1967:235). And then the story closes back onto his father's class/ethnic oppressions: "She could have been a Lindabury, don't you see? A daughter of my father's boss!" (1967:237). Moreover, he decides that her resistance to oral sex with him was an act of class prejudice: "My father couldn't rise at Boston & Northeastern for the very same reason that Sally Maulsby wouldn't deign to go down on me! Where was the justice in this world?" (1967: 238). And finally, explaining why he left her: "No, Sally Maulsby was just something nice a son once did for his dad. A little vengeance on Mr. Lindabury for all those nights and Sundays Jack Portnoy spent collecting down in the colored district. A little bonus extracted from Boston and Northeastern, for all those years of service, and exploitation" (1967:241).

Roth's sexism is certainly offensive. His female characters—from Portnoy's overcontrolling mother to a whole range of mostly characterless sex objects—leave a lot to be desired. Yet I think that a narrow analysis of Roth's works as texts on the bottomless sexism of a certain kind of male would miss precisely the point I have sought to make: there is sexism, to be sure, but it is all bound up with the narrator's experiences of (class) discrimination (or rather his pain over his father's experiences thereof), as well as with his own (rather feeble) efforts to do good in the world. This is not to reduce sexism to a kind of eroticized classism. But it is to say that, if Freud and Foucault have taught us that there is a sexual underside to all social difference, we must also recognize that there is at least potentially a social-power underside to all sexual difference. Without denying the possibilities of a systematic feminist critique of Roth and the more general patterns of masculinity that he may represent, this is what I have sought to show.

At the same time, as I said earlier, such displacements are not without their costs. If class is displaced into other arenas of social life, then to that extent these other arenas must be carrying a burden of what might be called "surplus antagonism," over and above whatever historical and structural frictions they embody in their own terms. We saw this clearly in the case of working-class gender relations, both black and white. Frictions between men and women had as much to do with their symbolic (and perhaps subjectively embraced) class alignments as with anything related to their gender roles as such. Women were seen as middle-class agents within the working class, a perception that emerged on the light side in jokes, but on the dark side in a kind of bitterness heard in many informants' comments about their marriages. A similar kind of surplus antagonism may be discovered, I think, in race and ethnic frictions, but these questions must be reserved for another paper.

A SHORT CONCLUSION

This paper represents an attempt both to draw upon and shift the emphases of certain contemporary theoretical trends, as represented in part in Marcus and Fischer's *Anthropology as Cultural Critique*, and in the work of the British cultural studies writers (Willis, Hall, Hebdige, etc.). A good part of *Anthropology as Cultural Critique*, and all of the British cultural studies work, focuses on the critical study of the researcher's own culture. Obviously this paper follows in this track. It is worth stressing, however, that "cultural critique" or a critical cultural studies perspective does not (or should not) primarily mean studying ourselves—either our own society as ethnographic object or our own modes of academic production. Indeed I am rather nervous about both these trends, which, when coupled with the powerful critique of anthropology as "orientalizing" or "essentializing" other cultures, threatens to undermine anthropology's commitment to getting beyond its own cultural boundaries. Thus despite my shift to American research, I continue to identify strongly with anthropology's mission of understanding other cultures. If we do not continue to do that, who will?

I define the cultural critique move, then, more broadly—as a sense of the importance of recognizing that, whether we are studying our own society or another, we and those we study are implicated in one another's lives. This is true in several senses—in the smallest sense because we as anthropologists go the field, enter into personal relationships with people, and derive our knowledge from that process; and in the largest sense because we are all by now part of, in Appadurai's telling phrase, a global ethnoscape. Even on this latter point, however, we must be careful: by focusing heavily on the points at which "we" and "they" intersect (whether in fieldwork, world-system studies, colonialism studies, studies of tourism, or whatever), we run the danger of implicitly denying the validity, or at least the interest, of the worlds of other peoples prior to, or apart from, the operations of capitalism, colonialism, or other forms of Western "penetration."[18]

The same general point applies to the study of American society. In the past there has been a strong tendency on the part of many anthropologists studying America to "ethnicize" (the domestic version of "orientalize") the various groups, classes, and even institutions (e.g., corporations) under study, to treat them as if they were in effect separate tribes. There are exceptions to this tendency, as discussed earlier, but in general, anthropologists studying America have mirrored anthropologists studying other peoples in this respect. There are indications now that the anthropology of America is shifting on this point (this study is part of that shift), and beginning to recognize the importance of studying the relationships between whatever unit one undertakes to study and the larger social and cultural universe within which it operates. This includes recognizing both the ways in which various pieces of the society or culture may be mutually constituting (as in the arguments about the middle class and the working class in this paper), and the ways in which all the pieces are at the same time constituted by the larger histories and structures that encompass them.

But just as I want, within this framework, to preserve the traditional mission of anthropology with respect to other cultures, so I want to preserve it with respect to our own. Traditionally, anthropology (and for the most part only anthropology) has attempted to achieve some understanding of the ways in which other cultural universes represent coherent and valuable systems of meaning and order for those who live within them. We have taken cultures to be authentic expressions of particular ways of life in particular times and places. However much we now recognize that cultures are riddled with inequality, differential understanding, and differential advantage, and however much we now recognize that cultures are at least partly constituted by forces external, and often inimical, to them, nonetheless they remain for the people who live within them sources of value, meaning, and ways of understanding—and resisting—the world. This is as true for disadvantaged groups in, say, a class system as for the far-flung people we more often went off to study in the past. As we study the ways in which the cultures of dominant and subordinate groups shape one another, or the ways in which a particular culture is reshaped through colonial encounters, capitalist penetration, or class domination, we must at the same time work against the denial of cultural authenticity that this may imply, and the related implication that the ethnography of meaningful cultural worlds is no longer a significant enterprise.[19]

─────── *Notes* ───────

This paper was written while I was a visiting member at the Institute for Advanced Study in Princeton, New Jersey, supported by funds from the University of Michigan and the National Endowment for the Humanities. Arjun Appadurai, Nicholas B. Dirks, and Elliot Shore read the first draft on short notice, and gave me extremely useful comments. Later drafts were read by Nancy Chodorow, Salvatore Cucchiari, Richard Fox, Abigail Stewart, and Peter van der Veer, all of whom provided excellent insights and suggestions. There was also very constructive and stimulating discussion of the paper in the Thursday night seminar of the Program in the Comparative Study of Social Transformations, which has been both nourishing and provoking me intellectually at the University of Michigan for the past three years.

1. I have laid out in greater detail these transformations in myself and in the field more generally in Ortner (1984). Marcus and Fischer (1986) cover similar ground.

2. I expect the project to have a major historical dimension as well. This is not addressed in the present paper, and the theoretical literature relevant to it is thus not invoked.

3. Ethnographic work by sociologists began to diminish in the 1950s, presumably coinciding with the achievement of hegemony of quantitative research in that field.

4. Schneider and Smith's *Class Differences and Sex Roles in American Kinship and Family Structure* (1973) is one of the rare anthropological works on America with "class" in its title, but it is not a monograph. There are also some older

review articles by Goldschmidt (1950, 1955). A recent review article by Raymond Smith on "Anthropological Studies of Class" (1984) focuses largely on the study of Third World societies.

5. Television sitcoms of both white and black lower-class families ("All in the Family," "Sanford and Sons," etc.) have long followed the tradition of representing both groups as endearing ethnic others.

6. It will be no surprise to the anthropologists that Lloyd Warner, whose work with Australian aborigines focused on kinship terms—that is, on native categories of social relationships—was essentially the founding father of the second—native category—approach.

7. It might be argued that "middle class" is not a class term at all, since it is not generally seen as part of a class *structure*, that is, as a positional or relational category vis-à-vis other classes. In ordinary discourse it seems simply to mean a general allegiance to the nation and to large, overarching values like freedom and individualism.

8. This is the so-called multiple domination position, with which I am in basic agreement. One of the clearest statements of this position is to be found in Cohen (1982). Another version is developed in Laclau and Mouffe (1985). Feminist theory in general also tends toward a multiple domination position; see, for example, Sacks (1989).

9. There is a problem of terminology here. The terms for the lower end of the class structure seem to be racially coded. The term "working class" seems normally to refer to whites. For blacks, one more often sees "lower class." I will use the terms interchangeably for both.

10. There seems to have been more introjection in the nineteenth century, where the split between the middle class and the working class was played out *within* middle-class gender relations (see Smith-Rosenberg 1986).

11. The authors also identify an important ethnographic category: "nobody," as in, "Her? Oh, she's nobody." More work needs to be done on nobodies. For example, the organizers for my high-school reunion did not locate about 50 percent of the addresses in the class. This included all the blacks and virtually all of the non-Jews. It also included some percentage of the Jewish kids, and I suspect that those not located were distinguished from those who were, as "nobodies" are to "somebodies."

12. In Willis's account of the discourse of the nonconformist (i.e., the most "hoody") working-class lads, they claim this greater sexual experience and knowledgeability for themselves, and Willis thinks it is probably true that they have more active sexual lives than the ear'oles.

13. I am indebted to Arjun Appadurai for putting these particular pieces together. Some of my students at Michigan think that this sexual-cum-class division no longer applies, because even middle-class kids are having a lot of sex in high school. Although I accept my students as valid informants, the question needs to be investigated more closely. I suspect that the situation is similar to that described by Eckert in her high-school study with respect to drugs: both middle-

class and working-class kids do drugs, but the use of drugs plays an entirely different role in their respective symbolic economies (Eckert 1989).

14. The phrase is from Claude Lévi-Strauss (1966).

15. A little known but very interesting example is Raymond Sokolov's 1975 novel, *Native Intelligence*.

16. This also suggests that they were socialists, but Roth does not develop the political contrasts in the story.

17. Another painful irony with respect to hidden injuries of class: while the middle class endows the working class with a free and imaginative sexuality, sociologists tell us that sex as actually practiced in the working class is just the opposite: repressed, unimaginative, and—according to informants—largely un-satisfying (see Reiche 1971).

18. I tried to avoid that in my recent study of Sherpa history (Ortner 1989a).

19. After this paper had gone to press, a student brought to my attention the 1990 book by Benjamin DeMott, *The Imperial Middle: Why Americans Can't Think Straight about Class* (New York: William Morrow and Company). As the subtitle indicates, the book makes arguments very similar to those made in this paper. I regret not having had access to it before the paper reached the point of editorial untouchability.

Chapter 10

GLOBAL ETHNOSCAPES

Notes and Queries for a Transnational

Anthropology

Arjun Appadurai

IN my title, I use the term *ethnoscape*. This neologism has certain
ambiguities deliberately built into it. It refers, first, to the dilemmas of
perspective and representation that all ethnographers must confront, and
it admits that (as with landscapes in visual art) traditions of perception
and perspective, as well as variations in the situation of the observer, may
affect the process and product of representation. But I also intend this
term to indicate that there are some brute facts about the world of the
twentieth century that any ethnography must confront. Central among
these facts is the changing social, territorial, and cultural reproduction of
group identity. As groups migrate, regroup in new locations, reconstruct
their histories, and reconfigure their ethnic "projects," the *ethno* in ethnography takes on a slippery, nonlocalized quality, to which the descriptive practices of anthropology will have to respond. The landscapes of
group identity—the ethnoscapes—around the world are no longer familiar anthropological objects, insofar as groups are no longer tightly territorialized, spatially bounded, historically unselfconscious, or culturally
homogenous. We have fewer cultures in the world and more "internal
cultural debates" (Parkin 1978).

By *ethnoscape*, I mean the landscape of persons who make up the shifting world in which we live: tourists, immigrants, refugees, exiles, guestworkers, and other moving groups and persons constitute an essential feature of the world and appear to affect the politics of and between nations to a hitherto unprecedented degree. This is not to say that nowhere are there relatively stable communities and networks of kinship, friendship, work, and leisure, as well as of birth, residence, and other filiative forms. But it is to say that the warp of these stabilities is everywhere shot through with the woof of human motion, as more persons and groups deal with the realities of having to move or the fantasies of wanting to move. What is more, both these realities and these fantasies now function on large scales, as men and women from villages in India think not just of moving to Poona or Madras, but of moving to Dubai and Houston; and refugees from Sri Lanka find themselves in South India as well as in Canada; and the Hmong are driven to London as well as Philadelphia. As the needs of international capital shift, as production and technology generate different consumer needs, as nation-states change their policies on refugee populations, these moving groups can never afford to let their imaginations rest too long, even if they wished to.[1]

In this paper, I seek, through a series of notes, queries, and vignettes, to reposition some of our disciplinary conventions, while trying to show that the ethnoscapes of today's world are profoundly interactive.

ALTERNATIVE MODERNITIES
AND ETHNOGRAPHIC COSMOPOLITANISM

A central challenge for current anthropology is to study the cosmopolitan (Rabinow 1986) cultural forms of the contemporary world without logically or chronologically presupposing either the authority of the Western experience or the models derived from that experience. It seems impossible to fruitfully study these new cosmopolitanisms without analyzing the transnational cultural flows within which they thrive, compete, and feed off one another in ways that defeat and confound many verities of the human sciences today. One such verity concerns the link between space, stability, and cultural reproduction. There is an urgent need to focus on the cultural dynamics of what is now called *deterritorialization*. This term applies not only to obvious examples such as transnational corporations and money markets, but also to ethnic groups, sectarian movements, and political formations, which increasingly operate in ways that transcend specific territorial boundaries and identities. Deterritorialization (of which I offer some ethnographic profiles in another section of this paper) affects the loyalties of groups (especially in the context of complex diasporas), their transnational manipulation of currencies and other forms of wealth and investment, and the strategies of states. The loosening of the bonds between people, wealth, and territories fundamentally alters the basis of cultural reproduction.

Deterritorialization is one of the central forces of the modern world, since it brings laboring populations into the lower-class sectors of relatively wealthy societies, while sometimes creating exaggerated and intensified senses of criticism of, or attachment to, politics in the home state. Deterritorialization, whether of Hindus, Sikhs, Palestinians, or Ukranians, is now at the core of a variety of global fundamentalisms, including Islamic and Hindu fundamentalism. In the Hindu case, for example (Appadurai and Breckenridge: in press), it is clear that the overseas movement of Indians has been exploited by a variety of interests both within and outside India to create a complicated network of finances and religious identifications in which the problem of cultural reproduction for Hindus abroad has become tied to the politics of Hindu fundamentalism at home.

At the same time, deterritorialization creates new markets for film companies, impressarios, and travel agencies, which thrive on the need of the relocated population for contact with its homeland. But the homeland is partly invented, existing only in the imagination of the deterritorialized groups, and it can sometimes become so fantastic and one-sided that it provides the fuel for new ethnic conflicts.

The idea of deterritorialization may also be applied to money and finance, as money managers seek the best markets for their investments, independent of national boundaries. In turn, these movements of monies are the basis of new kinds of conflict, as Log Angelenos worry about the Japanese buying up their city, and people in Bombay worry about the rich Arabs from the Gulf States, who have not only transformed the price of mangos in Bombay but have also substantially altered the profile of hotels, restaurants, and other services in the eyes of the local population—just as they have in London. Yet most residents of Bombay are ambivalent about the Arabs there, for the flip side of their presence is the absent friends and kinsmen earning big money in the Middle East and bringing back both money and luxury commodities to Bombay and other cities in India. Such commodities transform consumer taste in these cities. They often end up smuggled through air- and seaports and peddled in the "gray" markets of Bombay's streets. In these gray markets (a coinage which allows me to capture the quasi-legal characteristic of such settings), some members of Bombay's middle classes and of its lumpen proletariat can buy goods, ranging from cartons of Marlboro cigarettes to Old Spice shaving cream and tapes of Madonna. Similar gray routes, often subsidized by moonlighting sailors, diplomats, and airline stewardesses, who get to move in and out of the country regularly, keep the gray markets of Bombay, Madras, and Calcutta filled with goods not only from the West, but also from the Middle East, Hong Kong, and Singapore. It is also such professional transients who are increasingly implicated in the transnational spread of disease, not the least of which is AIDS.

It is this fertile ground of deterritorialization, in which money, commodities, and persons unendingly chase each other around the world, that the group imaginations of the modern world find their fractured and fragmented counterpart. For the ideas and images produced by mass media often are only partial guides to the goods and experiences that deterritorialized populations transfer to one another. In Mira Nair's brilliant film, *India Cabaret* (discussed in greater detail in another section), we see the multiple loops of this fractured deterritorialization as young women, barely competent in Bombay's metropolitan glitz, come to seek their fortunes there as cabaret dancers and prostitutes, entertaining men in clubs with dance formats derived wholly from the prurient dance sequences of Hindi films. These scenes cater to Indian ideas about Western and foreign women and their "looseness," while dancing provides tawdry career alibis for these girls. Some of these girls come from Kerala, where cabaret clubs and the pornographic film industry have blossomed, partly in response to the purses and tastes of Keralites returned from the Middle East, where their diasporic lives away from women distort their very sense of what the relations between men and women might be. These tragedies of displacement could certainly be replayed in an analysis of the relations between Japanese and German sex tours to Thailand and the tragedies of the sex trade in Bangkok, and in similar loops that tie together fantasies about the Other, the conveniences and seductions of travel, the economics of global trade, and the violent fantasies that dominate gender politics in many parts of Asia and the world at large.

The vision of transnational cultural studies suggested by the discussion so far appears at first sight to involve only modest adjustments of anthropologists' traditional approaches to culture. In my view, however, a genuinely cosmopolitan ethnographic practice requires an interpretation of the terrain of "cultural studies" in the United States today, and of the status of anthropology within such a terrain.[2]

CULTURAL STUDIES IN A GLOBAL TERRAIN

Since this volume concerns anthropologies of the present, it may be important to ask about the status of anthropology in the present and, in particular, about its now-embattled monopoly over the study of "culture" (from now on, without quotation marks). The following discussion sets the stage for the critique of ethnography contained in subsequent sections.

As a topic, culture has many histories, some disciplinary, some that function outside the academy. Within the academy, there are certain differences between disciplines in the degree to which culture has been an explicit topic of investigation, and the degree to which it has been understood tacitly. In the social sciences, anthropology (especially in the United States; less so in England) has made culture its central concept, defining it as some sort of human substance—even though ideas about this substance have shifted, over the course of a century, roughly from Tylorean ideas about custom to Geertzian ideas about meaning. Some anthropologists have worried that the meanings given to culture have been far too diverse for a technical term; others have made a virtue of that diversity. At the same time, the other social sciences have not been unconcerned with culture: in sociology, Max Weber's sense of *verstehen* and Simmel's various ideas have mediated between the German neo-Kantian ideas of the late nineteenth century and sociology as a social science discipline. As in many other cases, culture is now a subfield within sociology, and the American Sociological Association has legitimized this segregation by creating a subunit in "the sociology of culture," where persons concerned with the production and distribution of culture, especially in Western settings, may freely associate with one another.

At the epicenter of current debates in and about culture, many diverse streams flow into a single, rather turbulent river: the many poststructuralisms (largely French) of Lacan, Derrida, Foucault, Bourdieu, and their many subschools. Some of these streams are self-conscious about language as their means and their model, others less so. The current multiplicity of uses that surrounds the three words *meaning, discourse*, and *text* should be sufficient to indicate that we are not only in an era of "blurred genres" (as Geertz [1980] said presciently a decade ago), but we are in a peculiar state that I would like to call "post-blurring," in which ecumenism has—happily in my opinion—given way to sharp debates about the word, the world, and the relationship between them.

In this post-blur blur, it is crucial to note that the high ground has been seized by English literature (as a discipline) in particular and by literary studies in general. This is the nexus where the word "theory," a rather prosaic term in many fields for many centuries, suddenly took on the sexy ring of a trend. For an anthropologist in the United States today, what is most striking about the last decade in the academy is the hijack of culture by literary studies—though we no longer have a one-sided Arnoldian gaze, but a many-sided hijack (where a hundred Blooms flower) with many internal debates about texts and antitexts, reference and structure, theory and practice. Social scientists look on with bewilderment as their colleagues in English and comparative literature talk (and fight) about matters which, until as recently as fifteen years ago, would have seemed about as relevant to English departments as, say, quantum mechanics.

The subject matter of cultural studies could roughly be taken as the relationship between the word and the world. I understand these two terms in their widest sense, so that *word* can encompass all forms of textualized expression, and *world* can mean anything from "the means of production" and the organization of life-worlds to the globalized relations of cultural reproduction discussed in this paper.

Cultural studies, conceived this way, could be the basis for a cosmopolitan (global? macro? translocal?) ethnography. To translate the tension between the word and the world into a productive ethnographic strategy requires a new understanding of the deterritorialized world that many persons inhabit and the possible lives that many persons are today able to envision. The terms of the negotiation between imagined lives and deterritorialized worlds are complex, and they surely cannot be captured by the localizing strategies of traditional ethnography alone. What a new style of ethnography can do is to capture the impact of deterritorialization on the imaginative resources of lived, local experiences. Put another way, the task of ethnography now becomes the unravelling of a conundrum: what is the nature of locality, as a lived experience, in a globalized, deterritorialized world? As I will suggest in the next section, the beginnings of an answer to this conundrum lie in a fresh approach to the role of the imagination in social life.

The master narratives that currently guide much ethnography all have Enlightenment roots, and all have been called into serious question. Foucault's searing critique of Western humanism and its hidden epistemologies has made it difficult to retain much faith in the idea of "progress" in its many old and new manifestations. The master narrative of "evolution," central to anthropology in the United States, suffers from a profound gap between its short-run, culturally oriented versions (as in the work of Marvin Harris) and its long-run, more appealing, but less anthropological versions such as the biogeological fables of Stephen Jay Gould. The "emergence of the individual" as a master narrative suffers not only from the counterexamples of our major twentieth-century totalitarian experiences, but also from the many deconstructions of the idea of self, person, and agency in philosophy, sociology, and anthropology (Parfit 1986; Giddens 1979; Carrithers, Collins, and Lukes 1985). Master narratives of the "iron cage" and the march of bureaucratic rationality are constantly refuted by the irrationalities, contradictions, and sheer brutality increasingly traceable to the pathologies of the modern nation-state (Nandy 1987). Finally, most versions of the Marxist master narrative find themselves embattled as contemporary capitalism takes on an increasingly "disorganized" and deterritorialized look (Lash and Urry 1987) and as cultural expressions refuse to bend to the requirements of even the least parochial Marxist approaches (see the debate between Frederic Jameson and Aijaz Ahmad in *Social Text* [Jameson 1986; Ahmad 1987]).

Cosmopolitan ethnography, or what might be called macroethnography, takes on a special urgency given the ailments of these many post-Enlightenment master narratives. It is difficult to be anything but exploratory about what such a macroethnography (and its ethnoscapes) might look like, but the following section seeks, by illustration, to point to its contours.

IMAGINATION AND ETHNOGRAPHY

We live in a world of many kinds of realism, some magical, some socialist, some capitalist, and some that are yet to be named. These generic realisms have their provinces of origin: magical realism in Latin American fiction in the last two decades; socialist realism in the Soviet Union of the 1930s; and capitalist realism, a term coined by Michael Schudson (1984), in the visual and verbal rhetoric of contemporary American advertising. In much aesthetic expression today, the boundaries between these various realisms have been blurred. The controversies over Salman Rushdie's *The Satanic Verses* (*Public Culture*, vol. 2, fall 1989:2), over the Robert Mapplethorpe photographic exhibition in Cincinnati, and over many other works of art in other parts of the world remind us that artists are increasingly willing to place high stakes on their sense of the boundaries between their art and the politics of public opinion.

More consequential for our purposes is that the imagination has now acquired a singular new power in social life. The imagination—expressed in dreams, songs, fantasies, myths, and stories—has always been part of the repertoire, in some culturally organized way, of every society. But there is a peculiar new force to the imagination in social life today. More persons in more parts of the world consider a wider set of "possible" lives than they ever did before.[3] One important source of this change is the mass media, which present a rich, ever-changing store of possible lives, some of which enter the lived imaginations of ordinary people more successfully than others. Important also are contacts with, news of, and

rumors about others in one's social neighborhood who have become in-
habitants of these faraway worlds. The importance of media is not so
much as direct sources of new images and scenarios for life possibilities,
but as semiotic diacritics of great power, which also inflect social contact
with the metropolitan world facilitated by other channels.

One of the principal shifts in the global cultural order, created by
cinema, television, and VCR technology (and the ways in which they
frame and energize other, older media), has to do with the role of the
imagination in social life. Until recently, whatever the force of social
change, a case could be made that social life was largely inertial, that
traditions provided a relatively finite set of "possible" lives, and that fantasy and imagination were residual practices, confined to special persons
or domains, restricted to special moments or places. In general, they were
antidotes to the finitude of social experience. In the last two decades, as
the deterritorialization of persons, images, and ideas has taken on new
force, this weight has imperceptibly shifted. More persons throughout the
world see their lives through the prisms of the possible lives offered by
mass media in all their forms. That is, fantasy is now a social practice; it
enters, in a host of ways, into the fabrication of social lives for many
people in many societies. I should be quick to note that this is not a
cheerful observation, intended to imply that the world is now a happier
place with more "choices" (in the utilitarian sense) for more people, and
with more mobility and more happy endings.

What is implied is that even the meanest and most hopeless of lives,
the most brutal and dehumanizing of circumstances, the harshest of lived
inequalities is now open to the play of the imagination. Prisoners of con-
science, child laborers, women who toil in the fields and factories of the
world, and others whose lot is harsh no longer see their lives as mere
outcomes of the givenness of things, but often as the ironic compromise
between what they could imagine and what social life will permit. The
biographies of ordinary people, thus, are constructions (or fabrications)
in which the imagination plays an important role. Nor is this role a simple
matter of escape (holding steady the conventions that govern the rest of
social life), for it is in the grinding of gears between unfolding lives and
their imagined counterparts that a variety of "imagined communities"
(Anderson 1983) is formed, communities that generate new kinds of politics, new kinds of collective expression, and new needs for social discipline and surveillance on the part of elites.

All this has many contexts and implications that cannot be pursued
here. But what does it imply for ethnography? It implies that ethnographers can no longer simply be content with the "thickness" they bring to

the local and the particular, nor can they assume that as they approach the local, they approach something more elementary, more contingent, and thus more "real" than life seen in larger-scale perspectives. For what is real about ordinary lives is now real in many ways that range from the sheer contingency of individual lives and the vagaries of competence and talent that distinguish persons in all societies to the "realisms" that individuals are exposed to and draw upon in their ordinary lives.

These complex, partly imagined lives must now form the bedrock of ethnography, at least of the sort of ethnography that wishes to retain a special voice in a transnational, deterritorialized world. For the new power of the imagination in the fabrication of social lives is inescapably tied up with images, ideas, and opportunities that come from elsewhere, often moved around by the vehicles of mass media. Thus, standard cultural reproduction (like standard English) is now an endangered activity that succeeds only by conscious design and political will, where it succeeds at all. Indeed, where insulation from the larger world seems to have been successful, and the role of the global imagination withheld from ordinary people—in places like Albania, North Korea, and Burma—what seems to appear instead is a bizarre state-sponsored realism, which always contains within it the possibility of the genocidal and totalizing lunacies of a Pol Pot or of long-repressed desires for critique or exit, as are emerging in Albania and Myanmar (Burma) as this paper is being written.

The issue, therefore, is not how ethnographic writing can draw on a wider range of literary models, models which too often elide the distinction between the life of fiction and the fictionalization of lives, but to figure out a way in which the role of the imagination in social life can be described in a new sort of ethnography that is not so resolutely localizing. There is, of course, much to be said for the local, the particular, and the contigent, which have always been the forte of ethnographic writing at its best. But where lives are being imagined partly in and through "realisms" that must be in one way or another official or large scale in their inspiration, then the ethnographer needs to find new ways to represent the links between the imagination and social life. This problem of representation is not quite the same as the familiar problem of micro and macro, small and large scale, though it has important connections to it. The connection between the problem of ethnographically representing imagined lives and of making the move from local realities to large-scale structures is implicit in Sherry Ortner's paper in this volume. Taken together, Ortner's argument and mine point to the importance of embedding large-scale realities in concrete life-worlds, but they also open up the possibility of divergent interpretations of what "locality" implies.

The link between the imagination and social life, I would suggest, is increasingly a global and deterritorialized one. Thus, those who represent "real" or "ordinary" lives must resist making claims to epistemic privilege in regard to the lived particularities of social life. Rather, ethnography must redefine itself as that practice of representation which illuminates the power of large-scale, imagined life possibilities over specific life trajectories. This is "thickness" with a difference, and the difference lies in a new alertness to the fact that ordinary lives today are increasingly powered not by the givenness of things but by the possibilities that the media (either directly or indirectly) suggest are available. Put another way, some of the force of Bourdieu's idea of the "habitus" can be retained (Bourdieu 1977), but the stress must be put on his idea of improvisation, for improvisation no longer occurs within a relatively bounded set of thinkable postures, but is always skidding and taking off, powered by the imagined vistas of mass-mediated master narratives. There has been a general change in the global conditions of life-worlds: put simply, where once improvisation was snatched out of the glacial undertow of habitus, habitus now has to be painstakingly reinforced in the face of life-worlds that are frequently in flux.

Three examples will suggest something of what I have in mind. In January 1988, my wife (who is a white American historian of India) and I (a Tamil Brahman male, brought up in Bombay and turned into *Homo academicus* in the United States), along with our son, six members of my eldest brother's family, and an entourage of his colleagues and employees, decided to visit the Meenaksi Temple in Madurai, one of the great pilgrimage centers of South India. My wife has done research there, off and on, for the last two decades.

Our purposes in going were various. My brother and his wife were worried about the marriage of their eldest daughter and were concerned to have the good wishes of as many powerful deities as possible in their search for a good marriage alliance. For my brother, Madurai was a special place, since he spent most of his first twenty years there with my mother's extended family. He thus had old friends and memories in all the streets around the temple. Now he had come to Madurai as a senior railway official, with business to conduct with several private businessmen who wished to persuade him of the quality of their bids. Indeed, one of these potential clients had arranged for us to be accommodated in a garish "modern" hotel in Madurai, a stone's throw from the temple, and drove him around in a Mercedes, while the rest of us took in our own Madurai.

Our eleven-year-old son, fresh from Philadelphia, knew he was in the presence of the practices of heritage and dove to the ground manfully, in the Hindu practice of prostration before elders and deities, whenever he was asked. He put up graciously with the incredible noise, crowding, and sensory rush that a major Hindu temple involves. For myself, I was there to embellish my brother's entourage, to add some vague moral force to their wishes for a happy marriage for their daughter, to reabsorb the city in which my mother grew up (I had been there several times before), to share in my wife's excitement about returning to a city and a temple that are possibly the most important parts of her imagination, and to fish for cosmopolitanism in the raw.

So we entered the fourteen-acre temple compound, an important entourage, though one among many, and were soon approached by one of the several priests who officiate there. This one recognized my wife, who asked him where Thangam Bhattar was. Thangam Bhattar was the priest she had been closest to and with whom she had worked most closely. The answer was "Thangam Bhattar is in Houston." This punch line took us all a while to absorb, and then it all came together in a flash. The Indian community in Houston, like many communities of Asian Indians in the United States, had built a Hindu temple, this one devoted to Meenaksi, the ruling deity in Madurai. Thangam Bhattar had been persuaded to go there, leaving his family behind. He leads a lonely life in Houston, assisting in the complex cultural politics of reproduction in an overseas Indian community, presumably earning some dollars, while his wife and children stay on in their small home near the temple. The next morning, my wife and niece visited Thangam Bhattar's home, where they were told of his travails in Houston, and they told the family what had gone on with us in the intervening years. There is a transnational irony here, of course: Carol Breckenridge, American historian, arrives in Madurai waiting with bated breath to see her closest informant and friend, a priest, and discovers that he is in faraway Houston, which is far away even from faraway Philadelphia.

But this transnational irony has many threads that unwind backward and forward in time to large and fluid structures of meaning and of communication. Among these threads are my brother's hopes for his daughter, who subsequently married a Ph.D. candidate in physical chemistry in an upstate New York university and recently came to Syracuse herself; my wife's recontextualizing of her Madurai experiences in a world that, at least for some its central actors, now includes Houston; and my own realization that Madurai's historical cosmopolitanism has acquired a new global dimension, and that some key lives that constitute the heart of the temple's ritual practices now have Houston in their imagined biographies.

Each of these threads could and should be unwound. They lead to an understanding of the globalization of Hinduism, the transformation of "natives" into cosmopolites of their own sort, and the fact that the temple is now not only a magnet for persons from all over the world but also itself reaches out. The goddess Meenaksi has a living presence in Houston.

Our son, meanwhile, has in his repertoire of experiences a journey of the "roots" variety. He may remember this, as he fabricates his own life as an American of partly Indian descent. But he may remember more vividly his sudden need to go to the bathroom while we were going from sanctum to sanctum in a visit to another major temple in January 1989, and the bathroom at the guesthouse of a charitable foundation in which he found blissful release. But here too is an unfinished story, which involves the dynamics of family, of memory, and of tourism, for an eleven-year-old hyphenated American who has to go periodically to India, whether he likes it or not, and encounter the many webs of shifting biography that he encounters there. This account, like the ones that follow, needs not only to be thickened but to be stirred, but it must serve for now as one glimpse of an ethnography that focuses on the unyoking of imagination from place.

My second vignette comes from a collection of pieces of one kind of magical realism, a book by Julio Cortázar called *A Certain Lucas* (1984). Since there has been much borrowing of literary models and metaphors in recent anthropology, but relatively little anthropology of literature, a word about this choice of example seems appropriate. Fiction, like myth, is part of the conceptual repertoire of contemporary societies. Readers of novels and poems can be moved to intense action (as with *The Satanic Verses* of Salman Rushdie), and their authors often contribute to the construction of social and moral maps for their readers. Even more relevant for my purposes, prose fiction is the exemplary province of the post-Renaissance imagination, and in this regard it is central to a more general ethnography of the imagination. Even small fragments of fantasy, such as Cortázar constructs in this brief story, show the contemporary imagination at work.

Magical realism is interesting not only as a literary genre but also as a representation of how the world appears to some people who live in it (for an interesting commentary on one aspect of this approach to literary narrative, see Felman 1989). Cortázar is doubtless a unique person, and not everyone imagines the world his way, but his vision is surely part of the evidence that the globe has begun to spin in new ways. Like the myths of small-scale society, as rendered in the anthropological classics of the past, contemporary literary fantasies tell us something about displace-

ment, disorientation, and agency in the contemporary world (for an excellent recent example of this approach, in the context of cultural studies,
see Rosaldo 1989: chapter 7).

Since we have now learned a great deal about the writing of ethnography (Clifford and Marcus 1986; Marcus and Fischer 1986; Geertz
1988), we are in a strong position to move to an anthropology of representation that would profit immensely from our recent discoveries about
the politics and poetics of "writing culture." In this view, we can restore
to the recent critiques of ethnographic practice the lessons of earlier critiques of anthropology as a field of practices operating within a larger
world of institutional policies and power (viz., Hymes 1969).

The Cortázar story in question, which is both more light-handed and
more heavy-hitting than some other, larger chunks of magical realism, is
called "Swimming in a Pool of Gray Grits." It concerns the discovery in
1964, by a certain Professor José Migueletes, of a swimming pool in
which, instead of water, there are gray grits. This discovery is quickly
taken note of in the world of sports, and, at the Ecological Games in
Baghdad, the Japanese champion, Akiro Tashuma, breaks the world record by "swimming five meters in one minute and four seconds" (Cortázar
1984:80). Corázar's piece goes on to speak of how Tashuma solved the
technical problem of breathing in this semisolid medium. The press then
enters the picture, and here is the rest of the vignette (pp. 82–83), in
Cortázar's own irreducibly spare words:

> Asked about the reasons why many international athletes show
> an ever-growing proclivity for swimming in grits, Tashuma would
> only answer that after several millenia it has finally been proven
> that there is a certain monotony in the act of jumping into the
> water and coming out all wet without anything having changed
> very much in the sport. He let it be understood that the imagi-
> nation is slowly coming into power and that it's time now to apply
> revolutionary forms to old sports whose only incentive is to lower
> records by fractions of a second, when that can be done, which
> is quite rare. He modestly declared himself unable to suggest
> equivalent discoveries for soccer and tennis, but he did make an
> oblique reference to a new development in sports, mentioning a
> glass ball that may have been used in a basketball game in Naga,
> and whose accidental but always possible breakage brought on
> the act of hara-kiri by the whole team whose fault it was. Every-
> thing can be expected of Nipponese culture, especially if it sets
> out to imitate the Mexican. But to limit ourselves to the West and

to grits, this last item has begun to demand higher prices, to the particular delight of countries that produce it, all of them in the Third World. The death by asphyxiation of seven Australian children who tried to practice fancy dives in the new pool in Canberra demonstrates, however, the limitations of this interesting product, the use of which should not be carried too far when amateurs are involved.

Now this is a very funny parable, and it could be read at many levels, from many points of view. For my purposes, I note first that it is written by an Argentine, born in Brussels, who lived in Paris from 1952 until his death in 1984. The link between magical realism and the self-imposed exile in Paris of many of its finest voices deserves further exploration—but what else does this vignette have to offer for the study of the new ethnoscapes of the contemporary world? The story is partly about a crazy invention that captures the faraway imagination of Tashuma, a person who believes that "the imagination is slowly coming into power." It is also about the transnational journey of ideas that may begin as playful meditations and end up as bizarre technical realities that can result in death. Here one if forced to think about the trajectory of *The Satanic Verses*, which began as a satiric meditation on good, evil, and Islam, and ended up a weapon in group violence in many parts of the world.[4]

The vignette is also about the internationalization of sport, and about the spiritual exhaustion that comes from technical obsession with small differences in performance. Different actors can bring their "imaginations" to bear on the problem of sport in different ways. The Olympic Games of the past are full of incidents that reveal complex ways in which individuals situated within specific national and cultural trajectories imposed their imaginations on global audiences. In Seoul in 1988, the defeated Korean boxer who sat in the ring for several hours to publically proclaim his shame as a Korean, and the Korean officials who swarmed into the ring to assault a New Zealand referee for what they thought was a biased decision, were bringing their imagined lives to bear on the official Olympic narratives of fair play, good sportsmanship, and clean competition. The whole question of steroids, including the case of Ben Johnson, the Canadian runner (see MacAloon 1990), is also not far from the technical absurdities of Cortázar's story, in which the body is manipulated to yield new results in a world of competitive and commoditized spectacle. The vision of seven Australian children diving into a pool of grits and dying also deserves to be drawn out into the many stories of individual abnegation and physical abuse that sometimes power the spectacles of global sport.

Cortázar is also meditating on the problems of imitation and cultural transfer, suggesting that they can lead to violent and culturally peculiar innovations. The adjective "cultural" appears gratuitous here, and needs some justification. That Tokyo and Canberra, Baghdad and Mexico City are all involved in the story does not mean that they have become fungible pieces of an arbitrarily shifting, delocalized world. Each of these places does have complex local realities, such that death in a swimming pool has one kind of meaning in Canberra, as do hosting large spectacles in Iraq and making bizarre technical innovations in Japan. Whatever Cortázar's idea about these differences, they remain cultural, but no longer in the inertial mode that the word previously implied. Culture does imply difference, but the differences now are no longer, if you wish, taxonomical; they are interactive and refractive, so that competing for a swimming championship takes on the peculiar power that it does in Canberra partly because of the way some transnational forces have come to be configured in the imagination of its residents. Culture thus shifts from being some sort of inert, local substance to being a rather more volatile form of difference. This is an important part of the reason for writing *against* culture, as Lila Abu-Lughod suggests in her paper in this volume.

There are surely other macronarratives that spin out of this small piece of magical realism, but all of them remind us that lives today are as much acts of projection and imagination as they are enactments of known scripts or predictable outcomes. In this sense, all lives have something in common with international athletic spectacle, as guestworkers strive to meet standards of efficiency in new national settings, and brides who marry into households at large distances from home strive to meet the criteria of hypercompetence which these new contexts often demand. The deterritorialized world in which many people now live—some moving in it actively, others living with their absences or sudden returns—is, like Cortázar's pool of grits, ever thirsty for new technical competences and often harsh with the unprepared. Cortázar's vignette is itself a compressed ethnographic parable, and in teasing out the possible histories of its protagonists and their possible futures, our own ethnographies of literature can become exercises in the interpretation of the new role of the imagination in social life. There is in such efforts a built-in reflexive vertigo, as we contemplate Cortázar inventing Tashuma, but such reflexivity leads not only into reflections on our own representational practices, as writers, but also into the complex nesting of imaginative appropriations that are involved in the construction of agency in a deterritorialized world.

But not all deterritorialization is global in its scope, and not all imagined lives span vast international panoramas. The world on the move affects even small geographical and cultural spaces. In several different ways, contemporary cinema represents these small worlds of displacement. Mira Nair's films capture the texture of these small displacements, whose reverberations can nevertheless be large. One of them, *India Cabaret*, is what I have called an ethnodrama.[5] Made in 1984, it tells about a small group of women who have left towns and villages, generally in the southern part of India, to come to Bombay and work as cabaret dancers in a seedy suburban bar-nightclub called the Meghraj.

The film contains (in the style of the early Godard) extended conversations between the filmmaker and a few of these women, who are presented facing the camera, as if they are talking to the viewer of the film. These interview segments, which are richly narrative, are intercut with dance sequences from the cabaret and with extended treatments of the sleazy paradoxes of the lives of some of the men who are regulars there. The film also follows one of the women back to her natal village, where we are shown the pain of her ostracism, since her occupation in Bombay is known to everyone. It is rumored that this scene was staged (replayed) for the benefit of the filmmaker, but if anything this replay adds to the awkwardness and pain of the sequence. The film is not about happy endings, and it leaves us with possibilities of various sorts in the lives of these women, all of whom are simultaneously proud and ashamed, dignified and defiant, de facto prostitutes who have fabricated identities as artists.

For the present purposes, what is most important about this film is the way in which it shows that the cabaret club is not simply a marketplace for desire but also a place where imagined lives are negotiated: the dancers act out their precarious sense of themselves as dancers; the second-rate band tries to work up its musical passions, which are fed by the aspiration of the Catholic community in Goa (western India) to play European and American instrumental music well. The men who come as customers clearly see themselves as participants in something larger than life, and they behave exactly like the customers in cabaret scenes in many Hindi commercial films. In fact, the scenario that provides the meeting ground for all these characters is provided by the cabaret sequences from Hindi commercial cinema.

In many such stock scenes, a tawdry nightclub quartet plays an oppressively sensuous melody, combining Western and Indian instruments and tonalities, while the villain and his cronies consume obviously nasty alcoholic drinks and watch a painfully explicit dance routine by a vamp-star. The hero is usually insinuated into the action in some way that simultaneously emphasizes his virility and his moral superiority over the tawdry environment. These scenes are usually filled with extras from the film studio, who struggle to maintain the sophisticated visage of persons

habituated to the high life. All in all, these scenes are stereotypically vi-
carious in their approach to drink, dance, and sound, and are somehow
depressing. The clients, the dancers, and the band at the Meghraj seem to
play out a slightly out-of-step, somnambulistic version of such classic
Hindi film sequences.

Life in the Meghraj is surely driven by commercial cinematic images,
but their force is inadequate to cover the anxieties, the self-abasement,
and the agonized drama of leisure in which the characters are all engaged.
Yet the characters in this ethnodrama have images and ideas of themselves
that are not simply contingent outcomes of their "ordinary" lives (or
simple escapes from them), but are fabrications based on a subtle complicity with the discursive and representational conventions of the Hindi
cinema.

Thus, though this film is a documentary in conventional terms, it is
also an ethnodrama, in the sense that it shows us the dramatic structure
and the characters that animate a particular strand of Bombay's ways of
life. These "actors" are also "characters," not so much because they have
obvious idiosyncracies attached to them but because they are fabrications
negotiated in the encounter between the efforts of cinema to represent
cabaret and of "real" cabarets to capture the excitement of cinema. It is
this negotiation, not only the negotiation of bodies, that is the real order
of business at the Meghraj. The women who work in the cabaret are deterritorialized and mobile: if you wish, they are guestworkers in Bombay.
It is hard to see in them the discourse of resistance (though they are
cynical about men, as prostitutes everywhere are), although their very
bodily postures, their linguistic aggressiveness, their bawdy, quasi-lesbian
play with each other does imply a kind of raunchy and self-conscious
counterculture. What we have is a sense that they are putting lives together, fabricating their own characters, using the cinematic and social
materials at their disposal.

There are individuals here, to be sure, and agency as well, but what
drives these individuals and their agency are the complex realisms that
animate them: a crude realism about men and their motives; a sort of
capitalist realism that animates their discourse about wealth and money;
a curious socialist realism that underlies their own categorizations of
themselves as dignified workers in the flesh trade, not very different from
the housewives of Bombay. They constitute a striking ethnographic example for this essay because the very displacement that is the root of their
problems (though their original departures turn out usually to be responses to even worse domestic horrors) is also the engine of their dreams
of wealth, of respectability, of autonomy.

Thus, pasts in these constructed lives are as important as futures, and the more we unravel these pasts, the closer we approach worlds that are less and less cosmopolitan, more and more local. Yet even the most local-ized of these worlds, at least in societies like India, has become inflected, even afflicted, by cosmopolitan scripts that drive the politics of families, the frustrations of laborers, the dreams of local headmen. Once again, we need to be careful not to suppose that as we work backward in these imagined lives, we will hit some local, cultural bedrock, constituted of a closed set of reproductive practices, untouched by rumors of the world at large (for a different, but complementary, angle on these facts, see Han-nerz 1989). Mira Nair's *India Cabaret* is a brilliant model of how ethnog-raphy in a deterritorialized world might handle the problems of "character" and "actor," for it shows how self-fabrication actually proceeds in a world of types and typification. It retains the tension between global and local that drives cultural reproduction today.

The vignettes I have used in this section have two purposes. One is to suggest the sorts of situations in which the workings of the imagination in a deterritorialized world can be detected. The second is to suggest that many lives are now inextricably linked with representations, and thus we need to incorporate the complexities of expressive representation (film, novels, travel accounts) into our ethnographies, not only as technical ad-juncts but as primary material with which to construct and interrogate our own representations.

CONCLUSION: INVITATIONS AND EXHORTATIONS

Although the emergent cosmopolitanisms of the world have complex local histories, and their translocal dialogue has a complex history as well (Is-lamic pilgrimage is just one example), it seems advisable to treat the pres-ent as a historical moment and use our understanding of it to illuminate and guide the formulation of historical problems. This is not perverse Whiggishness; it is rather a response to a practical problem: in many cases it is simply not clear at present how or where one would locate a chrono-logical baseline for the phenomena we wish to study. The strategy of "beginning at the beginning" becomes even more self-defeating when one wishes to illuminate the lived relationships between imagined lives and the webs of cosmopolitanism within which they unfold. Thus, not to put too fine a point on it, we need an ethnography that is sensitive to the historical nature of what we see today (which also involves careful com-parison, as every good historian knows), but I suggest that we cut into the problem through the historical present.

While much has been written about the relationship between history and anthropology (by practitioners of both disciplines) in the last decade, few have given careful thought to what it means to construct genealogies of the present. Especially in regard to the many alternative cosmopolitanisms that characterize the world today, and the complex, transnational cultural flows that link them, there is no easy way to "begin at the beginning." Today's cosmopolitanisms combine experiences of various media with various forms of experience—cinema, video, restaurants, spectator sports, and tourism, to name just a few—that have different national and transnational genealogies. Some of these forms may start out as extremely global and end up as very local—radio would be an example—while others, such as cinema, might have the obverse trajectory. In any particular ethnoscape (a term we might wish to substitute for earlier "wholes" such as villages, communities, and localities), the genealogies of cosmopolitanism are not likely to be the same as its histories: while the genealogies reveal the cultural spaces within which new forms can become indigenized (viz., tourism comes to inhabit the space of pilgrimage in India), the histories of these forms may lead outward to transnational sources and structures. Thus, the most appropriate ethnoscapes for today's world, with its alternative, interactive modernities, should confront genealogy and history with each other, thus leaving the terrain open for interpretations of the ways in which local historical trajectories flow into complicated transnational structures. Of course, this dialogue of histories and genealogies itself has a history, but for this latter history, we surely do not yet possess a master narrative. For those of us who might wish to move toward this new master narrative, whatever its form, new global ethnoscapes must be the critical building blocks. Michel-Rolph Trouillot, in chapter 2 of this volume, suggests that the historical role of anthropology was to fill the "savage slot" in an internal Western dialogue about utopia. A recuperated anthropology must recognize that the genie is now out of the bottle, and that speculations about utopia are everyone's prerogative. Anthropology can surely contribute its special purchase on lived experience to a wider, transdisciplinary study of global cultural processes. But to do this, anthropology must first come in from the cold and face the challenge of making a contribution to cultural studies without the benefit of its previous principal source of leverage—sightings of the savage.

─────── *Notes* ───────

An earlier version of this paper was presented at the advanced seminar on "Representing Anthropology" at the School of American Research. This considerably revised version is a response, partly indirect, to the many important issues raised there, to critical readings of a subsequent draft by Carol Breckenridge and Sherry Ortner, and to several suggestive observations by Richard Fox.

1. These ideas about the cultural economy of a world in motion, as well as the logic of terms such as "ethnoscape," are more fully developed in Appadurai (1990).

2. This is not the place for an extended review of the emergent field of cultural studies. Its British lineages are carefully explored in Hall (1986) and Johnson (1986). But it is clear that this British tradition, associated largely with the now-diasporic Birmingham school, is taking new forms in the United States, as it comes into contact with American cultural anthropology, the new historicism, and language and media studies in the American tradition.

3. This theme, as well as a series of related ideas, is more fully developed in a book in progress, *Imploding Worlds: Imagination and Disjuncture in the Global Cultural Economy*, which I am writing with Carol Breckenridge.

4. The Rushdie controversy is well on its way to becoming an industry. Some of the issues in this controversy are touched on in *Public Culture*, vol. 1, no. 2, and are followed up in a special section devoted to the Rushdie debate in *Public Culture*, vol. 2, no. 1, fall 1989).

5. The following discussion draws heavily on Appadurai and Breckenridge (in press).

REFERENCES

Abu-Lughod, Janet
  1989 *Before European Hegemony*. New York: Oxford University Press.
Abu-Lughod, Lila
  1986 *Veiled Sentiments: Honor and Poetry in a Bedouin Society*. New York: Oxford University Press.
  1988 Constructions of sexuality: public and private in Bedouin weddings. Paper presented at the conference, "Feminist Perspectives on Women in the Arabo-Islamic Culture," Cornell University.
  1989 Zones of theory in the anthropology of the Arab world. *Annual Review of Anthropology* 18:276–306.
  1990a Can there be feminist ethnography? *Women and Performance: A Journal of Feminist Theory* 5:7–27.
  1990b Shifting politics in Bedouin love poetry. In *Language and the Politics of Emotion*. C. Lutz and L. Abu-Lughod, eds. New York: Cambridge University Press.
  in press *Writing Women's Worlds*. Berkeley: University of California Press.
  n.d. Islam and the discourses of death. Unpublished manuscript.
Abu-Lughod, Lila, and Catherine Lutz
  1990 Introduction: discourse, emotion, and the politics of everyday life. In

Language and the Politics of Emotion. New York: Cambridge University Press.

Aguilar, John L.
1981 Insider research: an ethnography of a debate. In *Anthropologists at Home in North America: Methods and Issues in the Study of One's Own Society*, pp. 15–26. New York: Cambridge University Press.

Ahmad, Aijaz
1987 Jameson's rhetoric of otherness and the "National Allegory." *Social Text* 17:3–25.

Aijmer, Goran
1988 Comment in "Rhetoric and the authority of ethnography: 'postmodernism' and the social reproduction of texts," by P. Steven Sangren. *Current Anthropology* 29 (3):405–35.

Ainsa, Fernando
1988 L'invention de l'Amérique: signes imaginaires de la découverte et construction de l'utopie. *Diogènes* 145:104–117.

Altorki, Soraya, and Camillia El-Solh
1988 *Arab Women in the Field: Studying Your Own Society*. Syracuse, NY: Syracuse University Press.

Anderson, Benedict
1983 *Imagined Communities: Reflections on the Origin and Spread of Nationalism*. London: Verso.

André-Vincent, Philippe
1980 *Bartholomé de Las Casas, prophète du nouveau-monde*. Paris: Librarie Jules Tallandier.

Andrews, Charles M.
1937 Introduction. In *Famous Utopias*. New York: Tudor Publishing.

Appadurai, Arjun
1988 Putting hierarchy in its place. *Cultural Anthropology* 3:36–49.
1990 Disjuncture and difference in the global cultural economy. *Public Culture* 2(2):1–24.

Appadurai, Arjun, and Carol Breckenridge
in press. Marriage, migration and money: Mira Nair's cinema of displacement. *Visual Anthropology*.
in press. *A Transnational Culture in the Making: The Asian-Indian Diaspora in the United States*. London: Berg Press.

Applebaum, Herbert
1981 *Royal Blue: The Culture of Construction Workers*. New York: Holt, Rinehart, Winston.

Arac, Jonathan
1986 Introduction. In *Post-Modernism and Politics*. J. Arac, ed., pp. ix–xiii. Minneapolis: University of Minnesota Press.
1989 *Critical Genealogies: Historical Situations for Postmodern Literary Studies*. New York: Columbia University Press.

Arens, William
1979   *The Man-Eating Myth: Anthropology and Anthropophagy.* New York: Oxford University Press.
Arens, William, and Susan P. Montague, eds.
1976   *The American Dimension: Cultural Myths and Social Realities.* Port Washington, NY: Alfred Publishing Co.
Aronowitz, Stanley
1988   Post-modernism and politics. In *Universal Abandon? The Politics of Post-Modernism,* A. Ross, ed., pp. 46–62. Minneapolis: University of Minnesota Press.
Asad, Talal
1973   *Anthropology and the Colonial Encounter.* London: Ithaca Press.
1983   Anthropological conceptions of religion: reflections on Geertz. *Man* 18:237–59.
Ashmore, Malcolm
1988   The life and opinions of a replication claim: reflexivity and symmetry in the sociology of scientific knowledge. In *Knowledge and Reflexivity: New Frontiers in the Sociology of Knowledge.* S. Woolgar, ed., pp. 125–53. London: Sage Publications.
1989   *The Reflexive Thesis: Writing the Sociology of Scientific Knowledge.* Chicago: University of Chicago Press.
Atkinson, Geoffroy
1920   *The Extraordinary Voyage in French Literature Before 1700.* New York: Columbia University Press.
1922   *The Extraordinary Voyage in French Literature from 1700 to 1720.* Paris: Librarie Ancienne Edouard Champion.
1924   *Les relations de voyage du XVIIe siècle et l'évolution des idées.* Paris: Librarie Ancienne Edouard Champion.
Atkinson, Paul
1988   Ethnomethodology: a critical review. *Annual Reviews of Sociology* 14:441–65.
Barnes, Barry
1978   *Interests and the Growth of Knowledge.* London: Routledge and Kegan Paul.
1981a On the "hows" and "whys" of cultural change (response to Woolgar). *Social Studies of Science* 11:481–98.
1981b On the conventional character of knowledge and cognition. *Philosophy of the Social Sciences* 11:303–33.
Barnes, Barry, and David Bloor
1982   Relativism, rationalism and the sociology of knowledge. In *Rationality and Relativism.* M. Hollis and S. Lukes, eds., pp. 21–47. Oxford: Blackwell.
Barnes, Barry, and John Law
1976   Whatever should be done with indexical expressions? *Theory and Society* 3:223–37.

Barton, Roy Franklin
  1919   *Ifugao Law.* Reprint edition, 1969. Berkeley: University of California
         Press.
Baudet, Henri
  1959   *Some Thoughts on European Images of Non-European Man.* Reprint edi-
         tion, 1965. New Haven: Yale University Press.
Belenky, Mary, Blithe Clinchy, Nancy Goldberger, and Jill Tarule
  1986   *Women's Ways of Knowing.* New York: Basic Books.
Bell, Diane
  1983   *Daughters of the Dreaming.* Melbourne: McPhee Gribble/N. Sydney:
         George Allen & Unwin.
Bellow, Saul
  1975   *Humboldt's Gift.* New York: Viking Press.
Benson, Douglas, and John A. Hughes
  1983   *The Perspective of Ethnomethodology.* London: Longman.
Benveniste, Emile
  1969   *Le vocabulaire des institutions indo-européenes.* Paris: Editions de Minuit.
Berman, Marshall
  1982   *All that Is Solid Melts into Air.* New York: Simon and Schuster.
Bernal, Martin
  1987   *Black Athena: The Afroasiatic Roots of Classical Civilization, vol. 1, The
         Fabrication of Ancient Greece 1785–1985.* New Brunswick: Rutgers Uni-
         versity Press.
Bhaskar, Roy
  1979   *The Possibility of Naturalism.* Atlantic Highlands, NJ: Humanities Press.
Bilmes, Jack
  1976   Rules and rhetoric: negotiating the social order in a Thai village. *Jour-
         nal of Anthropological Research* 32:44–57.
Bloom, Harold
  1973   *The Anxiety of Influence: A Theory of Poetry.* New York: Oxford Univer-
         sity Press.
  1975   *A Map of Misreading.* New York: Oxford University Press.
Bloom, Howard
  1989   The importance of hugging. *Omni* 11(5):30, 116.
Bloor, David C.
  1976   *Knowledge and Social Imagery.* London: Routledge and Kegan Paul.
Boas, Franz
  1888   The aims of ethnography. In *Race, Language, and Culture,* pp. 626–38.
         Reprint edition, 1940. New York: MacMillan.
  1908   Decorative designs of Alaskan needlecases: a study in the history of
         conventional designs, based on materials in the US National Museum.
         In *Race, Language, and Culture,* pp. 564–92. Reprint edition, 1940.
         New York: Macmillan.
  1920   The methods of ethnology. *American Anthropologist* 22:311–21.

1927   *Primitive Art.* Oslo: Institute for Sammenlignende Kulturforskning.

1928   *Anthropology and Modern Life.* Reprint edition, 1962. New York: Norton.

Bowen, Elenore S.

1954   *Return to Laughter.* Reprint edition, 1964. Garden City, NY: Anchor Books.

Bourdieu, Pierre

1977   *Outline of a Theory of Practice.* Trans. R. Nice. Cambridge: Cambridge University Press.

1984   *Distinction: A Social Critique of the Judgement of Taste.* Trans. R. Nice. Cambridge, MA: Harvard University Press.

1989   Social space and symbolic power. *Sociological Theory* 7: 14–24.

Brannigan, Augustine

1981   *The Social Basis of Scientific Discoveries.* Cambridge: Cambridge University Press.

Brewer, David

1985   Diderot et l'autre feminin. In *L'Homme des Lumières et la découverte de l'autre.* D. Droixhe and P. Gossiaux, eds., pp. 81–91. Bruxelles: Editions de l'Université de Bruxelles.

Briggs, Jean

1970   *Never in Anger.* Cambridge, MA: Harvard University Press.

Burke, Peter

1980   *Sociology and History.* London: George Allen and Unwin.

Butler, Marilyn

1982   *Romantics, Rebels and Reactionaries: English Literature and its Background, 1760–1830.* Oxford: Oxford University Press.

1989   Repossessing the past: the case for an open literary history. In *Rethinking Historicism: Critical Readings in Romantic History.* M. Levinson, M. Butler, J. McGann, and P. Hamilton. Oxford: Basil Blackwell.

Caplan, Pat

1988   Engendering knowledge: the politics of ethnography. *Anthropology Today* 4(5):8–12.

Carrithers, Michael

1988   The anthropologist as author: Geertz's "Works and Lives." *Anthropology Today* 4(4):19–22.

Carrithers, M., S. Collins, and S. Lukes, eds.

1985   *The Category of the Person.* Cambridge: Cambridge University Press.

Cesara, Manda

1982   *Reflections of a Woman Anthropologist: No Hiding Place.* London and New York: Academic Press.

Childe, V. Gordon

1936   *Man Makes Himself.* Reprint edition, 1951. New York: Mentor Books.

Chinard, Gilbert

1934   *L'amérique et le rêve exotique dans la littérature française aux XVIIe et XVIII siècles.* Paris: Librairie de Medicis.

Chodorow, Nancy

1978   *The Reproduction of Mothering*. Berkeley: University of California Press.

Cixous, Helene

1983   The laugh of the Medusa. In *The Signs Reader*. K. Cohen and P. Cohen, trans., E. Abel and E. Abe, eds., pp. 279–97. Chicago: University of Chicago Press.

Clausewitz, Carl von

1968   *On War*. A. Rapoport, ed. Baltimore: Penguin Books.

Clifford, James

1980   Review of "Orientalism," by Edward Said. *History and Theory* 19: 204–23.

1983a Power in dialogue in ethnography. In *Observers Observed: Essays on Ethnographic Fieldwork*. G. W. Stocking, Jr., ed., pp. 121–56. Madison: University of Wisconsin Press.

1983b On ethnographic authority. *Representations* 1(2):118–46.

1986a Introduction: partial truths. In *Writing Culture: The Poetics and Politics of Ethnography*. J. Clifford and G. Marcus, eds., pp. 1–26. Berkeley: University of California Press.

1986b On ethnographic allegory. In *Writing Culture: The Poetics and Politics of Ethnography*. J. Clifford and G. Marcus, eds., pp. 98–121. Berkeley: University of California Press.

1988a On collecting art and culture. In *The Predicament of Culture: Twentieth-Century Ethnography, Literature, and Art*. James Clifford, pp. 215–51. Cambridge, MA: Harvard University Press.

1988b On ethnographic self fashioning. In *The Predicament of Culture: Twentieth-Century Ethnography, Literature, and Art*. James Clifford, pp. 92–113. Cambridge, MA: Harvard University Press.

1988c *The Predicament of Culture: Twentieth-Century Ethnography, Literature, and Art*. James Clifford. Cambridge, MA: Harvard University Press.

Clifford, James, and George E. Marcus, eds.

1986   *Writing Culture: The Poetics and Politics of Ethnography*. Berkeley: University of California Press.

Cohen, A. P., and J. L. Comaroff

1976   The management of meaning: on the phenomenology of political transactions. In *Transaction and Meaning*. B. Kapferer, ed., pp. 87–107. Philadelphia: Institute for the Study of Human Issues.

Cohen, Jean L.

1982   *Class and Civil Society: The Limits of Marxian Critical Theory*. Amherst, MA: University of Massachusetts Press.

Coleman, Richard P., and Les Rainwater

1978   *Social Standing in America: New Dimensions of Class*. New York: Basic Books.

Collini, Stefan

1978   Sociology and idealism in Britain, 1880–1920. *Archives Européenes de Sociologie* 19:3–50.

Collins, Harry M.
1983 An empirical relativist program in the sociology of scientific knowledge. In *Science Observed: Perspectives on the Social Study of Science*. K. Knorr-Cetina and M. Mulkay, eds., pp. 85–113. London: Sage Publications.

Comaroff, J. L.
1978 Rules and rulers: political process in a Tswana chiefdom. *Man* n.s. 13:1–20.

Connor, Linda
1984 Comment in "The thick and the thin: on the interpretative theoretical program of Clifford Gertz," by Paul Shankman. *Current Anthropology* 25(3):261–79.

Cortázar, Julio
1984 *A Certain Lucas*. G. Rabassa, trans. New York: Knopf.

Crane, Diana
1972 *Invisible Colleges: Diffusion of Knowledge in Scientific Communities*. Chicago: University of Chicago Press.

Crapanzano, Vincent
1977 On the writing of ethnography. *Dialetical Anthropology* 2:69–73.
1980 *Tuhami: Portrait of a Moroccan*. Chicago: University of Chicago Press.
1986 Hermes' dilemma: the masking of subversion in ethnographic description. In *Writing Culture: The Poetics and Politics of Ethnography*. J. Clifford and G. Marcus, eds., pp. 51–76. Berkeley: University of California Press.

De Certeau, Michel
1975 *L'Ecriture de l'histoire*. Paris: Gallimard.

de Lauretis, Teresa, ed.
1986 *Feminist Studies, Critical Studies*. Bloomington: University of Indiana Press.

de Leon, Arnoldo
1982 *The Tejano Community, 1836–1900*. Albuqurque: University of New Mexico Press.
1983 *They Called Them Greasers: Anglo Atitudes toward Mexicans in Texas, 1821–1900*. Austin: University of Texas Press.

Droixhe, Daniel, and Pol-P Gossiaux, eds.
1985 *L'Homme des Lumières et la découverte de l'autre*. Bruxelles: Editions de l'Université de Bruxelles.

Duchet, Michele
1971 *Anthropologie et histoire au siècle des Lumières*. Paris: Maspero.

Dumont, Jean-Paul
1978 *The Headman and I*. Austin: University of Texas Press.
1986 Prologue to ethnography or prolegomena to anthropology. *Ethos* 14:344–67.
1988 The Tasaday, which and whose? Toward the political economy of an ethnographic sign. *Cultural Anthropology* 3(3):261–75.

Dumont, Louis
  1970   Caste, racism and 'stratification': reflections of a social anthropologist. Appendix in *Homo Hierarchicus: the Caste System and Its Implications.* Chicago: University of Chicago Press.
Du Tertre, Jean-Baptiste
  1667   *Histoire générale des Antilles habitées par les François.* Reprint edition, 1973. Fort de France: Editions des Horizons Caraïbes.
Dwyer, Kevin
  1982   *Moroccan Dialogues: Anthropology in Question.* Baltimore: The Johns Hopkins University Press.
Eagleton, Terry
  1987   Awakening from modernity. *Times Literary Supplement,* February 20.
Echols, Alice
  1984   The taming of the id: feminist sexual politics 1968–83. In *Pleasure and Danger.* C. Vance, ed. Boston: Routledge and Kegan Paul.
Eckert, Penelope
  1989   *Jocks and Burnouts: Social Categories and Identity in the High School.* New York: Teachers College Press.
Ehrenreich, Barbara
  1989   *Fear of Falling: The Inner Life of the Middle Class.* New York: Pantheon.
Eliav-Feldon, Miriam
  1982   *Realistic Utopias: The Ideal Imaginary Societies of the Renaissance, 1516–1630.* Oxford: Clarendon Press.
Elkin, A. P.
  1974   Elliot Smith and the diffusion of culture. In *Grafton Elliot Smith, the Man and His Work.* A. P. Elkin and N. W. G. Macintosh, eds. Sydney, Australia: Sydney University Press.
Ellen, Roy, Ernest Gellner, Grazyna Kubica, and Janusz Mucha, eds.
  1988   *Malinowski between Two Worlds: The Polish Roots of an Anthropological Tradition.* Cambridge: Cambridge University Press.
Ellman, Richard, and Charles Feidelson, Jr.
  1965   *The Modern Tradition: Backgrounds of Modern Literature.* New York: Oxford University Press.
Erikson, Erik
  1950   *Childhood and Society.* New York: Norton.
Errington, Frederick
  1987   Reflexivity deflected: the Festival of Nations as an American cultural performance. *American Ethnologist* 14(4):654–67.
Fabian, Johannes
  1983   *Time and the Other: How Anthropology Makes Its Object.* New York: Columbia University Press.
Fahim, Hussein, ed.
  1982   *Indigenous Anthropology in Non-Western Countries.* Durham, NC: North Carolina Academic Press.

Felman, S.
  1989 Narrative as testimony: Camus's "The Plague." In *Reading Narrative: Form, Ethics, Ideology*. J. Phelan, ed., pp. 250–71. Columbus: Ohio State University Press.

Fernea, Elizabeth W.
  1965 *Guests of the Sheik: An Ethnography of an Iraqi Village*. Reprint edition, 1969. Garden City, NY: Anchor Books.

Fischer, Michael M. J.
  1984 Towards a third world poetics: seeing through short stories and films in the Iranian culture area. *Knowledge and Society* 5:171–241.

  1986 Ethnicity and the post-modern arts of memory. In *Writing Culture: The Poetics and Politics of Ethnography*. J. Clifford and G. Marcus, eds., pp. 194–233. Berkeley: University of California Press.

  1988 Aestheticized emotions and critical hermeneutics. *Culture, Medicine and Psychiatry* 12:31–42.

Fish, Stanley
  1980 *Is There a Text in This Class?: The Authority of Interpretive Communities*. Cambridge, MA: Harvard University Press.

Foley, Douglas
  1978 *From Peones to Politics: Ethnic Relations in a South Texas Town*. Austin: University of Texas, Center for Mexican American Studies.

Forde, C. Daryll
  1926 *Ancient Mariners: The Story of Ships and Sea Routes*. London: Howe Press.

Fortes, Meyer
  1976 Cyril Daryll Forde 1902–1973. *Proceedings of the British Academy* 62:458–83.

Foster, Hal, ed.
  1983 *The Anti-Aesthetic: Essays on Postmodern Culture*. Port Townsend, WA.: Bay Press.

Foucault, Michel
  1978 *Discipline and Punish*. New York: Pantheon.

  1984 What is enlightenment? In *The Foucault Reader*, P. Rabinow, ed. New York: Pantheon.

Fox, Richard G.
  1972 Rationale and romance in urban anthropology. *Urban Anthropology* 1:205–233.

  1985 *Lions of the Punjab: Culture in the Making*. Berkeley: University of California Press.

  1989 *Gandhian Utopia: Experiments with Culture*. Boston: Beacon Press.

Frank, Arthur W.
  1985 Out of ethnomethodology. In *Micro-sociological Theory: Perspectives in Sociological Theory*, vol. 2. H. J. Helle and S. N. Eisenstadt, eds., pp. 111–16. London: Sage Publications.

Friedl, Erika
  1989   *Women of Deh Koh: Lives in an Iranian Village*. Washington, DC: Smith-
         sonian Institution Press.
Friedman, Jonathan
  1987   Beyond otherness: the spectacularization of anthropology. *Telos* 71:
         161–70.
Fussell, Paul
  1983   *Class*. New York: Ballantine Books.
Gadamer, Hans-Georg
  1976   *Philosophical Hermeneutics*. Berkeley: University of California Press.
Gage, Thomas
  1648   *Travels in the New World*. J. E. S. Thompson, ed., 1958 edition. Nor-
         man: University of Oaklahoma Press.
Gans, Herbert
  1962   *Urban Villagers: Group and Class in the Life of Italian-Americans*. New
         York: The Free Press.
Garfinkel, Harold
  1967   *Studies in Ethnomethodology*. Englewood Cliffs, NJ: Prentice-Hall.
Geertz, Clifford
  1973a The impact of the concept of culture on the concept of man. In *The
         Interpretation of Cultures*. Clifford Geertz, pp. 33–54. New York: Basic
         Books.
  1973b *The Interpretation of Cultures*. New York: Basic Books.
  1975a Thick description: toward an interpretive theory of culture. In *The In-
         terpretation of Cultures*. Clifford Geertz, pp. 3–30. London: Hutchinson.
  1975b Deep play: notes on the Balinese cockfight. In *The Interpretation of Cul-
         tures*. Clifford Geertz, pp. 412–53. London: Hutchinson.
  1980   Blurred genres: the refiguration of social thought. *American Scholar*
         49:125–59.
  1984   Distinguished lecture: Anti anti-relativism. *American Anthropology* 86:
         263–78.
  1985   Waddling in. *Times Literary Supplement*. June 7:623–624.
  1988   *Works and Lives: The Anthropologist as Author*. Stanford: Stanford Uni-
         versity Press.
Gellner, Ernest
  1988   "Zeno of Cracow" or "Revolution at Nemi" or "The Polish revenge: a
         drama in three acts." In *Malinowski between Two Worlds: The Polish Roots
         of an Anthropological Tradition*. R. Ellen, E. Gellner, G. Kubica, J. Mu-
         cha, eds. Cambridge: Cambridge University Press.
Genette, Gérard, Hans Robert Jauss, Jean-Marie Schaffer, et al.
  1986   *Théorie des genres*. Paris: Editions du Seuil.
Giddens, Anthony
  1973   *The Class Structure of the Advanced Societies*. London: Hutchinson.
  1979   *Central Problems in Social Theory: Action, Structure and Contradiction in
         Social Analysis*. Berkeley: University of California Press.

Gilbert, G. Nigel, and Michael Mulkay.
  1984   *Opening Pandora's Box: a Sociological Analysis of Scientists' Discourse.*
          Cambridge: Cambridge University Press.
Gilligan, Carol
  1982   *In a Different Voice.* Cambridge, MA: Harvard University Press.
Gitlin, Todd
  1989   Postmodernism: roots and politics. *Dissent,* winter, 100–108.
Glissant, Edouard
  1989   *Caribbean Discourse: Selected Essays.* J. M. Dash, trans. Charlottesville:
          University of Virginia Press.
Godzich, Vlad
  1986   Foreword. In *Heterologies: Discourse on the Other.* M. De Certeau,
          pp. vii–xxi. Minneapolis: University of Minnesota Press.
Goldenweiser, Alexander
  1917   The autonomy of the social. *American Anthropologist* 19:447–49.
  1933   *History, Psychology and Culture.* New York: Alfred A. Knopf.
Goldschmidt, Walter
  1950   Social class in America—a critical review. *American Anthropologist*
          52:483–98.
  1955   Social class and the dynamics of status in America. *American Anthro-
          pologist* 57:1209–17.
Gonnard, René
  1946   *La légende du bon sauvage: contribution a l'étude des origines du socialisme.*
          Paris: Librarie de Medicis.
Gordon, Deborah
  1988   Writing culture, writing feminism: The poetics and politics of experi-
          mental ethnography. *Inscriptions* 3/4:7–24.
Graff, Gerald
  1977   The myth of the post-modernist breakthrough. In *The Novel Today:
          Contemporary Writers on Modern Fiction.* M. Bradbury, ed., pp. 217–
          249. Manchester: Manchester University Press, Rowan and Littlefield.
Habermas, Jürgen
  1984   *The Theory of Communicative Action, vol. 1, Reason and the Rationaliza-
          tion of Society.* Boston: Beacon Press.
Hale, J. R.
  1977   *Renaissance Europe: Individual and Society, 1480–1520.* Berkeley: Uni-
          versity of California Press.
Hall, S.
  1986   Cultural studies: two paradigms. In *Media, Culture, and Society: A
          Critical Reader.* R. Collins, et al., eds., pp. 33–48. London: Sage
          Publications.
Hall, Stuart
  1988   The toad in the garden: Thatcherism among the theorists. In *Marxism
          and the Interpretation of Culture.* L. Grossberg and C. Nelson, eds. Ur-
          bana: University of Illinois Press.

Halle, David
    1984   *America's Working Man: Work, Home, and Politics among Blue Collar Property Owners*. Chicago: University of Chicago Press.

Handelman, Don
    1978   Bureaucratic interpretation: the perception of child abuse in urban Newfoundland. In *Bureaucracy and World View: Studies in the Logic of Official Interpretation*. D. Handleman and E. Leyton, eds., pp. 15–69. St. John's, Newfoundland: Memorial University.

Handler, Richard
    1983   The dainty and the hungry man: literature and anthropology in the work of Edward Sapir. In *Observers Observed: Essays on Ethnographic Fieldwork*. G. W. Stocking, Jr., ed., pp. 208–232. Madison: University of Wisconsin Press.

Hannerz, Ulf
    1969   *Soulside: Inquiries into Ghetto Culture and Community*. New York: Columbia University Press.
    1989   Notes on the global ecumene. *Public Culture* 1(2):66–75.

Haraway, Donna
    1985   A manifesto for cyborgs: science technology and socialist feminism in the 1980s. *Socialist Review* 80:65—107.

Harding, Sandra
    1986   *The Science Question in Feminism*. Ithaca: Cornell University Press.
    1987   The method question. *Hypatia* 2:19–35.

Hartsock, Nancy
    1985   *Money, Sex, and Power: Toward a Feminist Historical Materialism*. Boston: Northeastern University Press.

Harvey, David
    1989   *The Condition of Postmodernity*. Oxford: Basil Blackwell.

Hebdige, Dick
    1979   *Subculture: The Meaning of Style*. London: Methuen.

Heritage, John C.
    1987   Ethnomethodology. In *Social Theory Today*. A. Giddens and J. Turner, eds., pp. 224–70. Oxford: Polity Press.

Herskovits, Melville J.
    1937a   The significance of acculturation for anthropology. *American Anthropologist* 39:259–64.
    1937b   *Life in a Haitian Valley*. Reprint edition, 1975. New York: Octagon Books.

Hollis, Martin, and Steven Lukes, eds.
    1982   *Rationality and Relativism*. Oxford: Blackwell.

Howells, William Dean
    1804   *A Traveler from Altruria*. New York: Harper and Brothers.

Hymes, Dell
    1969   *Reinventing Anthropology*. New York: Pantheon.
    1974   *Reinventing Anthropology*. Paperback edition. New York: Vintage.

Irigaray, Luce
    1985a *Speculum of the Other Woman.* G. C. Gill, trans. Ithaca: Cornell University Press.
    1985b *This Sex Which Is Not One.* C. Porter with C. Burks, trans. Ithaca: Cornell University Press.

Isaac, Jeffrey C.
    1987 *Power and Marxist Theory: A Realist Approach.* Ithaca, NY: Cornell University Press.

Jackson, Anthony, ed.
    1987 *Anthropology at Home.* London: Tavistock.

Jacob, François
    1988 *The Statue Within: An Autobiography.* F. Philip, trans. New York: Basic Books.

Jacobs, Jerry
    1974 *Fun City: An Ethnographic Study of a Retirement Community.* New York: Holt, Rinehart, Winston.

Jameson, Fredric
    1981 *The Political Unconscious: Narrative as a Socially Symbolic Act.* Ithaca: Cornell University Press.
    1984 Postmodernism, or the cultural logic of late capitalism. *New Left Review* 146:53–92.
    1986 Third World literature in the age of multinational capitalism. *Social Text* 15:53–92.

Jarvie, Ian
    1974 *The Revolution in Anthropology.* Chicago: Henry Regnery.
    1987 Comment in "Out of context: the persuasive fictions of anthropology," by Marilyn Strathern. *Current Anthropology* 28(3):251–81.
    1988 Comment in "Rhetoric and the authority of ethnography: 'postmodernism' and the social reproduction of texts," by P. Steven Sangren. *Current Anthropology* 29(3):405–35.

Jencks, Charles
    1986 *What is Post-Modernism?* London: Academy Editions, St Martin Press.

Johnson, R.
    1986 What is cultural studies anyway? *Social Text* 16:38–80.

Jones, Delmos J.
    1970 Towards a native anthropology. *Human Organization* 29:1–59.

Joseph, Suad
    1988 Feminization, familism, self, and politics: research as a *Mughtaribi.* In *Arab Women in the Field: Studying Your Own Society.* S. Altorki and C. El-Solh, eds., pp. 25–47. Syracuse, NY: Syracuse University Press.

Jules-Rosette, Bennetta
    1978 The veil of objectivity: prophecy, divination and social inquiry. *American Anthropologist* 80:549–70.

Kahn, Joel
    1989 Culture, demise, or resurrection? *Critique of Anthropology* ix:5–26.

Kamenka, Eugene, ed.
   1987   *Utopias.* Oxford: Oxford University Press.
Katznelson, Ira, and Aristide Zolberg
   1986   *Working Class Formation: Nineteeth-Century Patterns in Western Europe and the United States.* Princeton, NJ: Princeton University Press.
Keiser, R. Lincoln
   1969   *The Vice Lords: Warriors of the Streets.* New York: Holt, Rinehart and Winston.
Kondo, Dorinne
   1986   Dissolution and reconstitution of self: implications for anthropological epistemology. *Cultural Anthropology* 1: 74–88.
Krige, E. Jensen, and J. D. Krige
   1943   *The Realm of a Rain Queen: A Study of the Pattern of Lovedu Society.* Reprint edition, 1956. London: Oxford University Press.
Kristeva, Julia
   1981   Women's time. A. Jardine and H. Blake, trans. *Signs* 7: 13–35.
Kroeber, A. L.
   1915   Eighteen professions. *American Anthropologist* 17: 283–88.
   1917   The superorganic. Reprinted 1952 in *The Nature of Culture.* A. L. Kroeber, pp. 22–51. Chicago: University of Chicago Press.
   1919   On the principle of order in civilization as exemplified by changes of fashion. *American Anthropologist* 21: 231–63.
   1923   *The History of Native Cultures in California.* University of California Publications in American Archaeology and Ethnology, vol. 20. Berkeley: University of California Press.
   1935   History and science in anthropology. *American Anthropologist* 37: 539–69.
   1936a So-called social science. Reprinted 1952 in *The Nature of Culture.* A. L. Kroeber, pp. 66–84. Chicago: University of Chicago Press.
   1936b Kinship and history. Reprinted 1976 in *Selected Papers from the American Anthropologist 1921–1945.* G. W. Stocking, Jr., ed., pp. 226–29. Washington, D.C.: American Anthropological Association.
   1938   Historical context, reconstruction, and interpretation. Reprinted 1952 in *The Nature of Culture.* A. L. Kroeber, pp. 79–94. Chicago: University of Chicago Press.
   1954   The place of anthropology in universities. *American Anthropologist* 56: 764–67.
   1956   History of anthropological thought. In *Current Anthropology.* W. L. Thomas, ed. Chicago: University of Chicago Press.
Kuper, Adam
   1988   *The Invention of Primitive Society: Transformation of an Illusion.* Boston and London: Routledge and Kegan Paul.
Labat, Jean Baptiste
   1722   *Nouveau voyage aux isles de l'Amérique.* Fort de France: Reprint edition, 1972. Editions des Horizons Caraïbes.

LaCapra, Dominick
1985   *History and Criticism*. Ithaca, NY: Cornell University Press.
Laclau, Ernesto, and Chantal Mouffe
1985   *Hegemony and Socialist Strategy: Towards a Radical Democratic Politics*. London: Verso.
Lamont, Michele
1988   From Paris to Stanford, une reconversion sociologique: de la sociologie française a la sociologie américaine. *Politix* 3–4:29.
Langham, Ian
1981   *The Building of British Social Anthropology*. Dordrecht, Netherlands: D. Reidel.
Lash, S., and J. Urry
1987   *The End of Organized Capitalism*. Madison: University of Wisconsin Press.
Latour, Bruno
1988a The politics of explanation: an alternative. In *Knowledge and Reflexivity: New Frontiers in the Sociology of Knowledge*. S. Woolgar, ed., pp. 155–76. London: Sage Publications.
1988b *Science in Action*. Cambridge, MA: Harvard University Press.
Latour, Bruno, and Steve Woolgar
1979   *Laboratory Life: The Social Construction of Scientific Facts*. London: Sage Publications.
Lawrence, Peter
1975   The ethnographic revolution. *Oceania* 44:253–71.
Leach, Edmund
1965   *Political systems of Highland Burma: A Study of Kachin Social Structure*. Boston: Beacon Press.
1989   Writing anthropology. *American Ethnologist* 16(1):137–41.
Lepenies, Wolf, and Peter Weingart
1983   Introduction. In *Functions and Uses of Disciplinary Histories*. L. Graham, W. Lepenies, and P. Weingart, eds. Dordrecht, Netherlands: D. Reidel.
Lesser, Alexander
1933   The *Pawnee Ghost Dance Hand Game*. Columbia University Contributions to Anthropology, vol. 16. New York: Columbia University Press.
1935   Functionalism in social anthropology. *American Anthropologist* 37:386–93.
1981   Franz Boas. In *Totems and Teachers*. S. Silverman, ed., pp. 1–34. New York: Columbia University Press.
Levin, Harry
1967   *The Power of Blackness*. New York: Alfred A. Knopf.
LeVine, Robert, and Donald T. Campbell
1972   *Ethnocentrism: Theories of Conflict, Ethnic Attitudes and Group Behavior*. New York: John Wiley.
Levinson, Marjorie
1989   Introduction. In *Rethinking Historicism: Critical Readings in Romantic*

History. M. Levinson, M. Butler, J. McGann, and P. Hamilton. Oxford: Basil Blackwell.

Lévi-Strauss, Claude
1966   *The Savage Mind.* Chicago: University of Chicago Press.

Liberman, Kenneth
1985   *Understanding Interaction in Central Australia: An Ethnomethodological Study of Australian Aboriginal People.* London: Routledge and Kegan Paul.

Limón, José E.
1973   Stereotyping and Chicano resistance: an historical dimension. *Aztlán* 4:257–70.
1980   Américo Paredes: a man from the border. *Revista Chicano-Requeña* 5:1–5.
1981   The folk performance of *chicano* and the cultural limits of political ideology. In *". . . and Other Neighborly Names": Social Process and Cultural Image in Texas Folklore.* R. Bauman and R. D. Abrahams, eds., pp. 197–225. Austin: University of Texas Press.
1990   Américo Paredes and the Mexican ballad: the creative anthropological text as social critique. In *Creativity: Self and Society.* S. Lavie, K. Narayan, and R. Rosaldo, eds. Ithaca: Cornell University Press.

Lipset, Seymour Martin, and Reinhard Bendix
1957   *Social Mobility in Industrial Society.* Berkeley: University of California Press.

Livingston, Eric
1986   *The Ethnomethodological Foundation of Mathematics.* London: Routledge and Kegan Paul.

Lowie, Robert
1911   A new conception of totemism. *American Anthropologist* 13:189—207.
1937   *The History of Ethnological Theory.* New York: Farrar and Rinehart.

Lukacs, Georg
1910   On the nature and form of the essay. In *Soul and Form.* Reprint edition, 1974, pp. 1–18. A. Bostock, trans. Cambridge: MIT Press.

Lukes, Steven
1973   *Emile Durkheim: His Life and Work. A Historical and Critical Study.* London: Allen Lane.

Lyotard, Jean François
1979   *La Condition post-moderne.* Paris: Editions de Minuit.
1984   *The Postmodern Condition: A Report on Knowledge.* G. Bonnington and B. Massumi, trans. Minneapolis: University of Minnesota Press.
1986   *Le Post-moderne expliqué aux enfants.* Paris: Editions Galilee.

MacAloon, J.
1990   Steroids and the state: Dubin, melodrama and the accomplishment of innocence. *Public Culture* 2(2):41–64.

MacKinnon, Catherine

1982   Feminism, Marxism, method, and the state: an agenda for theory. *Signs* 7:515—44.

Malinkowski, Bronislaw

1922   *Argonauts of the Western Pacific: An Account of Native Enterprise and Adventure in the Archipelagoes of Melanesian New Guinea.* Reprint edition, 1961. New York: E. P. Dutton.

1935   *Coral Gardens and Their Magic.* 2 vols. Reprint edition, 1978. New York: Dover Publications.

1967   *A Diary in the Strict Sense of the Term.* New York: Harcourt, Brace and World.

Manuel, Frank E., and Fritzie P. Manuel

1979   *Utopian Thought in the Western World.* Cambridge, MA: Belknap Press of Harvard University Press.

Marcus, George E.

1980   Rhetoric and the ethnographic genre in anthropological research. *Current Anthropology* 21:507–10.

Marcus, George E., and James Clifford

1985   The making of ethnographic texts: preliminary report. *Current Anthropology* 26:267–71.

Marcus, George E., and Dick Cushman

1982   Ethnographies as texts. *Annual Reviews of Anthropology* 11:25–69.

Marcus, George, and Michael M. J. Fischer

1986   *Anthropology as Cultural Critique: An Experimental Moment in the Human Sciences.* Chicago: University of Chicago Press.

Martin, Emily

1987   *The Woman in the Body: A Cultural Analysis of Reproduction.* Boston: Beacon Press.

Martin, Randy

1985   Dance as a social movement. *Social Text* 12:54–70.

Maruyama, Magorah

1974   Endogenous research vs. delusions of relevance and expertise among exogenous academics. *Human Organization* 33:318–22.

McCrea, Frances B., and Gerald E. Markle

1989   *Minutes to Midnight, Nuclear Weapons Protest in America.* London: Sage Publications.

McDonald, Maryon

1988   Comment in "Rhetoric and the authority of ethnography: 'postmodernism' and the social reproduction of texts," by P. Steven Sangren. *Current Anthropology* 29(3):405–35.

Mead, Margaret

1928   *Coming of Age in Samoa.* Reprint edition, 1949. New York: Mentor Books.

Meis, Maria

1983   Towards a methodology for feminist research. In *Theories of Women's*

Studies. G. Bowles and R. D. Klein, eds. Boston and London: Routledge and Kegan Paul.

Miller, James
1986   C. Wright Mills reconsidered. *Salmagundi* 70–71:82–101.

Mintz, Sidney
1960   *Worker in the Cane*. New Haven: Yale University Press.
1971   Le rouge et le noir. *Les Temps modernes* 299–300:2354–61.
1985a   *History, Evolution and the Concept of Culture*. Cambridge: Cambridge University Press.
1985b   *Sweetness and Power: The Place of Sugar in Modern History*. New York: Viking.
1990   Introduction. In *The Myth of the Negro Past*. M. J. Herskovits, pp. ix–xxi. Boston: Beacon Press.

Mitchell, Timothy
1988   *Colonizing Egypt*. Cambridge: Cambridge University Press.

Moerman, Michael
1968   Being Lue: uses and abuses of ethnic identification. In *Essays on the Problem of Tribe: Proceedings of the 1967 Annual Spring Meeting of the American Ethnological Society*. J. Helm, ed., pp. 153–69.
1988   *Talking Culture: Ethnography and Conversation Analysis*. Philadelphia: University of Pennsylvania Press.

Moffat, Michael
1989   *Coming of Age in New Jersey: College and American Culture*. New Brunswick, NJ: Rutgers University Press.

Mohanty, Chandra
1988   Under Western eyes: feminist scholarship and colonial discourses. *Feminist Review* 30:61–88.

Montaigne, Michel Eyquiem de
1952   *Essays*. Chicago: Encyclopedia Britannica, Great Books of the Western World.
1983   *Travel Journals*. D. M. Frame, trans. Berkeley: North Point Press.

Montejano, David
1987   *Anglos and Mexicans in the Making of Texas, 1836–1986*. Austin: University of Texas Press.

Morsy, Soheir
1988   Fieldwork in my Egyptian homeland: toward the demise of anthropology's distinctive-other hegemonic tradition. In *Arab Women in the Field: Studying Your Own Society*. S. Altorki and C. El-Solh, eds., pp. 69–90. Syracuse: Syracuse University Press.

Mudimbe, Valentine Y.
1988   *The Invention of Africa: Gnosis, Philosophy and the Order of Knowledge*. Bloomington: Indiana University Press.

Mulkay, Michael

1984   The scientist talks back: a one act play, with a moral, about replication in science and reflexivity in sociology. *Social Studies of Science* 14:265–82.

Myerhoff, Barbara
1978   *Number Our Days*. New York: Simon and Schuster.

Nader, Laura
1969   "Up the anthropologist"—perspectives gained from studying up. In *Reinventing Anthropology*. D. Hymes, ed., pp. 284–311. New York: Random House.

Nandy, Ashis
1987   *Traditions, Tyranny and Utopias*. Delhi: Oxford University Press.

Narayan, Kirin
1989   *Saints, Scoundrels, and Storytellers*. Philadelphia: University of Pennsylvania Press.

Neville, Gwen Kennedy
1987   *Kinship and Pilgrimage: Ritual of Reunion in American Protestant Culture*. New York: Oxford University Press.

Newman, Katherine S.
1988   *Falling from Grace: The Experience of Downward Mobility in the American Middle Class*. New York: The Free Press.

Newton, Esther
1972   *Mother Camp: Female Impersonators in America*. Englewood Cliffs, NJ: Prentice-Hall.

Nieboer, Hermann J.
1900   *Slavery as an Industrial System*. The Hague: Martinus Nijhoff.

Ohnuki-Tierney, Emiko
1984   "Native" anthropologists. *American Ethnologist* 11:584–86.

Ortner, Sherry B.
1973   On key symbols. *American Anthropologist* 75:1338–46.

1984   Theory in anthropology since the sixties. *Comparative Studies in Society and History* 26:126–66.

1989a   *High Religion: A Cultural and Political History of Sherpa Buddhism*. Princeton: Princeton University Press.

1989b   Categories of un-modernity: community. Paper delivered at the 88th annual meeting of the American Anthropological Association, Washington, DC.

Ortner, Sherry B., and Harriet Whitehead, eds.
1981   *Sexual Meanings: The Cultural Construction of Gender and Sexuality*. Cambridge: Cambridge University Press.

Overing, Joanna
1985   Introduction. In *Reason and Morality*. J. Overing, ed., pp. 1–28. London: Tavistock Publications.

Pagden, Anthony
> 1982 *The Fall of Natural Man: The American Indian and the Origins of Comparative Ethnology.* Cambridge: Cambridge University Press.

Paredes, Américo.
> 1958 *"With His Pistol in His Hand": A Border Ballad and Its Hero.* Reprint edition, 1971. Austin: University of Texas Press.

Parfit, Derek
> 1986 *Reasons and Persons.* Oxford: Clarendon Press.

Parkin, David
> 1978 *The Cultural Definition of Political Response.* London: Academic Press.
> 1982 *Semantic Anthropology.* London: Academic Press.

Parsons, Elsie Clews, ed.
> 1925 *American Indian Life.* New York: Viking.

Peña, Manuel H.
> 1980 Ritual structure in a chicano dance. *Latin American Music Review* 1: 47–73.
> 1985 *The Texas-Mexican Conjunto: History of a Working Class Music.* Austin: University of Texas Press.

Pfaelzer, Jean
> 1984 *The Utopian Novel in America, 1886–1896: The Politics of Form.* Pittsburgh: University of Pittsburgh Press.

Pilcher, William
> 1972 *The Portland Longshoremen.* New York: Holt, Rinehart and Winston.

Pitt-Rivers, George Henry Lane-Fox
> 1927 *The Clash of Culture and the Contact of Races: An Anthropological and Psychological Study of the Laws of Racial Adaptability, with Special Reference to the Depopulation of the Pacific and the Government of Subject Races.* London: Routledge.

Polier, Nicole, and William Roseberry
> 1989 Tristes tropes. *Economy and Society* 18:245–64.

Pollner, Melvin
> 1974 Mundane reasoning. *Philosophy of Social Sciences* 4:35–54.

Porter, Joseph C.
> 1986 *Paper Medicine Man: John Gregory Bourke and His American West.* Norman: University of Oklahoma Press.

Poulantzas, Nicos
> 1974 *Classes in Contemporary Capitalism.* London: New Left Books.

Powdermaker, Hortense
> 1939 *After Freedom: A Cultural Study in the Deep South.* New York: Viking Press.
> 1950 *Hollywood, The Dream Factory: An Anthropologist Looks at the Movie Makers.* Boston: Little, Brown.

Pratt, Mary Louise
> 1986 Fieldwork in common places. In *Writing Culture: The Poetics and Politics*

of Ethnography. J. Clifford and G. Marcus, eds., pp. 27–50. Berkeley: University of California Press.

Quiggin, A. Hingston

1942   *Haddon the Headhunter: A Short Sketch of the Life of A. C. Haddon.* Cambridge: Cambridge University Press.

Rabinow, Paul

1977   *Reflections on Fieldwork in Morocco.* Berkeley: University of California Press.

1986   Representations are social facts: modernity and post-modernity in anthropology. In *Writing Culture: The Poetics and Politics of Ethnography.* J. Clifford and G. Marcus, eds., pp. 234–61. Berkeley: University of California Press.

1988   Beyond ethnography: anthropology as nominalism. *Cultural Anthropology* 3(3):355–64.

Radcliffe-Brown, A. R.

1935   Kinship terminologies in California. Reprinted 1976 in *Selected Papers From the American Anthropologist 1921–1945.* G. W. Stocking, Jr., ed., pp. 221–25. Washington, DC: American Anthropological Association.

1964   *The Andaman Islanders.* New York: Free Press of Glencoe.

Radin, Paul

1929   History of ethnological theories. *American Anthropologist* 31:9–33.

1933   *The Method and Theory of Ethnology.* New York and London: McGraw Hill.

Reiche, Reimut

1971   *Sexuality and Class Struggle.* S. Bennett, trans. New York: Praeger.

Reinharz, Shulamit

1983   Experimental analysis: a contribution to feminist research. In *Theories of Women's Studies.* G. Bowles and R. D. Klein, eds., pp. 162–91. London and Boston: Routledge and Kegan Paul.

Rich, Adrienne

1979   Toward a woman-centered university. In *On Lies, Secrets and Silence,* pp. 125–56. New York: W. W. Norton & Co.

Ricoeur, Paul

1965   *History and Truth.* C. A. Kelbley, trans. Evanston: Northwestern University Press.

1984   *The Reality of the Historical Past.* Milwaukee: Marquette University Press.

1986   *Lectures on Ideology and Utopia.* G. H. Taylor, ed. New York: Columbia University Press.

Riesman, Paul

1977   *Freedom in Fulani Social Life.* Chicago: University of Chicago Press.

1982   Fieldwork as initiation and as therapy. Paper presented at the 81st annual meeting of the American Anthropological Association, Washington, DC.

Rivers, W. H. R.

1913 Anthropological research outside America. In *Reports on the Present Condition and Future Needs of the Science of Anthropology*. W. H. R. Rivers, A. E. Jenks, and S. G. Morley. Carnegie Institution of Washington, publication no. 200. Washington, DC.

Rosaldo, Renato

1986 From the door of his tent: the fieldworker and the inquisitor. In *Writing Culture: The Poetics and Politics of Ethnography*. J. Clifford and G. Marcus, eds., pp. 77–97. Berkeley: University of California Press.

1989 *Culture and Truth: The Remaking of Social Analysis*. Boston: Beacon Press.

Rose, Hilary

1983 Hand, brain and heart: a feminist epistemology for the natural sciences. *Signs* 9: 73–90.

1986 Women's work: women's knowledge. In *What Is Feminism? A Re-Examination*. J. Mitchell and A. Oakley, eds., pp. 161–83. New York: Pantheon Books.

Roseberry, William

1989 *Anthropologies and Histories: Essays in Culture, History, and Political Economy*. Rutgers, NJ: Rutgers University Press.

Ross, Andrew

1988a Introduction. In *Universal Abandon? The Politics of Post-Modernism*. A. Ross, ed., pp. vii–xviii. Minneapolis: University of Minnesota Press.

1988b (Ed.) *Universal Abandon? The Politics of Post-Modernism*. Minneapolis: University of Minnesota Press.

Roth, Philip

1960 *Goodbye, Columbus and Five Short Stories*. New York: Meridian Books.

1967 *Portnoy's Complaint*. New York: Random House.

1988a *The Counterlife*. New York: Penguin Books.

1988b *The Facts: A Novelist's Autobiography*. New York: Penguin Books.

Ruby, Jay

1982a (Ed.) *A Crack in the Mirror: Reflexive Perspectives in Anthropology*. Philadelphia: University of Pennsylvania Press.

1982b Ethnography as trompe l'oeil. In *A Crack in the Mirror: Reflexive Perspectives in Anthropology*. J. Ruby, ed., pp. 121–31. Philadelphia: University of Pennsylvania Press.

Ruddick, Sara

1980 Maternal thinking. *Feminist Studies* 6(2): 342—67.

Rudwick, Martin

1985 *The Great Devonian Controversy: The Shaping of Scientific Knowledge among Gentlemanly Specialists*. Chicago: University of Chicago Press.

Rupp-Eisenreich, Britta

1984 (Ed.) *Histoire de l'anthropologie (xvie–xix siècles)*. Paris: Klincksiech.

1985 Christophe Meiners et Joseph-Marie de Gerando: un chapitre du comparatisme anthropologique. In *L'Homme des Lumières et la découverte de l'autre.* D. Droixhe and P. Gossiaux, eds., pp. 21–47. Bruxelles: Editions de l'Universite de Bruxelles.

Sacks, Karen Brodkin
  1989   Toward a unified theory of class, race, and gender. *American Ethnologist* 16(3):534–50.

Sahlins, Marshall
  1985   *Islands of History.* Chicago: University of Chicago Press.

Said, Edward
  1978   *Orientalism.* New York: Pantheon.
  1989   Representing the colonized: anthropology's interlocuters. *Critical Inquiry* 15:205–25.

Sangren, P. Steven
  1988   Rhetoric and the authority of ethnography: "postmodernism" and the social reproduction of texts. *Current Anthropology* 29(3):405—35.

Sanjek, Roger, ed.
  1990   *Fieldnotes: The Makings of Anthropology.* Ithaca: Cornell University Press.

Sapir, Edward
  1917   Do we need a "Superorganic?" *American Anthropologist* 19:441–47.

Sartre, Jean-Paul
  1963   *Search for a Method.* H. E. Barnes, trans. New York: Alfred A. Knopf.

Schneider, David M.
  1980   *American Kinship: A Cultural Account.* Chicago: University of Chicago Press.

Schneider, David M., and Raymond T. Smith
  1973   *Class Differences and Sex Roles in American Kinship and Family Structure.* Englewood Cliffs, NJ: Prentice-Hall.

Schudson, M.
  1986   *Advertising, The Uneasy Persuasion.* New York: Basic Books.

Schwartz, Gary, and Don Merten
  1975   Social identity and expressive symbols. In *The Nacirema: Readings on American Culture.* J. P. Spradley and M. A. Rynkiewich, eds. Boston: Little, Brown.

Sennett, Richard, and Jonathan Cobb
  1972   *The Hidden Injuries of Class.* New York: Vintage Books.

Shankman, Paul
  1984   The thick and the thin: on the interpretive theoretical program of Clifford Geertz. *Current Anthropology* 25(3):261–79.

Sharrock, W. W., and R. J. Anderson
  1982   On the demise of the native: some observations on and a proposal for ethnography. *Human Studies* 5:119–35.

Sharrock, Wes, and Rod Watson
  1988   Anatomy among social theories: the incarnation of social structures. In *Actions and Structures: Research Methods and Social Theory.* N. G. Fielding, ed., pp. 56–77. London: Sage Publications.

Shostak, Marjorie
  1981   *Nisa: The Life and Words of a !Kung Woman.* Cambridge, MA: Harvard University Press.
Silverman, David
  1985   *Qualitative Methodology and Sociology: Describing the World.* Aldershot, England: Gower Publishing.
Slobodin, Richard
  1978   *W. H. R. Rivers.* Leaders of Modern Anthropology Series. New York: Columbia University Press.
Smith, Dorothy
  1987   *The Everyday World as Problematic.* Boston: Northeastern University Press.
Smith, Marian W.
  1959   Boas' 'natural history' approach to field method. In *The Anthropology of Franz Boas.* W. Goldschmidt, ed., pp. 44–60. American Anthropological Association Memoir 89.
Smith, Raymond T.
  1984   Anthropology and the concept of social class. *Annual Reviews of Anthropology* 13:467–94.
Smith-Rosenberg, Carroll
  1986   Writing history: language, class and gender. In *Feminist Studies, Critical Studies.* T. de Lauretis, ed. Bloomington: University of Indiana Press.
Sokolov, Raymond
  1975   *Native Intelligence.* New York: Harper and Row.
Somers, Margaret Ramsay
  1989   Workers of the world, compare! *Contemporary Sociology* 17(3): 325–29.
Spaulding, Albert C.
  1988   Distinguished lecture: Archaeology and anthropology. *American Anthropologist* 90(2):263–71.
Spiro, Melford E.
  1986   Cultural relativism and the future of anthropology. *Cultural Anthropology* 1:259–86.
Spradley, James P.
  1980   *Participant Observation.* New York: Holt, Rinehart, and Winston.
Spradley, James P., and Michael A. Rynkiewich, eds.
  1975   *The Nacirema: Readings on American Culture.* Boston: Little, Brown.
Stack, Carol B.
  1974   *All Our Kin: Strategies for Survival in a Black Community.* New York: Harper and Row.
Stanley, Liz, and Sue Wise
  1983   *Breaking Out: Feminist Consciousness and Feminist Research.* London: Routledge and Kegan Paul.
Stocking, George W., Jr.
  1968   *Race, Culture, and Evolution.* New York: The Free Press.

1974   *The Shaping of American Anthropology, 1883–1911: A Franz Boas Reader.* Washington, DC: American Anthropological Association.

1976   Ideas and institutions in American anthropology: toward a history of the interwar period. In *Selected Papers from the American Anthropologist 1921–1945.* G. W. Stocking Jr., ed., pp. 1—42. Washington, DC: American Anthropological Association.

1983   The ethnographer's magic: fieldwork in British anthropology from Tylor to Malinowski. In *Observers Observed: Essays on Ethnographic Fieldwork.* G. W. Stocking, Jr., ed. History of Anthropology Series, no. 1. Madison: University of Wisconsin Press.

1984   Radcliffe-Brown and British social anthropology. In *Functionalism Historicized: Essays on British Social Anthropology.* G. W. Stocking, Jr., ed. History of Anthropology Series, no. 2. Madison: University of Wisconsin Press.

1987   *Victorian Anthropology.* New York: The Free Press.

Strathern, Marilyn

1985   Dislodging a worldview: challenge and counter-challenge in the relationship between feminism and anthropology. *Australian Feminist Studies* 1: 1–25.

1987a   An awkward relationship: the case of feminism and anthropology. *Signs* 12: 276–92.

1987b   Out of context: the persuasive fictions of anthropology. *Current Anthropology* 28: 251–281.

Taussig, Michael T.

1987   *Shamanism, Colonialism, and the Wild Man.* Chicago: University of Chicago Press.

Tedlock, Dennis

1983   *The Spoken Word and the Work of Interpretation.* Philadelphia: University of Pennsylvania Press.

1987   Questions concerning dialogical anthropology. *Journal of Anthropolgical Research* 43: 325–37.

Thompson, E. P.

1968   *The Making of the English Working Class.* Harmondsworth, England: Penguin Books.

Thornton, Robert

1983   Narrative ethnography in Africa, 1850–1920. *Man* 18: 502–20.

Tibbetts, Paul

1988   Representation and the realist-constructivist controversy. *Human Studies* 11: 117–32.

Tinker, Chauncey Brewster

1922   *Nature's Simple Plan: A Phase of Radical Thought in the Mid-Eighteenth Century.* Princeton, NJ: Princeton University Press.

Todorov, Tzvetan

1982   *La Conquête de l'Amérique: la question de l'autre.* Paris: Editions du Seuil.

Tompkins, Jane
  1985   *Sensational Designs: the Cultural Work of American Fiction, 1790–1860.*
         New York: Oxford University Press.
Trollope, Anthony
  1859   *The West Indies and the Spanish Main.* Reprint edition, 1985. Allan Sutton, Hippocrene Books.
Trouillot, Michel-Rolph
  1988   *Peasants and Capital: Dominica in the World Economy.* Baltimore: Johns Hopkins University Press.
  1989   Discourses of rule: the acknowledgement of the peasantry in Dominica, W.I., 1838–1928. *American Ethnologist* 16(4): 704–18.
  1990   Goodbye Columbus: silences, power and public history (1492–1892). *Public Culture* 3(1): 1–24.
Trousson, Raymond
  1975   *Voyages aux pays de nulle part: histoire littéraire de la pensée utopique.* Bruxelles: Editions de l'Université de Bruxelles.
Turner, Edith
  1987   *The Spirit and the Drum: A Memoir of Africa.* Tucson: University of Arizona Press.
Tyler, Stephen
  1986   Post-modern ethnography: from document of the occult to occult document. In *Writing Culture: The Poetics and Politics of Ethnography.* J. Clifford and G. Marcus, eds., pp. 122–140. Berkeley: University of California Press.
Urry, James
  1985   W. E. Armstrong and social anthropology at Cambridge, 1922–26. *Man* n.s. 20: 412–33.
Vanneman, Reeve, and Lyn Weber Cannon
  1987   *The American Perception of Class.* Philadelphia: Temple University Press.
Varenne, Hervé
  1977   *Americans Together: Structured Diversity in a Midwestern Town.* New York: Columbia University Teachers College Press.
Vincent, Joan
  1984   Law in action: an appreciation of Malinowski's theoretical approach. A Malinowski Retrospective. Barnard College.
  1986a System and process, 1974–1985. *Annual Review of Anthropology* 15: 99–119.
  1986b Functionalism revisited: an unsettled science. *Reviews in Anthropology* 13: 331–39.
  1987   Romance and realism in the ethnography of Ifugao law. Paper presented at the 86th annual meeting of the American Anthropological Association, Chicago.
  1989   Evolution and history in Edwardian anthropology. Columbia University Seminar on Ecological Systems and Cultural Evolution, 6 February.

1990 *Anthropology and Politics: Visions, Traditions, and Trends.* Tucson: University of Arizona Press.

n.d.   *Romance and Realism in the Anthropology of Law.* Work in progress.

Walkover, Andrew

1974 *The Dialectics of Eden.* Stanford, CA: Stanford University Press.

Wallace, Anthony F. C.

1972 *Rockdale: The Growth of an American Village in the Early Industrial Revolution.* New York: W. W. Norton.

Warner, W. Lloyd, and Paul S. Lunt

1941 *The Social Life of a Modern Community.* New Haven, CT: Yale University Press.

Watson, Graham

1981 The reification of ethnicity and its political consequences in the North. *Canadian Review of Sociology and Anthropology* 18:453–69.

1984 The social construction of boundaries between social and cultural anthropology in Britain and North America. *Journal of Anthropological Research* 40:351–66.

1987a Make me reflexive—but not yet: strategies for managing essential reflexivity in ethnographic discourse. *Journal of Anthropological Research* 43(1):29–41.

1987b What is "effective intercultural communication?" *Canadian Ethnic Studies* 19(1):118–22.

1989 Definitive Geertz. *Ethnos* 54(1–2):23–30.

Weber, Max

1915 Religious rejections of the world and their directions. In *From Max Weber: Essays in Sociology.* H. H. Gerth and C. W. Mills, eds., pp. 323–59. Oxford: Oxford University Press.

Weil, Françoise

1984 La relation de voyage: document anthropologique ou texte littéraire? In *Histoire de l'anthropologie (xvie–xix siècles).* B. Rupp-Eisenreich, ed., pp. 55–65. Paris: Klincksiech.

Weiner, Annette

1976 *Women of Value, Men of Renown.* Austin: University of Texas Press.

Wheeler, Gerald Camden

1926 *Mono-Alu Folklore (Bougainville Strait, Western Solomon Islands).* London: George Routledge & Sons.

Wieder, D. Lawrence

1971 On meaning by rule. Reprinted 1973 in *Understanding Everyday Life: Toward the Reconstruction of Sociological Knowledge.* J. D. Douglas, ed., pp. 107–35. London: Routledge and Kegan Paul.

1974 *Language and Social Reality: The Case of the Convict Code.* The Hague: Mouton.

Williams, Raymond

1977 *Marxism and Literature.* Oxford: Oxford University Press.

Willis, Paul
   1977   *Learning to Labor: How Working Class Kids Get Working Class Jobs*. New York: Columbia University Press.

Wissler, Clark
   1923   *Man and Culture*. New York: Thomas Y. Crowell.

Wittgenstein, Ludwig
   1922   *Tractatus logico-philosophicus*. London: Routledge and Kegan Paul.

Wolf, Eric R.
   1956   Aspects of group relations in a complex society: Mexico. *American Anthropologist* 58: 1065–78.
   1964   *Anthropology*. Princeton Studies in the Humanities. Englewood Cliffs, NJ: Prentice-Hall.
   1969   American anthropologists and American society. In *Concepts and Assumptions in Contemporary Anthropology*. S. Tyler, ed., pp. 3–11. Proceedings of the Southern Anthropological Society, no. 3. Athens: University of Georgia Press.
   1982   *Europe and the People without History*. Berkeley: University of California Press.

Wolf, Margery
   1968   *The House of Lim*. New York: Appelton-Century-Crofts.

Woolgar, Steve
   1981   Interests and explanation in the social study of science. *Social Studies of Science* 2: 365–94.
   1988   (Ed.) *Knowledge and Reflexivity: New Frontiers in the Sociology of Knowledge*. London: Sage Publications.

Wright, Erik Olin
   1985   *Classes*. London and New York: Verso.

Wynne, Anna
   1988   Accounting for accounts of the diagnosis of multiple sclerosis. In *Knowledge and Reflexivity: New Frontiers in the Sociology of Knowledge*. S. Woolgar, ed., pp. 101–22. London: Sage Publications.

Yearley, Steven
   1981   Textual persuasion: the role of social accounting in the construction of scientific arguments. *Philosophy of the Social Sciences* 11: 409–35.

INDEX

SCHOOL OF AMERICAN RESEARCH ADVANCED SEMINAR SERIES

Published by SAR Press	*Published by Cambridge University Press*
Chaco & Hohokam: Prehistoric Regional Systems in the American Southwest P. L. CROWN & W. J. JUDGE, eds.	Dreaming: Anthropological and Psychological Interpretations BARBARA TEDLOCK, ed.
Recapturing Anthropology: Working in the Present RICHARD G. FOX, ed.	The Anasazi in a Changing Environment GEORGE J. GUMERMAN, ed.
War in the Tribal Zone: Expanding States and Indigenous Warfare R. B. FERGUSON & N. L. WHITEHEAD, eds.	Regional Perspectives on the Olmec R. J. SHARER & D. C. GROVE, eds.
Ideology and Pre-Columbian Civilizations A. A. DEMAREST & G. W. CONRAD, eds.	The Chemistry of Prehistoric Human Bone T. DOUGLAS PRICE, ed.
Dreaming: Anthropological and Psychological Interpretations *(reprint)* BARBARA TEDLOCK, ed.	The Emergence of Modern Humans: Biocultural Adaptations in the Later Pleistocene ERIK TRINKAUS, ed.
Historical Ecology: Cultural Knowledge and Changing Landscapes CAROLE L. CRUMLEY, ed.	The Anthropology of War JONATHAN HAAS, ed.
Themes in Southwest Prehistory GEORGE J. GUMERMAN, ed.	The Evolution of Political Systems STEADMAN UPHAM, ed.
Memory, History, and Opposition under State Socialism RUBIE S. WATSON, ed.	Classic Maya Political History: Hieroglyphic and Archaeological Evidence T. PATRICK CULBERT, ed.
Other Intentions: Cultural Contexts and the Attribution of Inner States LAWRENCE ROSEN, ed.	Turko-Persia in Historical Perspective ROBERT L. CANFIELD, ed.
	Chiefdoms: Power, Economy, and Ideology TIMOTHY EARLE, ed.

Published by University of California Press

Writing Culture: The Poetics and Politics of Ethnography
J. CLIFFORD & G. E. MARCUS, eds.

SCHOOL OF AMERICAN RESEARCH ADVANCED SEMINAR SERIES

Published by University of New Mexico Press

Reconstructing Prehistoric Pueblo
Societies
WILLIAM A. LONGACRE, ed.

New Perspectives on the Pueblos
ALFONSO ORTIZ, ed.

Structure and Process in Latin America
A. STRICKON & S. M. GREENFIELD, eds.

The Classic Maya Collapse
T. PATRICK CULBERT, ed.

Methods and Theories of Anthropological
Genetics
M. H. CRAWFORD & P. L. WORKMAN, eds.

Sixteenth-Century Mexico:
The Work of Sahagun
MUNRO S. EDMONSON, ed.

Ancient Civilization and Trade
J. A. SABLOFF & C. C. LAMBERG-KARLOVSKY, eds.

Photography in Archaeological Research
ELMER HARP, JR., ed.

Meaning in Anthropology
K. H. BASSO & H. A. SELBY, eds.

The Valley of Mexico: Studies in Pre-
Hispanic Ecology and Society
ERIC R. WOLF, ed.

Demographic Anthropology:
Quantitative Approaches
EZRA B. W. ZUBROW, ed.

The Origins of Maya Civilization
RICHARD E. W. ADAMS, ed.

Explanation of Prehistoric Change
JAMES N. HILL, ed.

Explorations in Ethnoarchaeology
RICHARD A. GOULD, ed.

Entrepreneurs in Cultural Context
SIDNEY M. GREENFIELD, A. STRICKON, &
R. T. AUBEY, eds.

The Dying Community
ART GALLAHER, JR., & H. PADFIELD, eds.

Southwestern Indian Ritual Drama
CHARLOTTE J. FRISBIE, ed.

Lowland Maya Settlement Patterns
WENDY ASHMORE, ed.

Simulations in Archaeology
JEREMY A. SABLOFF, ed.

Chan Chan: Andean Desert City
M. E. MOSELEY & K. C. DAY, eds.

Shipwreck Anthropology
RICHARD A. GOULD, ed.

Elites: Ethnographic Issues
GEORGE E. MARCUS, ed.

The Archaeology of Lower Central
America
F. W. LANGE & D. Z. STONE, eds.

Late Lowland Maya Civilization:
Classic to Postclassic
J. A. SABLOFF & E. W. ANDREWS V, eds.

Director of Publications and Editor: Jane Kepp

Designer: Deborah Flynn Post

Indexer: Douglas J. Easton

Typographer: G&S Typesetters, Inc.

Printer: Bookcrafters

This book was set in Linotron Berkeley Old Style Book.

The book paper is made from acid free, recycled fibers.

Participants in the advanced seminar

RECAPTURING ANTHROPOLOGY.

Left to right: Richard G. Fox

Michel-Rolph Trouillot

José E. Limón

Joan Vincent

Lila Abu-Lughod

Paul Rabinow

Sherry B. Ortner

Arjun Appadurai

Graham Watson

Bruce Kapferer.